NEW DIRECTIONS IN DREAM INTERPRETATION

SUNY Series in Dream Studies
Robert L. Van de Castle, editor

NEW DIRECTIONS IN DREAM INTERPRETATION

edited by
Gayle Delaney

STATE UNIVERSITY OF NEW YORK PRESS

Published by
State University of New York Press, Albany

© 1993 State University of New York

For information, address State University of New York Press,
State University Plaza, Albany, N.Y., 12246

Production by Marilyn P. Semerad
Marketing by Theresa A. Swierzowski

Library of Congress Cataloging-in-Publication Data

New directions in dream interpretation/edited by Gayle Delaney.
     p.   cm.—(SUNY series in dream studies)
   Includes bibliographical references.
   ISBN 0-7914-1605-4 (hard).—ISBN 0-7914-1606-2 (pbk.)
   1. Dream interpretation.   I. Delaney, Gayle M. V.   II. Series.
 BF1078.N45   1993
   154.6′3—dc20   92-33941
                                                                    CIP

10   9   8   7   6   5   4   3   2   1

CONTENTS

Introduction   *Gayle Delaney*   1

1. Dreams, the Dreamer, and Society
                         Montague Ullman   11

2. Dreams: The Gateway to Consciousness
                      Joseph M. Natterson   41

3. A Jungian Approach to Working with Dreams
                              John Beebe   77

4. Phenomenological Challenges for the Clinical
   Use of Dreams
              P. Erik Craig and *Stephen J. Walsh*   103

5. Dream Translation: An Approach to
   Understanding Dreams
                         Milton Kramer   155

6. The Dream Interview
                         Gayle Delaney   195

7. The Dream Interview Method in a Private
   Outpatient Psychotherapy Practice
                         Loma Flowers   241

8. An Integrated Approach to Dream Theory
and Clinical Practice
Ramon Greenberg and *Chester Pearlman*   289

List of Contributors   307

INTRODUCTION

Contemporary methods of dream interpretation have changed a great deal in the last few decades. Most effective therapists and dream specialists no longer rigidly follow the seminal, but often limiting, doctrines of Sigmund Freud, Carl Jung, or Fritz Perls. Today's leading dreamworkers have taken the best from Freud, Jung, Medard Boss, and recent sleep and dream research to synthesize new and fresh approaches. These methods de-emphasize theoretical purity and focus more attention on finding approaches that promote the greatest practical application of insights gained from dream interpretation.

This book is designed as a basic text on modern methods of interpretation for mental health students and professionals, as well as the general public. It presents seven hands-on approaches as they are actually practiced by highly skilled psychologists and psychiatrists today, each of whom have worked with dreamers for at least two decades. Each chapter serves both as an introduction to a given method as well as an example of an evolution of classical approaches. Thus the reader who is new to dream study will be able to follow each author's description of his or her work and note its evolution from classical perspectives to contemporary practice. Meanwhile, the professional who may have extraordinary expertise in a particular method will find easy access to unfamiliar approaches that may complement and strengthen his or her current dreamwork. As the founding president of the Association for the Study of Dreams, an international forum for the interdisciplinary study of dreaming, and as a director of the Delaney and Flowers Dream and Consultation Center, a dream-skills training center, I have been consistently and disappointingly impressed by the fact that it is a rare professional in dreamwork who has anything more than a very superficial and usually prejudiced knowledge of more than one method of dream interpretation. This situation has been fostered by the fact that it is extraordinarily difficult for the professional or the student to make his

1

or her way through the relevant and most useful literature describing alternative methods of dream interpretation. This book is intended to serve as a handy and informative resource and is aimed at encouraging both amateurs and professionals to explore and experiment with a variety of new interpretive perspectives and techniques.

This collection is not a superficial summary. Our publisher has provided us the rare, if not unique, opportunity to bring together in one volume rich descriptions of seven different approaches to dreams. Instead of the usual practice of limiting the authors to ten or fifteen pages, each was invited to take the space needed to give the reader a tangible, practical description and demonstration of his or her approach that could be put to use to enrich the reader's study and work with dreamers. Thus the reader can take a close look at how eight masters in the field really work as they present practical advice and procedures rather than rehash war-weary dream theories. The reader can sample radically different approaches from different schools of interpretation and gain the tools by which he or she can make meaningful comparisons. In these pages several authors also had enough space to answer questions and give suggestions for dealing with a variety of situations which arise as one progresses and matures in more advanced levels of dream interpretation.

Several contributors have provided edited nearly "verbatim" examples of their work with dreamers. I think the reader will find such examples to be extremely useful in understanding and experimenting with a given approach. In describing their theoretical roots and how they have departed from them when confronted with the real world of real dreamers, our contributors show the reader in very practical terms what to do and say when trying to understand a dream. Our authors take the reader behind the curtain of theory into the consultation room where the work of interpretation and of generating specific insights takes place.

Most modern interpretive methods can be easily understood once one has grasped the basic principles of interpretation described by Freud, Jung, and the existentialists such as Medard Boss. Freud was able to convince us that dreams relate to the conflicts of our personal lives, and that they reflect aspects of our development from childhood. Freud was the first one in the long history of dream interpretation to ask dreamers for their associations to the dream imagery and for the feelings the imagery and the associations evoked. In the preceding five thousand years, priests and other professional dream interpreters had relied on traditional or superstitiously fixed symbolic meanings, at worst, and, at best (as in the case of the second-century Greek Artemidorus), on the insight, associations, and projections of the interpreter. Freud believed that dreams disguise their real or latent meaning in benign details called "day residue," and that a specialized knowledge of dream symbolism was necessary so that the therapist could give interpretations to the dreamer whether or not the dreamer's associations led to the same conclusion. Freud's symbolic substitution, which he used to complement his association method, was based not on ancient traditions but upon his metapsychology, i.e., his beliefs about the structure and function of the male and the female psyche. Contemporary dreamwork owes much to Freud. Many have insufficiently appreciated his many contributions, which include showing how dreams can reveal not only unresolved childhood issues but also how they can elucidate the dreamer's resistances and transferences when personal associations are elicited in a safe, nonjudgmental atmosphere.

Carl Jung, a Swiss psychiatrist and one-time student of Freud's, took issue with many aspects of classical psychoanalytic dreamwork as developed by Freud and some of his followers. While Jung agreed that dreams expressed the individual's psychological development and blocks to that development, he emphasized that dreams offer to help the dreamer transcend the conflicts of childhood and develop a fuller psychological growth process within the dreamer. He insisted that dreams reveal rather than conceal, and that the symbolic language of dreaming called not for a decoding of an internal unconscious censor's effort to hide latent meaning, but for an appreciation of the revelatory and expressive power of symbols. Rather than gathering what he found to be too lengthy and often tangential lists of associations to dream images, he would ask the dreamer to elaborate on the images but keep close to thoughts directly related to them. He would also suggest possible parallels and interpretations to the dreamer, drawing from his specialized knowledge based upon his own metapsychology and his reading of the history of mythology, religion, and alchemy, among other subjects. Jung aimed at being less authoritarian than Freud. He insisted that any interpretation he offered could only be a working hypothesis until such time as the dreamer was able to confirm its emotional fit or appropriateness.

Medard Boss, a Swiss psychiatrist who studied for a time with both Freud and Jung, went on to develop an existential-phenomenological perspective and added yet another vocabulary to the study of dreams. Freud was a good writer and is easy to read. Jung is not easy to read, and Boss is almost impossible to understand unless one has a predilection for Germanic philosophical writing styles. Thus, Boss is not well known in the United States. His influence, which is much greater in Europe, has come to us more subtly in the spirit of the times. For example, there are elements of the existential perspective in the work of Freud and Fritz Perls, among others.

Briefly, Boss argued that all metapsychologies and their attendant conceptualizations of how the unconscious works are as unnecessary as they are contradictory and unprovable. He insisted that if the dreamer were only assisted in fully reexperiencing the dream and in reflecting upon the realities of being an experience to which the dream (in the mind of the dreamer or the analyst) seems to allude, the individual would become open to states of being and awareness to which he or she had previously been closed. Thus a greater openness and perhaps insight could be gained.

Boss eschewed Freud's and Jung's associative phase of exploration and entirely rejected both versions of symbol substitution. Instead, he asked the dreamer to "explicate" the dream, or to retell the dream or various parts of it several times in greater and greater detail. The dreamer was to describe the qualities of feeling and experiencing in the dream as well as in the retelling of the dream.

From this stage of explication, one moves into the elucidation phase. Here the analyst, who may or may not invite the dreamer to participate, searches for an intuitive grasping of the meaning in the manifest content. Neither the bases of this intuitive grasping nor the procedural method for achieving it are clearly described. We are told, however, that the searchers formally reject both the symbol substitution and metapsychologies of Freud and Jung. The analyst and the dreamer seek to apprehend both the dream as dream and as allusion to what Craig calls "the fundamental meaning structure of the manifest dream" as well as to some aspect of the dreamer's waking existence. It has been argued that any intuitive search for meaning related to a dream experience must draw upon one's metapsychology or belief about how the psyche operates. Certain aspects of Boss's metapsychology can be deduced by the patterns of his interpretations.

Erik Craig and Stephen Walsh's chapter on the existential-phenomenological approach derived from Boss's work provides some interpretive dialogues that demonstrate both the emphasis on staying closer to the actual dream imagery and the way meanings are derived from the dream. This classical tripod from which we can view all modern dreamwork will assist the reader in recognizing the three tremendously important influences on the theory and practice of contemporary dreamwork.

Our first chapter, "Dreams, the Dreamer, and Society," by Montague Ullman demonstrates how very far some psychoanalysts have come from early psychoanalytic procedures and theory. Ullman has developed a method for working with dreams in group settings. Instead of having the dreamer associate to the dream imagery, each group member is asked to describe his or her projections of meaning by answering the question, "What would this dream mean if it were mine?" The dreamer then comments to the degree he or she wishes on which projections from the group struck a responsive cord and seem to have shed light on the meaning of the dream.

After further clarification and discussion, and after the dream has been read back to the dreamer, one or more members of the group offer their "orchestrating projections." In this phase, members try to pull together what has been said and organize it according to the dramatic structure of the dream while relating the whole or parts of the dream to their metaphorical references. Thus Ullman proposes neither an authoritative symbolic substitution system nor a lengthy associative or descriptive procedure. While the dreamer is free to associate to the dream imagery after having heard the group's projections of meaning, the associative-descriptive material tends to be briefer than that found in other methods. Perhaps this is due to the tantalizing allure of responding to the projected meanings presented by the group. Although Ullman describes his as an atheoretical approach, the metapsychologies underlying the group's projected or orchestrated meanings are likely to be many and may or may not be consciously formulated, depending upon the makeup of the group.

A major safety factor of this approach is the clearly stated rule that the dreamer always has authority over the dream and the degree of self-revelation with which he or she chooses to participate. Group members are told to minimize intrusiveness especially in the form of telling the dreamer what his or her dream means. Although the orchestrating projections may sound like declarative interpretations, the dreamer is reminded that they are meant more as questions or hypotheses, which may well carry an overload of projections. Ullman greatly values the stimulation and social support which group work offers the dreamer, and he underlines the usually ignored social realities that dreams present to individuals. He argues that by reflecting our social beliefs and prejudices, dreams challenge "not only our personal but our social myths as well."

Ramon Greenberg and Chester Pearlman challenge a few Freudian and scientific myths about dreaming in, "An Integrated Approach to Dream Theory and Clinical Practice." Citing recent laboratory research on REM deprivation, the REM responsiveness to various waking/learning situations and the study of dream content of analytic patients collected in sleep labs, Greenberg and Pearlman reject the old Freudian notions that dreams use benign day residue to disguise meaning. Instead, they argue that dreams serve an information processing function which helps the dreamer deal with recently aroused emotional material and to promote new learning, creative thinking, and problem-solving.

Their method of interpretation makes liberal use of the dreamer's associations but is far more collaborative than Freud's. They comment and focus upon the central problem presented in the manifest dream scenario. They encourage the dreamer to look for parallels both to the problem and to ways of coping in childhood and in current waking life.

This growing respect for the revelatory power of the manifest dream, triggered by Jung and much more emphatically proclaimed by Boss, is also expressed in the work of Joseph Natterson. In his chapter, "Dreams: The Gateway to Consciousness," Natterson describes his contemporary psychoanalytic style and discusses both the effects of dreamwork in therapy and the changes in dream type and quality over the course of time in therapy.

John Beebe, in "A Jungian Approach to Working with Dreams," provides us with a rare glimpse of the actual dialogue that takes place between a dreamer and a Jungian analyst. While adhering to the classical Jungian metapsychology and to the belief that analysts must learn and give the dreamer special knowledge of dream symbolism (at appropriate times), he warns of the dangers therein. Beebe encourages the analyst to keep Jungian jargon to a minimum and to avoid letting the metapsychological ideas of Jung overshadow the dream itself as the topic of concern.

In "Phenomenological Challenges for the Clinical Use of Dreams" by Erik Craig and Stephen Walsh, we see a modern modification and organization of Medard Boss's approach. Craig and Walsh are more careful than Boss was in monitoring their comments on the manifest dream, avoiding Boss's sometimes limiting and rather authoritative statements. Craig and Walsh, like most modern dreamworkers owe a debt to psychoanalyst Walter Bonime in calling for a more collaborative stance with the dreamer.

After demonstrating how the analyst works through the explication, elucidation, and allusion phases of exploring a dream, Craig and Walsh discuss the influences of Irvin Yalom's work in using dreams to explore the existential givens of death, freedom/responsibility, isolation, and meaninglessness. The chapter closes with a description of how phenomenological dream work, with its emphases on the here and now of the dream experience, can evoke a greater sense of immediacy and of presence in both the dreamer and the therapist leading to viscerally experienced insights which have enhanced impact on the dreamer.

In "The Dream Interview" I present a systematized method of interpretation which is based on a minimalist metapsychology and aims at minimizing the expression and influence of the analyst-turned-interviewer's associations, projections, and conceptualizations. Like Bonime, Natterson, Ullman and Kramer, I focus on approaching the dream as a metaphoric statement about the dreamer's subjective life.

The dream interviewer is very active in asking the dreamer to describe the images, actions, and feelings in the dream as if he or she were describing them to someone from another planet who has little knowledge of earthly realities. This description phase is a very concrete and highly focused combination of explication and association. It is followed by the interviewer's recapitulation of the dreamer's responses.

Next, the dreamer is asked to bridge from the dream to waking experience with specific questions like, "Does the shoemaker in your dream whom you describe as _____ remind you of any part of yourself or of anyone or anything in your life?" If the dreamer's response is yes, the interviewer asks, "How so?" and thereby invites the dreamer to confirm or reject the bridge with greater specificity. These bridging steps are aimed at achieving both the elucidation and allusion goals described by Craig and Walsh.

As the dreamer progresses through the various scenes of the dream, as well as at the end of the dream, the interviewer or the dreamer makes summaries of the dream as told, including the descriptions and bridges made so far. The retelling of the dream which Ullman, Beebe, and Craig and Walsh encourage emphasizes the shared belief that "the dream says it best." Including the descriptions and bridges in the retelling is peculiar to the dream interview approach.

Throughout the interview, the interviewer is to use the dreamer's descriptions and bridges to discover the metaphors of the dream imagery. The interviewer is to keep his or her own projections and formulations out of the way to the greatest extent possible. This is much the same attitude of the phenomenologists and differs markedly from Ullman's and Beebe's approaches.

Loma Flowers in her chapter, "The Dream Interview Method in a Private Outpatient Psychotherapy Practice," describes her application of this method to a variety of therapeutic situations, including individual psychotherapy, consultation liaison, brief psychotherapy, and couples and group therapy. She also examines the various uses of dreams in the different stages of long-term psychotherapy as well as applications to psychosomatic symptoms, depression, anxiety, borderline traits, addictions, and decision-making. Flowers also considers the indications for and contradictions of using dream interviews in psychotherapy.

In "Dream Translation: An Approach to Understanding Dreams," Milton Kramer suggests a method that, at first glance, may seem to be the exact opposite of the Delaney and Flowers's dream interview, which so highly prizes the dreamer's very personal associations and concrete descriptions. Kramer presents a method of interpretation that can be practiced without any explicit associations from the dreamer—in fact, without any knowledge of the dreamer beyond age and sex. While Kramer acknowledges that collaborative dreamwork which employs the associations of the dreamer encourages engagement of the patient in the therapeutic process and lends specificity to interpretations, he demonstrates that there is much to be learned from the dream text itself.

Kramer looks at the structure of the dream report and relates it to his past experience in the analysis of dreams using the methods of various depth psychological approaches. He also compares the dream imagery to scientific studies of dream content and its relation to personality variables, and of the relation between dreamers' waking and sleeping personality traits and moods.

The dream translation method is based on the hypotheses that the manifest dream report is strictly determined, that the order of elements in the dream is also strictly determined, and that the sequence of these elements are causally related. Dream "translators" approach the dream as a metaphorical statement of the dreamer's inner life and use their own associations in attempting to discover its metaphoric meaning. Translators are encouraged to make their best guess as to what the dream is about. Kramer emphasizes that much can be learned about the dreamer in this fashion and that the diagnostic value of the dream report itself can be very useful.

The respect given the meaning inherent in the structure of the dream, the three working hypotheses used, and the search for metaphoric expression of Kramer's method are important elements of the dream interview as well. The differing goals of the two methods explain the more obvious methodological differences. Kramer seeks understanding of a more general nature from a dream report which can be used in studies or consultations without the presence of the dreamer, or in therapeutic situations in which there is an impasse or the need for early diagnostic hypotheses. Delaney and Flowers, whether using the dream in or out of a therapeutic or diagnostic setting, always work with the dreamer and seek the most specific metaphoric parallels possible. Both methods place particular emphasis on the metaphorical meaningfulness of the structure of the dream as a whole.

As you read the following chapters you may find it interesting to explore how different approaches address such basic questions as : How is depth defined? How active and how suggestive should the analyst be? Who best determines the subjective or objective level of interpretation? How does one know when a dream has been understood? How best does one encourage the integration of dream-generated insight?

The various approaches to the understanding of dreams presented in the following pages offer the reader new and synthetic perspectives on, and methods of entering into the world of dream interpretation which has too long been oppressed by parochial thinking. It is my hope that this collection will assist in furthering the establishment of more thorough, integrative, and practical education in this fascinating field.

1

Montague Ullman ▬▬▬▬▬▬▬▬▬▬▬▬▬

Dreams, the Dreamer, and Society

Many, if not most, people have a natural curiosity about their dreams. However, there are very few resources at hand to help them pursue this interest in a serious way. Dreams have a low priority in our society (in all civilized societies) and, as a consequence, little or no attempt is made to encourage their pursuit or to provide the necessary means to do so. The only socially sanctioned arrangement available is to seek a professional who, for a fee, will offer the help necessary to interpret the dream. In this respect, we have not advanced much from the way dreams were handled in ancient times. The skills and prerogatives around dreamwork continue to be vested in a small group of people who are acknowledged as experts by virtue of their specialized knowledge. The question I wish to explore is whether the skills necessary for dreamwork can and should be shared with the public at large. Can we transform dreamwork from a therapeutically valuable operation in the hands of specialists to a universally accessible experience that is available to anyone who wishes to take the time and trouble to learn how to go about it?

In recent years, many books have appeared for the general public which address this issue (Delaney, 1988, 1991; Faraday, 1974 and 1979; Sanford, 1968; Taylor, 1983; Ullman and Zimmerman, 1979; and Ullman and Limmer, 1988). They speak of the benefits to be gained by working with dreams and offer several approaches to them. My own work

---

The author wishes to acknowledge permission from the American Journal of Psychoanalysis for the reproduction of a passage from "The Social Roots of the Dream," a paper originally published in Vol. XX, No. 2, 1960 and to Contemporary Psychoanalysis, the journal of the William Alanson White Institute and the William Alanson White Psychoanalytic Society, New York, for permission to reproduce a passage from "Societal Factors in Dreaming," a paper which originally appeared in Vol.9, No. 3, May 1973.

emphasizes the skills necessary for dreamwork and the importance of a small group as the optimal supportive and helping agency. I will present what I consider the basic information that is needed if serious dreamwork is contemplated and a description of how I structure a small group setting to meet the needs of the dreamer. Finally, I will explore dream images in a larger social frame of reference, seeing them as pointers not only to personal issues but to related social issues as well.

In our society we grow up rather ignorant about the nature of our dream life. This is unfortunate because it leaves us without any understanding of a language we have been speaking all our lives and, therefore, without the means to connect to our dream life. We fail to introduce dreamwork into the family system, the educational system, or any natural system. For the most part, we come together only as adults to find a way to work with dreams. Much learning has to take place before we are ready to proceed.

The new recruit to dreamwork needs several different kinds of information, namely, clarity about the distinction between dreaming and what we call the dream, a grasp of those qualities of dreaming that make the dream a significant event in our lives, an understanding of the dreamer's predicament, the kind of help the dreamer needs, and the way that help can be provided.

Dreaming and the Dream

Dreaming and the dream refer to two different, though closely related, events. Dreaming is an intrinsic part of the sleep cycle that recurs every ninety minutes during sleep and is associated with distinct psychological changes that signify a state of arousal. The dream is a remembrance in the waking state of whatever we can bring back from the previous night's dreaming episodes. The two are not the same. The dream originates in the dreaming experience, but it is that experience transformed into the waking mode of expression. These two modes of consciousness resort to different languages to say different things about the same organism. In order to understand the dream, we must begin with an understanding of the way in which the two languages differ and what it is we are saying when we use dream language.

Our Two Languages

Waking language appears to have evolved as a way of speaking to each other about the world and the way we experience ourselves in that world. The world is broken down into manageable and agreed-upon categories which can then be communicated through a structured grammar that conveys the way our experiences are organized in space and time in a logical manner. Language is a way of categorizing reality to be able to talk about our experiences.

But our needs go beyond what can be transmitted in this fashion through language. We seem to need a more direct way of encountering and expressing the impact upon us of the world in which we live. We need a more effective language for the expression of feelings. In waking life we resort to the arts, music and poetry. While asleep and dreaming, a pictorial, figurative language takes over and reflects our feelings. This dream language has much in common with poetry in that both rely on metaphor for their expressive effect. There are, however, at least three significant differences in the way the poet and the dreamer use metaphor. The poet rearranges words to create the metaphorical quality he or she needs to best convey the feelings he or she wishes to communicate to others. The dreamer shapes images into metaphorical statements. The poet addresses an audience outside himself or herself. The dream is a private message to oneself. Finally, writing poetry is a task of greater or lesser difficulty. Dreaming and the creation of visual metaphors is something that *happens* to us through no deliberate or volitional effort on our part.

The neophyte in dreamwork has to learn to look at these images not as photographic reproductions of reality but as metaphorical ways of conveying the nature of the predicament felt by the dreamer. We have adapted what, in all likelihood, is a primitive imaging capacity that we probably share with animals lower on the evolutionary scale, and we use this as an instrument for symbolic rather than literal expression. Our sleeping self is concerned with managing certain residual feelings. Metaphorical imagery is a most suitable symbolic vehicle for containing and conveying feelings. A person who pictures himself or herself in a dream driving down a steep hill and having the brakes suddenly fail will experience the sensation of being in an uncontrollably dangerous situation far more powerfully than ordinary language could convey. In the dream we are part of the metaphor we ourselves are creating, a fact that places us in an immediate relationship to the feelings being generated. We are the actors, not the reporters, of the scene taking place. There is no way out except through terminating the dream either by generating feelings strong enough to awaken us or by somehow resolving the issue so there is a natural passage back into dreamless sleep. The concept of the visual metaphor is basic to dreamwork, and its importance cannot be overly stressed. We are more like poets than scientists when we sleep. We express our personal poetry in a language we have been using since childhood, yet this language continues to feel strange and unfamiliar to us as adults. To understand this fully we must also take into account the content of our dreams, what is being expressed through this language.

Dream Content

When we use this pictorial language what are we saying that makes the remembered dream so potentially illuminating when awake? Our imaging capacity provides the form that our consciousness takes, but where does the content come from?

As we fall asleep we close off our input channels. No new information is coming in, so whatever we become conscious of during this period of dreaming has its origin some time before falling asleep. Freud spoke of the "day residue" as the starting point of the dream. Some recent event sets up a lingering tension that surfaces at the onset of a dreaming period and acts as a shaping influence on the content to be developed. What gives this recent residual feeling its extraordinary power lies in the fact that, regardless of how trivial or insignificant it may seem at the time, it connects with unresolved issues from the past. It touches on vulnerable areas still being worked over. We are unaware of this connection when awake, but when we are asleep, it comes clearly into view. The first important point, then, is that the dream starts in the present. The issue it addresses derives from our past but continues to be of some importance for us in the present.

What we do with this residue while dreaming is quite extraordinary when judged by waking standards. We seem able to do many things at once. We scan our entire life history for events and experiences that are emotionally related to it; we explore our past ways of coping with whatever vulnerable areas may have been exposed; we mobilize the resources at our disposal and try to come to some resolution. In short, while dreaming we are reassessing the significance of recent events in the context of our past. In a rather clever way we express it all through pictorial metaphors that highlight the feelings evoked in the course of this self-exploratory adventure. And it is all done effortlessly and seemingly instantaneously. We have brought a current residue into a relationship with past residues. In so doing we bring together important information relevant to what we are struggling with now. The range and extent of that information is not easily available to us in the waking state. If aspects of it are available, they are not readily seen in relation to the current issue. This is the second significant feature of our dream life that contributes to its value as a potentially healing instrument.

This brings us to the most important quality of our dream life, particularly in its relation to the question of healing. We are alone when we sleep and dream, perhaps more alone than at any other time in our life. We have temporarily disconnected from the world around us. We have temporarily suspended our social roles and our social façades. We no longer are in need of our social defenses, those various ways of protecting ourselves from truths we cannot or do not wish to see. In the act of going to sleep we undress not only physically but psychically as well. When our brain gets the signal to start dreaming we are emotionally nude.

What happens next is best described by analogy. There is a magical mirror in this place where we find ourselves. It is a mirror capable of reflecting a profoundly honest picture of who we are rather than who we would like to think we are or who we would like others to think we are. Another bit of magic in this mirror is that only the dreamer can use it. No one else can look into it. Being alone and confronted with a mirror that provides a private view, the dreamer risks looking into it himself. The view reflected back is the view rendered by the imagery of the dream. It is a view without pretense. It is the truth. In a sense it is a privileged portrait of intrinsic value to the dreamer in search of a more honest self-concept. For the most part, our dreams are not understood or appreciated in their individual and social significance, and we are largely unaware of the personal and social choices and opportunities offered through our dream life. Once we are awake, there is an overwhelming tendency to slip back into a familiar character structure and behavioral pattern. At a social level the dream is also of dubious value to the dreamer who is concerned more with fitting *in* than with whatever he or she is fitting *into*.

It is much easier to adapt to the social blinders we have grown up with and are accustomed to than to challenge and reevaluate them in terms of the social truths they may be hiding from us. Both the individual and society are the losers. This will be considered further in a later section.

The Dreamer's Predicament

What about dreamers who want to become active agents in relation to their dreams and to repossess in the waking state all that they have to offer? They have at hand a potentially healing instrument. It deals with an issue of concern in the present. It mobilizes relevant information from the past that is honest and reliable. Taken together, these three aspects of the dream image speak to the essence of what emotional healing is. It means becoming more whole, more in touch with ourselves. It means shedding light on characteristics that would otherwise continue to operate autonomously in the dark.

At some level, there seems to be an awareness of this. Perhaps this is what lies behind the universal curiosity about dreams. The dreamer senses that there is something important about the dream, but whatever it is, it eludes one's grasp. A person is in a difficult position. The dream does not readily yield its secrets. It appears challenging and frustrating in its strangeness and disregard for time, space, logic, and causality. It uses a language that is difficult to understand.

To better appreciate the dreamer's situation let us take a closer look at what happens in the change from sleeping to waking. On awakening the dreamer does not simply engage in a change in physical state. There is also a profound change in his or her psychological state. The person resumes his or her social role and reenters the world of other people and the world of social responsibility. In order to carry out this role he or she has adopted a social façade that serves as a protective device and wards off truths about the outer and inner world that the person is not yet prepared to face. We are all quite clever at warding off certain truths when we are awake. We fashion a set of blinders that keep us from seeing things as they really are. These blinders take the form of what we refer to as defense mechanisms. We hide from the truth by denying, suppressing, rationalizing, and engaging in various other defensive maneuvers.

We are in a better position now to understand the difficulties the dreamer has. In finding oneself awake and in possession of a dream, a person has, without being aware of it, moved from a realm of profound honesty, the dreaming state, to a state in which his or her defenses are once again activated and where he or she is somewhat handicapped in the ability to be completely honest. The way of seeing things when awake tends to be a mixture of honest and expedient perceptions in relation to the outside world. The view a person now has of himself or herself and others is different from the one he or she confronted while asleep. The blinders have been restored, and so the person is now capable of seeing himself or herself only as his or her own defensive operations permit. We screen information in or out as suits our waking needs. We have dispensed with this screening device while dreaming. Looked at through these screening devices, the images we have created now strike us as strange, mysterious, and intrusive. They offer little or no hint of the valuable information they contain, and they convey their message in language that is foreign to our waking way of thinking.

There are, then, two reasons why the dreamer is in trouble when confronting a dream. The first has to do with the clarity and honesty of his perception of himself while dreaming as compared with being awake. The second is related to his or her unfamiliarity with the language of the dream. Since serious dreamwork is not among our priorities, nor is it socially encouraged, we are not prepared to relate to the metaphorical language of the dream. We try to teach children to appreciate the poetic metaphor but we do not acquaint them with the dream metaphor.

So there the dreamer stands, more or less helpless before his her dream, blinded by the honesty in the pictures being reflected, and a victim of social neglect that failed to teach him or her anything about the language of the dream.

First Aid for the Dreamer

The dreamer needs help. He or she has to turn to other people for that help, and herein lies the paradox of the dream and the nature of the dreamer's dilemma. On the one hand, the person has created a most personal and intimate representation of an aspect of his or her inner life. On the other hand, he or she has to go public with the dream to realize fully the information communicated by the imagery. The dream has to be transformed from a remembrance of a private experience to a public communication. When a personal experience is transformed into a social one the question of risk arises. When a person is asleep and alone, the initial risk is taken. When the person is awake and visible to others the sense of risk, vulnerability and exposure is experienced differently. To transform the dream into a social experience means facing possible social implications. Since the dreamer is dealing with something unknown, the social implications are also unknown and unpredictable.

In order to help a dreamer, the others involved must have a clear understanding of the dreamer's predicament and be able to respond to the needs that arise from it. The two overriding needs are, first, for the dreamer to feel safe and secure in sharing the dream and, second, for the dreamer to be helped to remove the blinders so that a clear and honest vision can emerge.

The need for safety is obvious. The dreamer is risking exposure of vulnerable parts of the psyche, which he or she can do only in an atmosphere of trust and safety. The most important factor in achieving the necessary level of safety and trust means giving the dreamer total control of the situation and making sure that all the interactions taking place between the dreamer and the group are nonintrusive in nature. As we will see later, this element of control is built into each stage of the process. It implies that sharing a dream is a voluntary decision made by the dreamer. At no time is anyone under constraint to share a dream. Any existing constraint is experienced equally by the entire group. Only the dreamer determines the level of self-disclosure he or she feels comfortable with, and no one pushes him or her beyond that level. Finally, the dreamer can stop the process at any point.

While the safety factor is a necessary condition it is not sufficient by itself. The dreamer needs active help from the group to make discoveries that are difficult to make alone. How the group does this will be described in connection with the various stages of the process as they unfold.

The process is structured to meet both of these needs. It rests on the premise that if a person remembers a dream, he or she is ready to be confronted by the information in that dream, aside from the question of whether the person wishes to or not. The dream is not a threat but an opportunity. Dreams are communications to oneself and as such imply that the dreamer is ready to confront, if not resolve, the issue being dreamed about. All dreams can serve as an aspect of the healing process. Through dreamwork the dreamer becomes more whole in the sense of being more in touch with oneself. Even profoundly frightening dreams have a healing aspect, and in a supportive social context the dreamer can find the courage to face what the dream is saying. Once this happens, his or her relation to the issue changes, regardless of the time it may take for the issue to ultimately be resolved.

Stage IA: Eliciting the Dream

The following question is put to the group: Who has a dream he or she would like to share with the group? Let us assume that someone volunteers to tell a dream. He or she is asked to speak slowly enough so that those who wish to can take notes. The person is asked to tell all he or she can about what was in the dream, but not to add his or her own thoughts and later associations.

The dreamer is asked to limit himself or herself to the manifest content of the dream, including any feelings connected with the imagery. Were he or she to give associations at this point, the dreamer would influence the way the group handles the dream in the next stage. Personal associations can limit the group's responses and the range of their imagination.

Although the dreamer is free to share any dream that is deemed important, emphasis is placed on recent dreams. It is important to discover the immediate life situation that triggered the dream, the life context that shaped the dream. It is the context that defines the issue that will be dreamed about. Only by identifying that context can the dreamer find the answer to the question why he or she had the dream on that particular night. The further back in time that a dream goes, the more difficult it usually is to reconstruct the context and the emotional climate arising out of that context.

Stage IB: Clarifying the Dream

When the dreamer has finished his or her account of the dream the members of the group can ask questions to clarify what they have heard, but they cannot pressure the dreamer beyond what is in the dream. The group is entitled to know:

1. Are the characters in the dream real people?
2. If real, what is their relationship to the dreamer (without going into the details)?
3. What are the dreamer's feelings in the dream?
4. Are there any colors in the dream?
5. Was the dreamer his or her present age?

With a new group there is often a tendency to ask more questions than necessary, either in an attempt to get the dreamer to give more associations or to make something more concrete and clearer than it actually was in the dream. Vague and illogical sequences must simply be accepted as such. No account can ever be perfect, and no attempt should be made to make it so. If there are complex spatial arrangements in the dream a diagram can often be helpful.

The Safety Factor in Stage I. It is the dreamer's choice whether or not to share the dream. He or she is not apt to do so unless the person has enough trust in the process and the atmosphere generated by the process.

The Discovery Factor in Stage I. Occasionally, the act of sharing a dream is associated with a sudden burst of insight. The willingness to share a dream means that there has been some lowering of defenses. A direct relationship exists between lowering defenses and the emergence of insight.

Stage II: The Group Makes the Dream Its Own

In this stage the dreamer does not participate actively but is asked to listen to the responses of the group while others make the dream their own. The dreamer is encouraged to jot down anything of interest so that it is available when he or she does respond later. In making the dream their own, the group members are asked first to sensitize themselves to any feelings or moods, that they connect with the imagery (Stage IIA). They are cautioned to speak of the dream as if it were their own and to address their comments to each other, not to the dreamer. Listening to the dream may have aroused various feelings in others or they may share feelings that might have arisen if they had created those particular images themselves.

When this phase is finished, the group is asked to consider each element in the dream symbolically and to link that element metaphorically to some actual or imagined life situation (Stage IIB). They are also told that they are free to share any other feelings that may arise when working with the meaning of the metaphors. Again, stress is placed on the importance of offering everything they say as their own projection.

It is particularly important that the group's comments are not addressed directly to the dreamer. In this way the dreamer feels free to accept or reject what is offered. The group's contributions can be generated in a number of ways. Members can work with the imagery as if it came from their own lives. They can scan their past and present to give the images a personal meaning or to identify the feelings connected with them. They can try to think of the feelings or meanings they might have were they to give their imagination free rein. They may place themselves into their imagined view of the dreamer's life, identify with the dreamer and come up with projections based on this identification. Regardless of how they come about, none of these projections is to be seen as applicable to the dreamer's situation until he or she later validates them. The important point is not how the projections are arrived at but how to create the largest number of them in the hope that some of them will resonate with the dreamer and leave him or her feeling that he or she has encountered a significant truth.

As the group begins to offer its projections, the dreamer undergoes a number of interesting reactions. When a group member presents feelings that resonate with the dreamer, the dreamer may not have been aware of these feelings until someone else conceptualizes them. By the same token, a metaphorical translation offered as a projection may feel right and lead to an insightful response. Even when the dreamer cannot identify with the projections from the group, they still may be of help by defining what the image is not. This may then bring the dreamer closer to what the image is about. The interest shown in the dream, the way the group members share their projections, and the help the dreamer feels when some of these meanings strike home all have the effect of facilitating the dreamer's concordant efforts at self-exploration.

The Safety Factor in Stage II. When the group members share feelings and meanings as their own projections the nonintrusive character of the process is maintained. Throughout this stage the dreamer remains in a safe position and is the guardian of his or her own reactions. Should the dreamer experience something coming from the group as true, he or she is free to deal with it either to acknowledge it (which usually happens) or to distance himself or herself from it (rare under the conditions of safety and freedom that exists). At a later stage, the dreamer can decide whether or not to share it with the group.

The Discovery Factor in Stage II. This has already been alluded to, but it is surprising how often the projections of the group are meaningful to the dreamer and how many levels of the personality are touched.

Stage III: The Dreamer's Response and Working Toward Closure

The second stage is only a game. It runs its course, after which the attention shifts back to the dreamer (Stage IIIA). It is important that the dreamer has a clear idea of what is expected at this point. He or she is invited to respond and is free to do so in any way. The dreamer can begin either with his or her associations and thoughts about the dream or with the impact of the group's input on him or her. He or she is free to carry it to any degree of self-disclosure that is comfortable. The dreamer is given all the time needed and is asked to tell the group when he or she is finished. It is important that he or she not be interrupted during the response.

The dreamer usually is appreciative of the concern shown by the group, the sharing of projections and the occasional bull's-eyes that come through. All of this leads to the desire to give something back to the group. Often he or she is amazed at how many of the group's responses were meaningful. The group's projections come in a random fashion and often have an impact at different levels of his psyche. In some cases the group's work has helped the dreamer come into good contact with the dream, and no further work is needed. The dream has made the connections between the images and the life situation. He or she feels in touch with the issues involved and is aware of why the dream occurred when it did.

In most instances, however, more work is needed, work that takes place in the form of a dialogue between the group and the dreamer (Stage IIIB). The purpose of the dialogue is twofold. If the dreamer has not fully developed the immediate life context that shaped the dream, the initial questions should be directed to elucidating that context. The dialogue then shifts to help the dreamer focus on any element in the dream that he or she has not yet commented on.

There is a clear structure within which the dialogue is conducted so that the dreamer's control over the process is maintained and any tendency to be intrusive is curbed. The dreamer is told he or she has complete freedom to decide whether or not to respond to a given question. If he or she does respond, then the level of self-disclosure he or she feels comfortable with is determined by the dreamer.

Specific instructions are given to the group about the kind of questions that may be asked in order to invite a response from the dreamer (without demanding one) and to ensure the dreamer's privacy. Intrusiveness would elicit defensiveness and would interfere with the dreamer's ability to connect with the imagery. To maintain the optimal milieu in which the dreamer feels the safety and freedom to continue exploring the dream, the questions have to be based obviously on the dream or on whatever the dreamer has shared with the group. If the questions are not obvious they are apt to heighten the dreamer's anxiety and defenses. The questions have to be open-ended so that they do not demand an answer but leave the dreamer free to go wherever he or she wishes with the question. The questions serve only to help the dreamer focus on an aspect of the dream that has not yet been developed.

The questioning continues until the dreamer, along with the group, experiences a sense of closure. This comes about at a point where the dreamer feels the connection of the dream to his or her present life and, in some measure, to the past, and feels able to develop further insight into the dream on his or her own if he or she wishes.

Orchestration. When this step is necessary it is considered part of the dialogue. It is treated separately here because the exchange with the dreamer now takes a different turn. Up to this point information-eliciting questions have been asked to clarify the dream content and to build bridges between the imagery and waking life. The dialogue may have given the dreamer a great deal, but he or she may not yet have an overall grasp of the dream and its meaning. Further questioning elicits no new data and leaves the dreamer still puzzled. There is a random quality to the game in Stage II and the dialogue, so whatever the impact they may have had, the insights still remain disconnected. The relevant data may have been elicited but are not yet seen in their relation to the dream. What is needed now is an effort to pull together the information that has been made available and to organize it as it applies to the sequential arrangements of the imagery of the dream. But this should not be attempted before all the relevant data have been elicited. It is an attempt at integration which takes the form of a playback by someone in the group, usually the leader, of what the dreamer has shared, put together now in its metaphorical reference to the sequential arrangement of the imagery of the dream. The person who offers the integration makes it clear that he is trying to put together (orchestrate) what he heard the dreamer share with the group, but inasmuch as it is filtered through his own psyche it is likely to include some of his own fantasies and distortions. It is therefore offered as his own projection, and although not put as a question, it is meant as a question for the dreamer to respond to as he or she sees fit. When this is done well, it often adds a finishing touch to the process and brings about a closure that might not have occurred otherwise. The dreamer, of course, is given an opportunity to respond.

The dialogue is the part of the process that requires the most skill and the most experience. It also requires some advance preparation. Careful listening to all that has been shared is an essential precondition for formulating helpful questions in the dialogue. This is not easy to do. The group members have pretended that the dream was their own and often listen to the dreamer more in the hope of validating or developing their own ideas of what the dream means instead of paying full attention to all that the dreamer shares and the way he or she is connecting the dream to his or her life. Listening is a skill that has to be learned. It means taking seriously everything the dreamer says, particularly those things that are emphasized or said with feeling. It also involves listening to what the dreamer does not say, that is, elements in the dream the dreamer has not mentioned.

The questions directed to the dreamer should be simple, clear, and obvious. They should be information-eliciting questions and not used to offer information or an interpretation to the dreamer. The information embedded in the imagery has come out of the life history of the dreamer, not out of the lives of the group members. The questions are attempts to externalize this information. Once the relevant facts are brought out, the dreamer often is able to see their connection to the imagery.

By calling attention to elements in the dream not addressed by the dreamer the group assumes an advocacy role for the dream. This helps the dreamer to go beyond the waking tendency to stay with the most immediate and obvious connections that come to mind. Once the dreaming experience is transformed into the dream as a waking memory it is seen from a waking perspective, which often results in a limited and distorted view of the dream. There is a tendency to recognize and deal with those elements in the dream that fit most readily into the waking mood and to neglect other elements. The group's responsibility is to consider all of the elements in the dream and to ensure that they are all called to the dreamer's attention. The dreamer still retains the freedom to respond to the question or not. In practice questioning along these lines is helpful for someone who has already been launched on the road to self-discovery in Stage II. When the nonintrusive atmosphere is maintained in the question period, the dreamer's desire to get deeper into the dream is stronger than any tendency toward avoidance. It is up to the group to keep that curiosity alive without invading the dreamer's privacy. The group has to develop a sensitivity as to when a dreamer is inviting them in or out. They learn to follow, never to lead, the dreamer. The group must always remember that its mission is to close the gap between the dreamer awake and the dreamer asleep. The group is never to test its own interpretive ability or to deal with personal reactions experienced during the process. There are occasions when these reactions do intrude, in which case the leader stops the dream process and opens up a group process in order to deal with the issue. However, this is rare if the structure is adhered to. Group members are generally able to contain their own reactions.

The important point about the orchestration is that, to the extent possible, it should be based solely on data coming from the dreamer and not from the theories and fantasies of the person doing the orchestration. In this way it differs from the projections offered to the dreamer during Stage II. Although the orchestration remains a projection, it is built upon what the dreamer has shared with the group rather than what comes out of the psyche of the person offering it. It should not be taken as an opportunity for free play of the one doing the orchestration.

Sometimes there is the feeling that an orchestration is needed, but either the time has run out or the data appear too profuse and too complex to be put together at the time. When that is the case a delayed orchestration may be attempted. The data offered by the dreamer are reviewed some time after the group has met but before the next group meeting. A delayed orchestration can best be done if all the data from the dreamer are available. It is usually helpful to have that information available in written form. The procedure is the same as before, scanning the data to identify the context and the metaphorical relation of the data to the sequential arrangement of images in the dream. This is then offered to the dreamer at the next meeting as a projection and a question, as previously described. The dreamer is given time to respond if he or she so wishes.

The Safety Factor in Stage III. The safety factor rests on the dreamer's right to decide what to share or not to share in his or her initial response and later in the dialogue. When the dreamer is tempted to withold something too private to share, he or she must be reassured by the leader that he or she has the right to do so and need not feel guilty. The primary goal of the process is to help the dreamer connect to the dream. While the sharing is important, it always remains secondary. As experience with the process is gained it becomes apparent that the freer the dreamer is in sharing his or her reactions the more data the group members have to work with and the more helpful they can be.

The Discovery Factor in Stage III. The same mechanism operates here as in Stage I. As the dreamer responds, spontaneous connections and insights occur. Often in the questioning period a simple information-eliciting question—such as "What thoughts or feelings did you have just before falling asleep?"—can immediately alert the dreamer to a sense of why the dream occurred when it did. By the same token direct questions about elements in the dream not mentioned by the dreamer can elicit a flow of relevant information.

Stage IV: The Dreamer's Review of the Dream

The dreamer is encouraged to review the dream in light of the work done by the group before the next meeting. Alone, but having had the benefit of the group work, the dreamer may now find that some things he or she had rejected while in the group may not fit. By the same token, the dreamer may reject some things he or she thought did fit while with the group.

These four stages define the process. They are fashioned to meet the dreamer's need to feel safe while being helped to connect with his or her dream images. The process should be experienced as nonintrusive and respectful of the dreamer's privacy as well as his or her authority over the dream. By allowing a safe public airing of the dream, there is a release from much that was secret and burdensome, which results in a greater capacity for honest self-scrutiny and a deeper sense of communion with fellow dreamers.

Example

The following example of a workshop experience was chosen because it illustrates the four stages of the process and also refers to socially relevant issues. The dreamer, Else, is a Norwegian photographer in New York on an assignment. While here she had an affair with a black musician who worked in Harlem. The dream occurred toward the end of her stay in New York. The group, of course, was not privy to any of this information at the point when Else volunteered to share her dream.

Stage IA: Else's Dream. "There was a small pond of dirty brown water. It seemed to be connected with industrial waste or farming. I was passing it on my way somewhere. There was a man bathing in the pond. To me he seemed white. He is drunk. There are others with him. It's a kind of party. They are all drunk. A voluptuous woman is also in the pond bathing. She is very white and naked. The man dives down. He doesn't come up. I know he has drowned. The woman tries to find him.

"I have almost passed by as this was happening. The thought came to me that perhaps I should go back and try to rescue him but I don't.

"Then one day later someone who I think is my mother or secretary phones the drowned man's mother on my behalf to offer my condolences. Then I see that his mother is black, an African, so at this point I realize the man was black. His mother is dressed like an African. She has a lot of people around her and says she doesn't need my condolences."

Stage IB. The following additional information came out in the questioning:

1. In the dream no one was recognized except for the possibility it was Else's mother who made the phone call.

2. At some point in the dream she realized there was shit in the pond.

3. It was dark as if the scene were taking place at night.

Stage IIA. The group made the dream their own and shared the following feelings evoked by the imagery:

"I have a feeling of dissipation and disgust at that drunken party and the dirty pond."

"I feel as though I'm denying something, as though I don't want to have anything to do with it."

"The feelings I have are those of confusion, disease, and death."

"I have an innocent feeling. I'm just passing by. There is a feeling of detachment."

"I feel ambivalent. I feel distant but involved."

"I feel powerless."

"A feeling of degredation."

"It leaves me with a feeling of foreigness."

"His mother makes me feel rejected."

Stage IIB. The group then considered the metaphorical possibilities of the images. Some of what they came up with follows:

"The woman is voluptuous. I'm expressing something both sexual and motherly."

"I feel self-righteous."

"There is a triangle in my dream arousing envy and jealousy. She can't save him but is willing to endure horrible things to be with him."

"The scene suggests an orgy."

"There is a sense of something going on on a large scale, a feeling of excesses."

"Work and nature converge and result in contamination."

"My feelings about the man change completely."

"Women dominate in my dream, first the voluptuous woman, then the mother."

"I have problems around a black man I'm going with."

"In the kind of bathing I'm doing it's the opposite of cleansing."

"Industrial waste is something occurring on a large scale and is toxic. There is a lack of caring as evidenced by the drunkenness and the shit."

"I'm not a part of his world."

"The women have the strength."

Stage III: The Dreamer's Response. The dream was given back to the dreamer and her response invited:

"I got lots of new ideas. I felt a lot while you were talking. I still can't put it together.

"When I went to sleep I felt very relieved. I had made a decision. My boyfriend here is black. I'm doing a photographic piece on Harlem. I sent a first draft to my agent and he was critical. I thought of trying another approach and started to do some preparation for it, but then the thought occurred to me that maybe I should just not do it. I felt so relieved.

"I didn't want to deal with half-truths in the article. That would be to betray by boyfriend. His life is rough right now. Perhaps I can't help him. I'm realizing more and more how different we are. I can't reach him."

Stage III: The Dialogue. It was evident that beginning contact with the dream had been made, but there was more work to be done. The work was carried further through the dialogue that ensued.

Why the voluptuous woman?
"I'm sure it was me. She is shining white there in the moonlight. I'm sure he finds me attractive. She is the Madonna and the Whore."

What were your last thoughts as you were about to fall asleep?
"I had a fantasy conversation with my boyfriend. I feel he is in deep trouble."

The scene at the pond?
"It was of Norwegian nature. It feels like where I grew up. I connect the pond to a well that was there. The water was brown and dirty. As a child I was scared of falling into it. There was a bull roaming around there that also scared me. I was afraid the bull might push me down the well."

Else volunteered more about the woman:
"The woman is the feminine part of me that I thought could help him. The dream tells me this is not so. Even with my femininity, I can't help him. And, do I really want to help him?"

Why the shitty water?
"I love New York but there are also ponds full of shit. I drink too much in New York."

Else went back to the image of herself walking away.
"It's really so simple. I'm walking away as if I'm just looking. That's what I do. I go places and do things but *I'm just looking*. It's been my whole life. On my tombstone they'll put: 'No thank you, I'm just looking' like I always say to the salesgirl at Bloomingdales."

Why is his mother in the dream?

"I have been in Africa. African women do all the work—they are strong."

Why is your mother in the dream?

"I would like her to help me. It would be good to have a mother who could help, an archetypal kind of mother."

Stage III: Orchestration. The session ended here with a partial sense of closure about the dream and an awareness of the connection of the feeling of relief, which came not only from her deciding to give up the idea of the piece she had set out to do but, more significantly, her awareness of the limitations in relation to her boyfriend and her inability to rescue him. With all that Else had shared spontaneously and all that came out in the dialogue there was a sense that more could be done with the dream if more time had been available. Under these circumstances a "delayed" orchestration can be attempted. It simply is an effort to bring together the highlights of what the dreamer shared in the group with the possible metaphorical meaning of the images and the sequential development of these images in the dream. Else left for Norway shortly after she presented the dream, so there was no opportunity to share any afterthoughts with her in person.

I reviewed the work that had been done on the dream, developed some additional ideas about the imagery, and mailed them to Else, indicating that they represented an orchestrating projection on my part and were being addressed to her as a question. I invited her to share any further thoughts she might have had about the dream. Briefly, I suggested that the two situations she was in (with regard to the article and her boyfriend) reawakened the feeling of helplessness and terror she experienced as a child in relation to the bull and the well. The dream brought home the growing realization that her boyfriend was drowning in the "shit" that goes on in New York City. There is the powerful statement in the dream that the man, displaced from his roots, symbolized by the archetypal black mother, becomes a lost soul. The dream ends with a sharper realization of the difference between them, a difference as sharp and unchangeable as the color of their skin.

Stage IV: Else's Additional Commentary. Else responded by mail:

"When I look back at that dream now, I see a few things more clearly than when it was new.

1. That dream marked a new phase in my relationship with Dave, my separation from him. From that day on, I started separating from him.

Before, I (the white female) had willingly joined in all his shit. I loved him and wanted to be with him. But in that dream I (the integrated me) passed by, worried and caring, but still passing by. There is nothing I can do but choose another life for myself.

2. Also, this dream made me realize other things. I can very well understand his reasons for not being nice (when he isn't) and also that he, in his own way, loves me and fights for us. But to understand is *not* to forgive and put up with. This I have lately realized. He cannot hurt me any longer. I am not mad at him. I just go away from him because he cannot give me the minimum I need in a relationship. And no one, for no reason, is allowed to treat me the way he does when I am needy and dependent.

3. The whole black and white story . . . In the dream his mother makes me realize that he is black and that she and the other black people don't need my condolences. Part of his not trusting me is because he doesn't trust women, but also that he doesn't trust whites. He never said so, but I am by now pretty sure that is the case. It makes me so depressed to see how much of our relationship has been a power struggle in which he cannot see my reality and deal with it; he sees only my strength. Male friends are what he relies on.

"My experience is that a relationship between whites and blacks is no problem as long as it is kept on a superficial level. It was wonderful for me with Dave in those little moments of love we were *united*. But as soon as we were in ordinary life, facing ordinary conflicts, the whole history—the slave trade, the Civil War, ghettoes, and the Third World stepped in between us. And the myths . . . but also, I am sure that with more time and money we could have worked things out."

The dreamwork led Else to a gradual unfolding of awareness into both the personal and the social meanings of the images. It exposed the fabric of her relationship with a black man, the problems posed by cultural differences, the problems she brought to the relationship (her "on-looker" mode of existence), and the social and historical roots of the problems he presented. The dream was triggered by events in the present. Having made a decision in one area (in relation to her job assignment), there was a readiness to make a decision in another, a readiness that hadn't been grasped in waking consciousness but that had surfaced during sleep to shape the dream. It was as if she were awakening to the fact that she could make decisions that were to her own best interest even though they might conflict with the expectations of others.

Once the decision had been clarified through the group work, many other things fell into place. The decision felt right and the reasons for it became clearer.

Else had little idea of the significance of the dream prior to the group work. Many of the group's projections touched her and made it easier for her to move into the dream.

In typical fashion the dream evoked childhood memories—the little girl and the bull, the contaminated well and the danger associated with it—memories related to the dangers facing her in the current relationship. She can now deal with the dangers through a deeper understanding of herself (she is no longer a helpless child facing the bull) and of her lover (his inability to extricate himself from the grip of historically and socially polluted circumstances).

Using Else's dream as an example, we may point to several images that have both significant personal and social referents. The black man drowning in polluted water represents a specific man in a specific relationship, but he also has a generic character. He is a member of a minority that has had a long history of persecution. There are still aftershocks of racism that continue to take a toll, a toll that can be disastrous at times. The image is there as a bridge, saying something about the personal reference to the social. Else was not just involved with a man, but with a black man in the Harlem ghetto, and the fear being expressed is that the cultural differences between them are contaminated by the toxic residues of racism.

In the dream there is also the combined image of the Madonna and the Whore and the broader social ramifications of such an image. It points to a personal and a social polarity. The Madonna is the ideal, pure nurturer. The Whore is the plaything, the pleasure-seeker living for the moment. The integration of these two polar opposites is not just the problem of the dreamer. To a greater or lesser degree, it is a problem of all women living in the twentieth century.

Here are some further brief examples of how social issues interdigitate with personal ones. Each plays into the other in a mutually reinforcing way.

Example

A young lawyer works for a prestigious law firm that handles large and powerful business accounts. Influenced in part by his wife, he has been moving toward a life-style quite different from his colleagues. In his own words, he is "trying to change from a left-brain creature to a right-brain one." During a recent sabbatical he became more and more disenchanted with his way of life and was drawn to a freer, more satisfying life-style, one not oriented toward increasing returns of status and money.

At the time of the dream he had just returned from his sabbatical and was more poignantly aware of his plight. He referred to the "golden handcuffs" tying him to the job being more evident.

The imagery of the dream evoked a painful childhood memory of an old injury, a deep cut on his cheek that came about because of his mother's carelessness. As a child he felt this was punishment for something bad he had done. Looking back at it, he felt the "bad" was the anger he felt toward his mother but couldn't express. One image in the dream reflected his displaced anger from his mother to his wife. In the dream he can't get his wife to do what he wants and ends up hurling two empty breadbaskets at her. They miss her but hit another woman (later identified as his mother) who was dining at their house.

Later in the dream he becomes aware that this woman has an evil-looking child who is holding a knife. He says to the boy, "That's dangerous. When I was a boy I got this bad cut on my right cheek, and now I have this big scar." The boy then points the knife at the dreamer's left cheek, and the dreamer jumps back in terror. Once again, but now as an adult, he would risk serious, perhaps life-threatening injury were he to buck the establishment.

Example

A woman in her late thirties is about to embark on a new relationship. She senses some hesitancy on her part and has a dream that displays some of the roots of her ambivalence. At one point in the dream she sees her father sitting on a swing with four female relatives, all in their heyday, dressed almost like cancan girls. What emerged from the dreamwork were two powerful images that surfaced from her childhood to influence her approach to a new relationship. One was that of the male, derived from the image of her father, as privileged to flirt and play around with other women. The other image was that of the female as victimized by the profligate male, as her mother was. These are images that she is still struggling with. In a larger sense they relate to the residues of sexism, a social issue not yet disposed. The privileged male and the victimized female are still available social stereotypes.

Example

The next dream also involves sexual stereotypes. The two significant images in the dream related to this are the image of a wounded bird unable to join the flock in flight that is picked on by a group of arrogant pheasants. The second image is one of a contractor who, in reality, is involved in remodeling her home. In the dream he tells the dreamer that he can't close off the basement for repairs without, at the same time, closing off the upstairs bedroom. What became clear from the dreamwork was that there was an unresolved tension between her husband and herself. The dreamer had recently gone into therapy to deal with her problems. What the dream seemed to be saying was that the focus couldn't be exclusively on her own problems but that she would have to confront the issues in her relationship with her husband at the same time. The vulnerable areas are those that arose from her own submissive and self-deprecatory tendencies and inclination to accept her husband as the stronger and dominant one. The pheasants who picked on the wounded bird were a string of older brothers in relation to whom these trends evolved. Again, we are seeing the personal impact of social stereotypes that support the notion of male dominance.

Example

A young woman, in the throes of feeling grown up and separate from her parents, dreams of wearing the kind of chic clothes that would appeal to her mother but which she feels don't suit her. In the dream she had put them on because her parents were coming to visit. The dreamwork explored the feeling of not being accepted for herself but only to the extent that she accepted her parent's values. The generational gap goes beyond the personal issue and speaks to the more general issue of the extent to which an older generation is out of touch with the values of the young.

Example

In Sweden, perhaps more so than in the States, there is considerable social pressure for a woman to pursue the dual roles of career professional and homemaker. A young Swedish social worker dreams of her one-year-old child falling off the back of a motorcycle and responds first with terror that he might be hurt. Then, finding that he was not seriously hurt, gets furious with her husband who was driving the motorcycle. The dreamer found it increasingly difficult to leave her young infant at eight in the morning and not see him again until she returned in the evening. She was particularly aware of this the day before the dream. "I felt like the worst mother in the world." The dream also portrayed her annoyance at her husband for not being as upset about this as she is. There doesn't seem to be enough room for women who want to be with their children at home for the first few years of their life. The social pressure to have an independent existence is too great.

Social Issues and Dreaming

Dreams tap into unsolved problems of living, and our first task is to rescue our dream life from the personal closeted existence to which it would otherwise be relegated. I would suggest that we go beyond this to develop a point of view that links the dream not only to our personal life but also to the way we cope with the social order of which we are an integral part. The individual is a point of concentration in a complicated arrangement of social forces, most of which operate outside his awareness and, to a considerable degree, beyond his control or understanding. They do, however, leave their mark, which is often at odds with the constructive potential of human nature.

There is a built-in connection of some sort between dream images and the fact that people participate in a complex social drama that goes on about them, with each person playing a role in it. There is, however, no simple ordered way of relating social issues to dreaming consciousness. The images we use have a social origin, having been created during humanity's long struggle to evolve as a social being. The dreamer borrows these images and then reshapes them to suit his immediate expressive needs. In the examples, we have noted a congruence between the way a dreamer uses a particular image and the existence of related problem areas in a broader social context. This relationship is generally not pursued in dream work. Cultural anthropologists have looked at dreams as mirroring aspects of primitive societies. But we have hardly begun to scrutinize the influence of our own social order on dream images. Were we to do so, I believe that interesting relationships would emerge.

A dream can express not only the personal and subjective but also the historical or current social referent that actually exists or did exist. The following example from Ullman (1960) is illustrative.

When a woman dreams of a reference to her sexual organs as a head of lettuce encased in the empty shell of a cantaloupe sitting on the shelf of a supermarket she is saying something about her own personal sexual problems and, at the same time, making a statement about an aspect of social life. The personal referents arouse our interest, but the social referents are generally not pursued to any great degree. Briefly, the personal referents are:

1. Sexual organs are seen as separate from her functioning self.
2. Sexual organs are seen as objects.
3. The object is made of completely closed leaves.
4. The object can be bought and sold.
5. There is an anonymity to objects on the shelf of a market.

The real-life situation to which this symbolism alludes may be noted as follows:

1. Involvement in a situation of incipient sexual activity that occurs apart from her own will and intent and at the instigation of her husband.
2. Reactions of irritation, guilt, and constraint.
3. A resolution through pseudo-acquiescence and preparatory sexual activity involving the use of a diaphragm.

The social referents may be similarly noted:

1. We live in a society where the capacities of people are sometimes treated as objects divorced from the person: labor, brains, beauty, talent, sex.
2. These separated capacities are bought and sold.
3. The exchange value and laws of the marketplace tend to make the transaction automatic and impersonal.
4. There exists in the nature of the external referents a detachment or separation of the individual from the commodity she needs or uses. Her real relation to the commodity is obscured and her relationship to it is determined by its manifest elements—the object exists as something apart from herself which may or may not be purchased.*

These external or social referents are not only of theoretical interest. They play a powerful role in maintaining a behavioral status quo. A dream may expose a particular behavioral trend that the dreamer may wish to change. He or she finds that change is not easy and is pulled back not only by the weight of his or her own past experiences but also by the external reinforcement that is always on hand in the surrounding social milieu. Stated another way, the trend pays off, that is, it has pragmatic value in a society that bathes and nurtures that particular behavior.

---

*From Ullman, M., "The Social Roots of the Dream," in the *American Journal of Psychoanalysis* 20(2): 1960, 187–88. Reprinted with the permission of the *American Journal of Psychoanalysis*.

In order to understand the possible connection between social forces and our dream life, we have to map our efforts along at least four dimensions:

1. What we know about our own life history, the kind of person we see ourselves as—our *personal consciousness*.

2. All that we do not know about our idiosyncratic life history and its impact on us—our *personal unconscious*.

3. What we know about the nature and operation of the world about us—our *social consciousness*.

4. All that we don't know about the laws and operations of the social system of which we are a part—our *social unconscious*.

Although these categories can be discretely defined, in practice there is much blurring and overlap. What it comes down to is that we know and don't know certain things about ourselves and the world about us. Growth is contingent upon experience that exposes areas of ignorance in either the personal or social sphere, providing we are ready for the changes that have to be made. Anxiety and other uncomfortable feelings arise when unconscious areas are intruded upon or gaps in our mastery are exposed. When we feel unable to deal with the issues raised by the gap, we try to brush it aside, deal with it in fantasy, or seek other solutions. Our dreams reflect whichever path we choose. What we come up with may be the precursor to a healthy solution or may represent an attempt to sidestep a healthy solution.

Discussion

In these examples I have tried to show that the private issue highlighted in the dream gains expression by attracting images that are taken from social experience and carry a congruent social valence. This generally escapes notice because we are not in the habit of extrapolating from the image to the social reality that lies beyond. Driving a car in a dream may deal with the paradoxical issue of personal power and control linked to the problem of dependency. At a social level the auto is a mixed blessing, linking us to a source of pollution while expanding our power of movement. This would simply be the surface thread which, if unravelled, might take us further into the world of giant corporations and their powerful impact on our environment and our lives.

As far as I know, there are no socially sanctioned, legitimate strategies for discovering our social unconscious. The reason is that exposure of our social unconscious would reveal the damage we pay in human terms for our social blindness. Nevertheless, a variety of approaches address themselves to the social unconscious, ranging from the pedantically scientific to the radically political. Some are to be found in scholarly treatises with little public fallout. Some of it is heralded by countercultural and progressive movements of one sort or another. Dreams are the only universally experienced phenomena that are linked actively each night to our social as well as our personal unconscious. Since they come at us as if they were purely personal, their social message, meaning, and impact are generally lost.

One might ask how these social factors can influence the dreams of people who are neither interested nor concerned about them. The fact is that they do impinge on our daily lives. Our personal interest and concern is relevant only to our consciousness of this influence, not to its occurrence. Most of us are dimly aware of the connection between toxins in the environment and cancer. The toxic fallout is becoming more and more palpable with measurable effects. If human misery were as easily identified and as objectionable as environmental pollution, then the emotional fallout consequent to the organization and evolution of particular aspects of our society would come back to haunt us in an oppressive way. This tends not to happen unless the conflict flares into the open. Then the emotional toxins, no longer containable, break out. Anyone who has ever witnessed a social crisis can bear witness to the speed and intensity with which violent feelings escalate out of all proportion to the issues involved. Only then does the emotional disorder become evident as a social problem. Something that has registered below the level of awareness congeals into consciousness.

The issues involved in social and political causes go far beyond the immediate participants of the drama to effect the lives of us all. For the most part, we live as if this were not so. That is why so many of us have an undeveloped sense of social consciousness, or conversely, huge unexplored areas of social unconsciousness. Interest in these areas is actively discouraged. Our feelings, however, can't be turned off, and these indicators surface time and again to make their presence felt in our dreams. In so doing they register the only form of protest that may be available to us.

Thus the dream makes us "political scientists of a progressive persuasion" if only we knew that it did. We become our own commentators of the social scene.

Coda

Our emphasis has been on dreamwork as a socializing process wherein the emotional thrust of the dream is recognized by the waking or social self. This process of engagement with feelings in a supportive and cooperative milieu makes for change. While the personal problems don't vanish, they are restructured to encompass the newly recognized aspects of the self more accurately. Created under conditions of the temporary suspension of the social self, the dream has been transformed into a communication that is meaningful to the social self. The process is difficult, uneven, troublesome, but infinitely rewarding. It is more than the negative process of ferreting out personal foibles and hypocrisies. It becomes a treasure hunt where one can discover an unsuspected quarry of human virtues. Our capacities for concern, courage, tenderness, and similar qualities confront us in our dreams, waiting to be recognized and validated by our social self. Paradoxically, often our unawareness of the existence and strength of these virtues serves to perpetuate the very myths that get us into psychological and emotional difficulty.

Using the notion of myth in the sense of a false or outworn belief system, our dreams can then be regarded as holding up a mirror that gives us a view of our personal myth-making propensity and talent. If we look deeply enough into the mirror, we can identify the sources of our personal myths in the prevailing social myths that continue to obscure certain aspects of society at large.

We have raised the question of the potential of dreamwork to get a deeper insight into the social scene and for social change. Dreams have been presented as bidirectional, pointing not only to still active issues in the life of the dreamer but also to still unresolved social issues. We further suggest that the relationship between the personal and the social is a mutually reinforcing one based on the congruence between prevailing social values and the meaning of the image for the dreamer.

We exist in a state of tension with a supraordinate system of social sanctions and constraints with which we cope as best we can, given our unique psychological endowment and history. Our uniquesness is the product of, and expressed through, the collective social forces that continuously impinge upon us. The dreamer pauses nightly to assess these influences, particularly in regard to their capacity to upset any preexisting equilibrium. We can seek help from others in searching for individual answers. Who can we take as a guide into the infinitely more complex and tangled underbrush of the social unconscious? Who but our own uncorrupted core of being, that part of us that can still invest in honesty? Fortunately, the dream is a kind of emotional range finder that locates this uncorrupted core in the sea of those influences, good and bad, known and unknown, that impinge on it. This is what makes their pursuit more than a game and more meaningful than fantasy.

It is my hope that a reexamination of the nature of our dream life and its importance to us will pave the way to the recognition that dreams can be more universally accessible and that the technology exists for placing dreamwork in the hands of the public. The skills needed can be identified, shared, and learned. It is to the interest of all of us to close the gap between the intrinsic value of dreamwork and the value accorded it in the social system.

Let me close with a quote from an earlier work:

> The technical skills needed to deal with dreams can be readily taught. One need only identify, refine, and help conceptualize certain intuitive faculties. At a time when expanded self-awareness seems to be the order of the day one wonders why the natural route of dream appreciation is not more popular. I would suggest that the socially reinforced privacy of the dream is not fortuitous and that our analysis of the objective and subjective sides of the dream may have some relevance here. As long as nothing of importance is allowed to find its way back to society *from the dream* the individual is left to his own devices and has no choice but to absorb its mysteries within his own personal consciousness or unconsciousness. No room is left for any challenge to the social order. There is room only for personal demons and the transformation of social demons into personal ones. Dream consciousness may indeed pose a danger to any bureaucratic or technologically supercharged society.*

References

Delaney, G. (1988). *Living Your Dreams*. New York: Harper and Row.

———. (1991). *Breakthrough Dreaming: How to Tap the Power of Your 24-hour mind*. New York: Bantam.

Faraday, A. (1974). *The Dream Game*. New York: Harper and Row.

———. (1979). *Dream Power*. New York: Berkely.

---

*From Ullman, M., "The Societal Factors in Dreaming," in *Contemporary Psychoanalysis* 9(3): 1973, 292. Reprinted with the permission of *Contemporary Psychoanalysis* (journal of the William Alanson White Institute and the William Alanson White Psychoanalytic Society, New York).

Krippner, S. and Dillard, J. (1988). *Dream Working*. Buffalo: Bearly Limited.

Sanford, J. (1968). *Dreams—God's Forgotten Language*. Philadelphia: Lippincott.

Taylor, J. (1983). *Dream Work*. New York: Paulist Press.

Ullman, M. (1960). The Social Roots of the Dream, *American Journal of Psychoanalysis* 20 (2): 187–88.

————. (1973). The Societal Factors in Dreaming, *Contemporary Psychoanalysis* 9 (3): 292.

Ullman, M., and Zimmerman, N. (1979). *Working With Dreams*. Los Angeles: Tarcher, J. P.

Ullman, M., and Limmer, C., eds. (1988). *The Variety of Dream Experience*. New York: Continuum.

2

Joseph M. Natterson ████████████████████

Dreams: The Gateway to Consciousness

The Central Position of Dreams in Psychotherapy

Dreams are situated near the very center of psychological activity. They are at once the most intimately revealing and the most cosmically expressive of psychological events. In his book titled *The Innocence of Dreams*, Charles Rycroft (1979) captures the naïve, ingenuous, uncalculated, even foolish revelation of self for which dreams are so valued by therapists. Of course, these qualities are usually more or less disguised in dreams, but when the disguise is penetrated, meanings of great power are exposed. In fact, dreams are often the most reliable and sensitive barometer of therapeutic action. Many times, the fact that the patient is reporting dreams informs me that the patient is appropriately engaged.

Some patients do good therapeutic work without bringing in dreams, but such therapy lacks the texture and ideational content provided by dreams. Therapy conducted nonintensively is more likely to be a therapy without dreams. However, many people work with dreams quite effectively in once-per-week psychotherapy. When no dreams are reported, the therapy is more likely to proceed without the idiosyncratic data provided by unconscious dream imagery. Thus, such therapy, while it may be very effective, may nevertheless lack the richness of themes and the clarity of problem definition that would be achieved through working with dreams. Such dreamless therapy tends to be relatively inelegant.

Conversely, some patients report dreams but are unable to work with their dreams. Such patients probably have magical expectations but no effective interest or motivation. They do not try to struggle with the meaning of their dreams. In general, those who do not report or work with their dreams are those who resist the hard work of therapy.

In a preliminary study, Cartwright and coworkers (1980) have found that prospective patients of types traditionally refractory to psychotherapy who are helped to recall their dreams in a dream laboratory tend to be more successful in their psychotherapy than similar patients who are not helped to recall their dreams.

Freud's assertion that dreams are the royal road to the unconscious certainly points to the centrality of dreams in therapy which is geared to the discovery of hitherto unrecognized truths. And it follows, then, that dreams are crucial to self-discovery, self-definition, and self-transformation, which are the legitimate goals of psychoanalytic psychotherapy.

A Review of the Classical Approach to Dreams

The Freudian position on the nature and meaning as well as the technical approach to dreams lends itself to a clear, internally consistent, and heuristically valuable exposition. This set of concepts can be presented with relative simplicity or with extensive elaboration. The present rendition inclines toward the former.

Freud developed the classical position, and its fullest enunciation occurred in *The Interpretation of Dreams* (1900). Certain fundamental assumptions are made. Human motivation always, ultimately, rests on a biological base. The biological processes produce instincts or drives. These, in turn, produce drive derivatives that are the psychological expression of the underlying instinctual drives. These drive derivatives consist of wishes whose obvious purpose is to direct the human animal to behavior that will permit the discharge of energy which otherwise accumulates within the organism, producing discomfort. This mounting discomfort pushes the individual into behaviors intended to relieve instinctual pressure.

These instinctual drives are essentially sexual and aggressive and consequently seem dangerous, base, and sinful to the conventional consciousness of most people. This circumstance requires that the base, and basic, wishes be repressed. The relentless pressure for expression against these repressive forces produces neurotic symptoms that are compromise formations, emerging from the clash of the basic instinctually derived wish and the secondary conventional conscious (and unconscious) repressive efforts. Originally, Freud employed a so-called topographic model, which essentially meant that the elemental wishes were pushing to emerge from the unconscious. The conscious found such wishes unacceptable, and a censor functioned to repress the unacceptable urges. This censor derived from unconscious guilt.

Later, Freud refined this formulation by dividing the psychic apparatus into three parts: (1) the id, which is the entirely unconscious repository of the instinctual wishes and the original matrix from which the other two parts of the psychic apparatus emerged; (2) the ego, partly conscious and partly unconscious, which serves the reality needs of the individual and is therefore continuously in conflict with the primitive drive derivatives emanating from the id; and (3) the superego, which is unconscious, affiliated with the ego's conflict with the id, but which paradoxically gains some of its power from the instinctual drives. Sometimes the superego is at war with the ego.

Not only are neurotic symptoms compromise formations resulting from the conflicts among these colliding parts of the person, but dreams are the sleeping version of the same process. During sleep the ego and superego regress and relax, and the repressive forces are correspondingly reduced. The instinctual forces therefore impinge more effectively on the barriers to consciousness. But the repressive forces, although diminished, retain some force.

Unacceptable wishes, the psychological derivatives of the instinctual drives, are more likely to become conscious, but the repressive forces retain enough power to cause these ideas to become manifest in a distorted or disguised form. This manifest content constitutes the compromise formation.

Since, according to Freud, the dream's primary purpose is the preservation of sleep, a dream has failed psychobiologically if the dream becomes flooded with anxiety and the dreamer awakens. This anxiety arises if the dream disguise is insufficient to deceive either the ego, which recognizes a real danger inherent in the wish, or the superego, whose moral standards are threatened, producing moral anxiety.

The production of a dream requires four major functions of the mind: symbolization, displacement, condensation, and secondary revision. These functions occur unconsciously, and they partake mainly of what Freud termed "primary process thinking." This would be true of displacement and condensation, both of which signify unusual motility of wishes, rendering them more likely to violate shamelessly the rules of conscious common sense and logic, known as secondary process. Symbolization, however, has an affinity to creative functions such as sublimation and cannot be seen simply as a variety of primary process thinking. And similarly, secondary revision is similar to the editorial work on an unpolished first draft and therefore also has qualities of secondary process thinking.

Freud recognized the existence of universal symbols appearing in dreams, and he also acknowledged the existence of typical dreams, such as dreams of flying, falling, being naked, losing teeth, or taking an examination for which one is unprepared. He also ventured general explanations of the meanings of such symbols and dreams. But he was ambivalent about these, and he inveighed strongly against interpreting dreams as though one were preparing a meal by strictly following instructions in a cookbook.

Instead, Freud insisted that free association is the correct method for discovering the important latent thoughts, ideas, and wishes situated beneath the manifest content, which is mainly a disguising façade. In free association, the dreamer starts with the dream as a whole, or any of its component parts, and lets his or her thoughts proceed, unguided by conscious control. The dreamer, if in analysis, utters aloud these seemingly anarchic and chaotic thoughts so that the analyst may also know them. If attended to carefully, patiently, and nontendentiously, these free associations eventually lead the analyst to at least an approximation of the unconscious wish-ideas that are contained but concealed within the dream. This understanding becomes the basis of the analyst's interpretation to the analysand.

In an authoritative paper, Rangell (1987) points out that the Freudian theory of dreams has required only minor changes over the years. Because of "the immensity of Freud's initial accomplishment new formulations were hardly necessary but were already mostly contained in the original."

Various questions about the Freudian theory of dreams frequently arise. Some will be considered here. As far as I know, none can be answered confidently on the basis of objective evidence, so my answers are perforce speculative.

First, are all dreams expressions of wish fulfillment? No one really knows. However, sensitive and effective therapists do know that it is a serious error to think about a dream with a primary determination to uncover the presumed unconscious wish. The first principle is for the therapist to be open to the dream, the dreamer, and the associations. Preoccupation with wishes in the clinical situation is tendentious and inevitably distorting.

If one chooses to think of a dream as a wish fulfillment, it is wise to defer the effort until after one has listened to the dream and the associations as open-mindedly as possible. From this, one's ideas about the dream are generated. At this point, it may become profitable to formulate the meaning of the dream in terms of a wish or wishes, manifest or latent.

Another important question is whether dreams are always disguised, and therefore, do the basic meanings of dreams always reside in the latent content? The answer here has to be both no and yes. No, because frequently many dream meanings are quite evident in the manifest content. However, manifest and latent are relative rather than absolute terms. To a person who has spent much time studying dreams and symbols, who is addicted to puns and double meanings, who is accustomed to noticing paraverbal as well as verbal communications, access to dream meanings will be much richer and easier than for other people who are much less sophisticated about such matters. So, a dream meaning that is initially inaccessible, that is, latent, for one person, may be quite readily apparent, that is, manifest, to another.

I think of degrees of latency or manifestness varying from dream to dream and from dreamer to dreamer. Freud referred to *manifest* content and *latent content*, whereas more recent thought tends toward *manifest* meaning and *latent meaning*. Breger (1980) has explored the important distinctions between the two concepts. He emphasizes that the dream meaning is established through the exploratory and the interpretive processes rather than resting in a preformed state in the dreamer's unconscious. Another important modification with regard to latent meanings has occurred. Latency of meaning may not necessarily be an exclusive function of repression. Psychobiological function while dreaming is qualitatively different than when the person is awake. Symbolic portrayal in dreams sometimes expresses the mind's activity without any repressing or disguising function. Spanjaard (1969) demonstrated that in Freud's illustrative dreams the issues being dealt with were actually expressed in the manifest dream.

It follows, then, that we should question Freud's insistence that the only creative thinking in dreams was directed to the construction of the dream itself. Dream thinking is different from waking thinking. However, it is no less creative than waking thought.

Another frequent question is whether dreams function as guardians of sleep. Freud believed so. This is a psychobiological question, and the definitive answer will have to come from that field. Personally, I doubt this is a major dream function. It is more appealing to me that dreaming occurs nightly to organize and situate the individual's experiences of the preceding day in that individual's hierarchy of memories. This function, in turn, would cause me to concur with Freud's impression that dreams always incorporate the preceding day's residue.

Finally, do dreams always deal with sex? This question is usually based on simplistic premises, and therefore, it probably deserves the equally simplistic answer: No! Usually, the question represents a thinly disguised criticism of Freud as being neurotically preoccupied with sex.

It is true that his libido theory accorded great importance to the sexual drive, but he did not regard sex as the exclusive motive force in human affairs. Furthermore, Freud's elaborate and masterful investigations of dreams shows that he was fully aware of the infinite richness of motives that drive human behavior.

General Attitudes toward Dreams

Informality and serious interest without authoritarian trappings are prominent elements in my interactions with patients. I try to convey the attitude that we are engaged in a joint enterprise, that I do not consider my patients sick or myself healthy, and that we all have times of trouble when it is necessary to have some help. This attitude of understanding and acceptance facilitates serious communication and dispels defensive compliance in many people. Others may be driven away by this stance. Such persons require more formality in the therapeutic environment and a more authoritative and formal role by the therapist. While such patients may, at a later time, develop a capacity for dreamwork, they must first resolve the defense requirements of this early stage. The more willing a patient is to assume responsibility for the progress of treatment, the more ready he or she is to work productively with dreams.

Does the patient translate the pain and suffering of life into a personal idiom (such as a dream) and thereby show a readiness to look at difficulties from an intrapsychic standpoint? Such a patient will produce and analyze dreams. Patients who are not thus oriented will have difficulty remembering and working with dreams. They are deeply defended against psychological intimacy and meaning. They require protection more than insight, and they regard the inevitable element of pain in interpretation as a cruel and unbearable attack.

With patients for whom an exploratory approach is suitable, "superficiality" or "depth" of communication is not the main point. The terms "depth" and "superficiality" are confusing. They denote both the degree of importance of a psychological phenomenon as well as its topographical location in the mind. The primary consideration is whether an important psychological truth of the person's life has become available for useful discussion, not whether it is deep or superficial.

It is remarkable how rapidly it becomes possible to discuss matters of surpassing intimacy without particular attention to the question of depth. A new patient reported several dreams in her second session with me. One of these dreams portrayed me in a sexual scene in which I was both insensitive and promiscuous. We employed the dreams to begin defining some of her important life issues. No serious question arose as to whether we were moving too quickly. I did silently speculate that the patient might be aware of my special interest in dreams, and I did ask whether any important life situations were being neglected in order to attend to the dreams. She and I both agreed that, instead, the dreams provided an avenue for reflection of her reality problems within the therapeutic relationship and that they thus facilitated the approach to her crucial concerns.

One of the great values of dreams lies in their portrayal of life problems in metaphorical form. Dreams are at their very best when this representation of basic life issues is accomplished in the context of the therapeutic relationship. Such very quickly became the case in this therapy. If a therapist is unduly focused on depth of repression, that is, how deeply buried a conflictual issue is, valuable therapeutic opportunities may be missed. The patient and I did not consider that discussion of her sexual, distrustful, and critical feelings to me were too "deep" for consideration in her second session, and we were correct.

Obviously, dreams do not function according to some marvelous principle of optimal comfort. Dreams may move faster than therapy. Here, a judicious therapist can use the depth concept advantageously. He or she may estimate that the issue is very deeply repressed, that it is "too hot to handle" at this time, even though the theme is revealed to the therapist via the dream. The therapist relies upon the therapeutic context and is guided to a large extent by the patient's associations. The dream, then, will be noted, and, if necessary, can be revisited in a month or a year. The therapist is best insured against using dreams for premature entry into supercharged areas by consistent viewing of the dream in the context of the total therapeutic situation rather than as an event occurring in splendid isolation.

What changes are likely to occur in the therapist's attitude toward a particular patient's dreams as the therapy progresses? I usually listen to early dreams with great enthusiasm. Many times I believe that I have discovered a profound insight in the dreams. But equally often, my understanding seems very limited, and I feel that the basic truths of the dream elude me. These early partial failures of discovery alert me to the possibility of my future disenchantment when the initial promise of very early dreams is not fulfilled. The therapist, I believe, regards the early reporting of dreams as a promise of trust, exuberant collaboration, and powerful revelation. As in the early excitement of love, the negative potentials are minimized. So it is a fortunate therapist who can perceive the early strands of ambivalence and weave them into the interpretive fabric.

A therapist's response to the patient's dreams should consist of interest, with a slight tension of uncertainty in a general climate of ease and receptiveness. If the patient's dream induces boredom, inattention, or worry over being unable to understand, then the therapist should be alerted to a substantial problem in the basic therapeutic situation. This can be described as a barometric function. The nature of the therapist's experience of the patient's dream is as satisfactory an indicator of the vitality of the therapeutic situation as any that I know.

Early Dreams

Several possibilities should be considered when a patient presents a dream very early in therapy. First, the patient may be bursting with the dream, recognizing its critical importance, as in the case of the woman who brought in a dream about me in the second session. This woman knows she is troubled. She has a number of specific problems bothering her, but she is not quite sure how or where to begin. She offered the dreams in the reasonable hope that they might help her and me see a clearer path to follow at the outset.

A second dream type that may be presented early in therapy is a frightening or otherwise very painful current dream, which is, in effect, the presenting symptom and which may be reported with considerable urgency. So, a new patient who begins therapy by reporting that a nightmare has propelled him or her into therapy is immediately establishing the possibility of dream analysis as one of the methods, par excellence, for the development of therapy.

A third type of early and emphasized dream is the dream from childhood—either it is a recurrent dream, or it is one that occurred only in childhood and has made a memorable impression. The dreamer remembers it as a definitely or presumably meaning-laden dream.

Most therapists no longer accept Gitelson's (1952) opinion that the therapist's undisguised appearance in an early dream augurs unfavorably for the future success of therapy. When my patient dreamed of me in that second session, it seemed to me that it reflected the good connection we had made; it also dramatized some of her problems. I saw no reason to dwell on the question of whether or why I was disguised or undisguised. Sometimes, however, such questions may become important in the course of therapy.

Two separate but interrelated questions arise in this regard. Is the transference a significant factor in the production of the dream? If so, how should the therapist respond? These questions address one aspect of a more general problem about how to evaluate and respond to transference. Gill (1982) has published a comprehensive discussion of this subject. The fundamental problem is that successful therapy depends on the therapist's understanding of the patient's communications. If the therapist misconstrues the meaning of dreams, and if the therapist insists upon the validity of these misconstructions, serious damage can thus be inflicted. I pointed out (1975) that this occurs by erroneously reading in transference meanings or by premature focus on the transference. Another kind of mistake is the neglect of transference that is crying out in the dream for recognition and discussion.

Theoretical and technical orientation of the therapist, clinical experience or inexperience of the therapist, personality-based considerations such as the therapist's inclination to a more intimate or remote stance—these are some of the factors that can influence the therapist's judgment about transference in dreams and its management. I hope that, thus far, I have conveyed an attitude of flexibility about such matters. Unfortunately, the immediacy of these questions tends to be greater early in therapy, when the resources for reliable answers are the most scant.

A young man had the following dream in a very early session: "I read a movie review written by you. It was shocking to see your name in print, as though it was in a psychiatric journal. You looked at the movie differently than the other critics."

Notice that while the patient dreams of me, he does not dream me. What are we to make of this? What, if any, are the distortions? To both the dreamer and to me, the dream addressed the fact that he had met with a number of other therapists in his search for a suitable person, and he had settled upon me. He felt that his characterization of me as a movie critic was somewhat disparaging of me in a defensive way, yet it was also an allusion to his desire to be one of the "beautiful people." His ambivalence was also evident in the fact that he was "shocked" and by his experience of me as "different," i.e., better. I told him that I thought the dream reflected his hope that in the therapy I would be able to make sense of his frightening symptoms but that in this very early period he was understandably anxious that I might not be able to meet his expectations. I thus attempted to condense and acknowledge his positive and negative feelings.

Recurrent and Traumatic Dreams

Recurrent and traumatic dreams are usually mentioned early in therapy. Traumatic dreams tend to be recurrent, but recurrent dreams are not invariably built upon traumatic themes. Recurrent dreams indicate that life conflict has caused particularly high levels of anxiety and an impairment of integrative ego functions. Therefore, dreaming becomes repetitive or recurring, rather than having the normal sequencing qualities. Cartwright (1979) has demonstrated this experimentally.

Here is a recurrent, traumatic dream reported in early therapy by a married man in his late fifties. He delayed reporting the dream, however, until he became confident that I would not become swamped by damaging countertransference reactions that had occurred in his previous therapy:

> I am in a beautiful glen with my mother, and Jimmy and his mother. The women are digging up Boston ferns. I am running around, calling for Jimmy, frantically trying to warn him that his mother is going to kill him. Then, a large, black snake rises out of the grass, menacingly. We all flee.

The dream had been recurring, with unremittent pain, since early childhood. It began after the death of his friend Jimmy, whose mother accidentally shot him in a hunting accident. The dreamer still recalls the horrible picture of the mother staggering down the mountainside, past his house, moaning, carrying the mutilated body of her son, with his blood and brains smeared over her hands, hair, face, and clothing. Jimmy, an only child, had been the dreamer's closest friend, even his alter ego. The dreamer was the first-born of his family and at the time of the tragedy was also an only child. The parents were also close friends. Jimmy had been conceived three years before the marriage of his parents, who were fanatical backwoods Baptists. The dreamer always knew that the death was really produced by the deep sexual guilt and rage in the family, as did everyone else in their small community. Nevertheless, the coroner ruled it an accidental death, while the minister consoled the mother and prayed for the soul of the dead boy, whose death, he proposed, was probably for the best.

The dreamer also knew that the psychology of Jimmy's family was paralleled in his own family. So his life became clouded with sadness and grief for Jimmy, fear that the same fate might befall him, and relief—heavily laced with guilt—that Jimmy and not he had been chosen for death. This traumatic complex became a developmental axis along which many other important life experiences organized themselves. Despite a high level of cultural development, varied life experiences, and even some previous psychotherapy, this dream and its surpassingly important life relevance had never previously been dealt with. Until the day he first reported the dream to me, whenever he masturbated he had a horrible illusion that the seminal ejaculate was blood, Jimmy's blood on his hands. Thereafter, the illusion no longer occurred. And in due time, the dream itself no longer recurred.

The most practical lesson learned from the preceding dream and its historical and therapeutic context is that the therapist should take nothing for granted. A trauma may persist unrelieved until middle age or later, a dream may become the most direct avenue to the trauma, and a history of psychotherapy does not necessarily mean that central problems have been recognized, let alone resolved or reduced.

This dream became the paradigmatic fantasy theme of the therapy. We initially approached it in terms of the awful reality trauma. Over several years the analytic emphasis shifted to the dream's unconscious meaning: from the mothers to the snake, from the fear of being punished or killed to the fear of inner destructiveness, from the past to the present. Once this dream was finally taken hold of in therapy, it disappeared relatively quickly. This change would be predictable as the previously high level of anxiety became lower and as integrative capabilities grew with increased insight and working-through.

The dreamer and I had already made an excellent beginning connection, so when the dream was presented, at a time of much anxiety and depression, he and I were able to collaborate very well, with a tremendous enhancement of our therapeutic alliance. The therapeutic discoveries, the events of the therapeutic experience, and the quality of the patient-therapist relationship are intricately interwoven. Dreams can be the axial phenomena for the integration of these varied elements.

Recurrence of dreams can vary from a dream that reappears virtually unchanged in its entirety to the repetition of certain elements large or small. Examples would be war dreams in which a beleaguered dreamer is struggling desperately against attacking forces, such "typical" dreams as flying or being lost in a building or a city, or dreams of failing an examination. Repetitive components can include almost anything: People or objects in miniature form, tanks or other war vehicles, or rejection by a desired woman. Repetitive dreams or dream parts are therapeutic communications that call for the therapist's attention and thought. Eventually, although often not soon, their meanings can be understood.

A married professional woman in her early thirties was in analysis with symptoms which included fear of flying, fear of vomiting, and painful gastrointestinal reactions of uncertain cause. In early childhood she had suffered a near-fatal encephalitis, which had obvious relevance for her later neurotic fears. She had recurring dreams involving destructive attacks from the air. Her fear of flying eventually became understandable as an outcome of her fears of death and burial in a coffin when she was a sick child. Airplanes, in her adult life, became symbolic of the coffin. She and her husband had been unable to decide whether to have children. Finally, they decided to become parents, and the patient promptly became pregnant. During pregnancy, the patient decided to reduce her analysis to once weekly. She then dreamed:

> A nuclear holocaust has occurred. I am in a room; I look out and see a mushroom cloud with multiple colors. I think, "Oh shit, someone finally did it." I decide I would rather die immediately than linger on with radiation sickness, yet I am attempting to survive. Then, due to the catastrophe, civilized restraint is gone in the world: I encounter people fighting, engaged in lethal combat—there were no more normal controls.

The patient's associations dealt mostly with her frightened feelings about reducing her visits to me to one time per week. We attributed this apocalyptic dream to a rather mundane and nonviolent concern: her fear of the possible symptomatic consequences of reducing the analytic frequency. So this patient had a pattern of vivid and violent dreams that symbolized her anxiety over ongoing life events. Of course, her profound dread of attack had other and deeper roots, which in turn powered her extreme fear of seeing me less often. However, my point is that a repetitive theme can be expressive of different levels of meaning.

Helping Patients Contact Their Dreams

While some patients begin recalling dreams early and amply in therapy, others are slow to remember and report their dreams. Some patients are simply so stringently defended that, until their sense of danger in the therapy abates, they cannot remember their dreams. Patience, which may have to extend over months or years, is often rewarded by the production of a significant number of illuminating dreams.

Some patients who do not report dreams early are much less refractory. Such patients often begin to bring dreams to the therapy when the therapist explicitly and/or implicitly indicates their usefulness. A middle-aged man came for intensive analytic therapy because of mild chronic depression, multiple phobias, and nagging feelings of inauthenticity. He expressed a profound wish to understand and normalize his inner relationship to the members of his family of origin and to the intimate others of his current adult life. He was also discouraged over a prior two-year static analytic experience with a very passive therapist. I asked about dreams in an early session, and he told me that he rarely recalled dreams. Shortly thereafter, I inquired again about dreams, this time coupling the inquiry with an explanation of the revelatory possibilities of dreams with respect to his analytic goals. He immediately responded with numerous dreams which included at least three discernible recurrent themes: nausea and vomiting, being in a complex and bewildering hotel setting fraught with anxiety, and playing bizarre games with dangerous consequences.

Exhortation and explanation are, of course, not enough. I had implicitly promised that his dreams would not go to waste as he felt had happened to his psychological productions in the previous therapy. The therapist should attempt to link the dream to current vexing life issues. The patient must permit this connection to be established, but when the therapist can demonstrate this linkage, the functional value of the dream has been demonstrated. In terms of therapeutic process, the patient has now had an experience of being understood rather than manipulated or directed. The empathic understanding of one's mental product, the dream, leads inevitably to the all-important sense of feeling subjectively understood, producing an increased sense of intimacy, trust, and meaning in the therapy.

On the other hand, as illustrated by the following vignette, some patients who may report dreams rarely are essentially unable to work with their dreams. The value of such dreams for the therapy is quite limited. A married man in his middle sixties had been in therapy once a week for about one year. He was chronically depressed, and he was angry with one of his sons and his wife, feeling unappreciated. Although intelligent and sensitive, he was psychologically naïve, and he had no one with whom he could share his feelings. His father had died as the result of a work accident when the patient was eight years old. He had never experienced grief over the father's death. He lived through puberty and adolescence resenting his mother for not being more loving and considerate.

In therapy, he reported no dreams during the first year, although I had indicated an interest in dreams on several occasions. After my summer vacation and one elapsed year of therapy, he entered my office and announced that in response to my wish for dreams, he now had some for me. Whereupon he took several sheets of paper from his pocket and proceeded to read a dozen dreams. For the most part, they were unpopulated landscapes or interiors, with only fragmentary references to people. One dream contained a body part or two, but the rest of the person was not visible. We discussed the dreams as an interesting corroboration of his isolation and his difficulties in relating to people. He has reported no further dreams in the several subsequent months.

The following case illustrates another variation of a therapeutic situation in which the patient is unaccustomed to remembering dreams. Here, we were able to integrate his initial dreams quickly into the therapeutic process and thereby facilitate optimal utilization of dreams in his therapy.

A married man in his early forties had been in psychotherapy for just a few weeks when, in two successive sessions, he reported his first dreams. At the outset of therapy he had said to me, "I never recall dreams." The patient had been referred to me by his internist because of a marital crisis.

In his first visit, he was extremely anxious, quite depressed and tearful, filled with hate toward his wife, and terrified over having to lose his young son. He had been an only child. His parents were unhappily married, and the father eventually killed himself. He felt that his mother had never been normally interested in or empathic toward him in childhood, and he became hostile to and distrustful of her, an attitude that persisted to the present. He had loved his father but became bewildered by his father's unhappiness and ultimate suicide.

Although rebellious, he did pursue higher education but entered a field different from the family business and was enjoying much success in his work.

After a few sessions of therapy, he disclosed that he had fallen in love with another woman and that he had now definitely decided to leave his wife. He expected this decision to be undermined by his mother. In this very early period of therapy we spent much time on parallel feelings and expectations toward his wife and his mother. As I would help him recognize that his anger, guilt, and fear to his wife were unconsciously linked to the same feelings to his mother, he began to enjoy the gratifying knowledge of which feelings belonged to which woman. Thus he began to feel stronger with diminishing anxiety and depression.

In the seventh week of therapy, he reported his first dream, and five days later, which was the next session, he reported his second dream. I will give an account of both sessions and how we worked. This reconstruction is derived from the detailed notes I took in both sessions.

He entered my office and almost immediately began to tell me the first dream enthusiastically. As usual, he was painfully preoccupied with his recent separation and its attendant difficulties. Nonetheless, he eagerly reported his dream:

> I am on the upper floor of a house. The police are coming, they are looking for me. Some event is going to happen, which is causing them to look for me. My friend, Harry, wants to take me away, to escape. But I want to remain for another event to occur—which has some interest for me. Then I hear the police coming to the house. I can think of two ways to hide: One is to crawl into an attic space, the other is to get into a big cardboard box. While this is going on, someone is calling for my old dog, but my dog doesn't respond because he is deaf.

The patient seemed quite pleased that he had recalled his first dream. He immediately stated that, indeed, his dog has become quite deaf in its old age. He asked me how to proceed with the dream, and I simply suggested that he tell me whatever came into his mind regarding any of the dream parts or about the dream as a whole.

So he now began associating. The police reminded him of authority, of his opposition to authority, especially in adolescence and younger adulthood. He smiled somewhat painfully, shook his head, and ruefully said, "I suppose I've done something wrong again." Then he thought of Harry, saying that Harry was his roommate in college. They remain friends, with occasional visits. Harry was the first person who encouraged the patient to talk about himself and to accept the value and legitimacy of talking about himself. Also, Harry's father died on the operating table in the same year that the patient's father died. (By this time I was silently thinking that in the dream Harry was a somewhat complex figure, symbolizing a very important alter ego relationship with the patient and even representing the patient himself, but I said nothing here about these thoughts).

He then began to describe himself harshly as having so much tension, as being superego-ridden. He feels he has "fucked up" again and has to get away but can't because of "other events." These other events remind him that he's always juggling stuff, trying to be perfect, as with his estranged wife and his child. He's furious with her for being away with his son just so that he will be unable to visit with them. He tries to behave impeccably with people, but when he doesn't get a fair response, he becomes furious, and he feels justified in leveling them.

I decided a simple interpretive comment about the therapeutic process would be useful at this point. So I stated that Harry's role in the dream seems like my role with the patient. I suggested that he sees me as helping him resolve the unconscious guilt which is such a problem for him and that possibly this connects with some continuing hope that his mother may respond empathically. (Harry's surname and his mother's maiden name are identical). The patient replied that my observations felt right and seemed to make sense. He became silent for a moment.

I then inquired about his deaf dog. He also thought that his dog's name indicated his impulses which opposed his superego. But then he wondered about the dog's deafness. I replied by telling him that Freud had said that the superego is mostly auditory. To this the patient replied that his new girlfriend told him that he is exceptionally "aural," that he hears much and talks a lot. He feels that his girlfriend's concern about his dependency on antianxiety medication can be taken seriously because she's basically nurturing. He responds quite differently to his mother's objections to the drugs because she is otherwise not nurturing.

The hour was rapidly drawing to a close, and I became more verbally active. First, I said that through his dreams he had made a very important metaphorical statement of our therapeutic task, namely, the resolution of his unconscious guilt. He replied that when he told his girlfriend about the dream, she had said it seemed "so confining," and he nodded to me that this seemed an appropriate observation about him. I replied with another interpretation: "As a corollary, this therapy should help you get rid of the constricting defenses against your unconscious guilt." He agreed and added, "I should have left the house [i.e., the marriage] sooner, but I always have to dot the fucking *i*'s and cross the fucking *t*'s." Furthermore, he said that he felt opened up, stimulated, and helped by the discussion today. I concluded the session by telling him, "I am happy that your first dream is so useful, that it helps define a basic problem, that it relates to the therapy, and that it shows certain resistances." He nodded and departed.

Four days later he returned. He immediately announced that he had had another dream which felt powerful, seemed important, but remained obscure in meaning. The dream:

> I am at my parents' house, at the pool behind the house. I see at the far end of the pool that a huge snake emerges from the water and crawls along the pool. It covers about half the pool. I have a single-shot .22 caliber rifle, which I have to keep reloading. I shoot at the snake, and I can actually see the trajectory of the bullets, and they are falling short of the snake. So I raise the gun level. Eventually, one of the bullets hits the

snake, I can see the hole it made in the snake. I also notice that some of the time the snake has a nondescript human shape, neither male nor female. But when the snake is hit, it is back in snake form. Then I am in a room. The snake and I are on different sides of the room. The snake is still coming after me, and I am very frightened. But now I have a .22 caliber revolver. I am still anxiously fumbling and reloading. I notice that now I have both the rifle and the revolver.

Here, the patient had apparently taken courage from the success of his work on the first dream, and I was quite silent during the first portion of the period after he related the dream. I will report the discussion as a dialogue, as I have reconstructed it from my notes.

Patient: I felt so good about the last session, I want to make good use of this dream.

Therapist: What about the revolver? [Here, I chose to pick up the very last item of the dream.]

Patient: The rifle was a gift from both my parents when I was ten years old. My father taught me to shoot. I loved the pool as a kid. Both dreams share the theme of someone coming after me, and I'm resisting or evading. At least in this snake dream it ends in a sort of standoff, but in the police dream they seem to be getting me. You know, another difference is that the snake isn't a superego symbol like the police. It's more like a female figure—it reminds me of Eve. And I shoot at it with something given to me by a male figure. My father would hunt and fish to escape from the rest of his adult life. It's a good feeling; I feel that I'm in a stronger position than my father ended up in—even though my father had a more powerful corporate position. The paradox is that by my age, he was already trapped, locked in by things that didn't make him happy. I've escaped this, and I feel good about it. I'm sure the snake is the incarnation of my mother—at least in her most judgmental aspects. [Here, he seems to be contradicting himself by attributing a superego quality to the snake.] So I shoot her with a weapon provided by my father. Mother was here last weekend. I expected her to be nice and sympathetic, and she was. However, I expected her also to be more implicitly judgmental than she turned out to be. I was glad my negative expectations were wrong. She was sympathetic to me over my leaving the marriage. But she did manage to criticize me for my error in judgment for marrying my wife in the first place.

Therapist: How about your own psychological set about your mother, that is, are *you* changed, are *you* different, are *you* letting her be different?

Patient: When I first saw my mother this weekend, she had just come from seeing my wife and my child, and she started crying. I thought, "Oh, God." It made me sad, and I popped two tranquilizers. But I helped pull her back to composure, and then she expressed sympathy. She hadn't realized the nature or the scope of the problems, and she had consequently felt baffled. I told her that it was understandable that without the necessary knowledge, she would be surprised and shocked over the breakup of the marriage. On Saturday, she, my child and I, had a nice day together. It's that old lack of normal motherly warm feelings. It still astounds me! She's concerned, but there's a real lack of mothering. (We are now about two-thirds through the session, and I now become more verbally active).

Therapist: I think you've taken a giant step in the intrapsychic relation to the internalized, archaic, insufficient mother. You are obviously less anxious, and you are more fluent in your psychological discussion. It's partly fallout from your separation, but also the inner change helps you deal with the separation.

Patient: No question about it. I feel better than I have for two years. I'm starting to take steps to improve my living arrangements. Also, I'm letting my girlfriend be nourishing. I'm feeling healed. I wasn't really eager to see my mother, but the whole experience was very helpful and in some ways painful. Oh yeah, she made another judgment: "Above all, don't get into another relationship quickly, because that's your pattern." When I objected to that simplistic judgment, she did accept my modifications. But then she said I should find a woman from the Northwest, that is, someone with a similar background.

Therapist: She is making an effort to help, but it's ineffectual because of her limited psychological understanding.

Patient: Yeah. My new girlfriend, who is quite unconventional, would be unacceptable to mother.

Therapist: The theme of your remarks is your mother's empathic insufficiency. But why do you dream of a snake, a snake emerging

	from water, a snake covering half the width of the pool, a snake in the house?
Patient:	You know, this dream reminds me of the first warm spring day. I would go swimming in the pool with my mother, and sometimes snakes would emerge from the nearby river—I've never been fond of snakes.
Therapist:	What color were the snakes?
Patient:	The real ones? They were water moccasins, the same as in the dream. I didn't like them. I'm not phobic about snakes. I once let a girl have her pet boa constrictor crawl on my arm and back. She was lesbian. I think the snake was huge in the dream, perhaps fifty or sixty feet long, and very thick—one shot hit it.
Therapist:	Did you or do you see your mother as frightening or large?
Patient:	I always saw her as large and lumpy. My father teased her about it. She wasn't very attractive physically.

(The session ended here).

Obviously, the analysis of the two dreams was very incomplete. Therapists should expect incompleteness of understanding, especially in the early phases of therapy. My goal was not to achieve comprehensive understanding of the dreams. My primary intent was to foster the therapeutic alliance, by enabling the patient to achieve an experiential conviction that dreams are very interesting and valuable in therapy. This goal was certainly accomplished, and the patient reported numerous dreams thereafter.

Dreams and Thematic Continuity

For most people, a haze surrounds their basic life themes. While this fogginess may be discouraging, it should stimulate the psychotherapist's curiosity and entice him or her to search further for meaning. I have repeatedly found that dreams convey crucial messages about the unfolding of basic life themes in psychotherapy.

A woman in her early forties entered therapy because she was in love with a homosexual man who showed no sign of changing his sexual orientation. She was quite fearful because several previous therapeutic experiences had not helped her avoid this painful situation. About a month after beginning therapy with me, she reported the following dream:

> I am in a beach house. People and children arrive with food, and a party is going on. Someone is keeping me quiet, and I am in bed a lot. I'm unable to talk. I am trying to communicate with someone by writing on the

bottom of my foot. This is related to a prior plan that if I needed to communicate with someone, the message would be on the bottom of my foot. But the others had wrapped my whole body in gauze. The beach house is being taken away from me.

Her associations took her to her early life difficulties in communicating with her parents and her fears of another therapeutic failure. Yet her dreams revealed her hope that despite her handicaps, she and I would find an effective avenue of communication.

This concern about communication itself was of basic importance because she felt her parents were false communicators, and most of her subsequent therapists also did not help her reach a crucial truth. So a life theme dealing with communication was conveyed through an early dream.

Dreams thus provide thematic continuity for therapy. While this is not a new idea, it cannot be overstated. A bewildering profusion of diverse manifest details is often reduced to simple coherence through the agency of a dream. The rhythm of therapy allows for a period of relatively disorganized expression of thought, feeling, and action, which gradually—but sometimes rapidly—develops to a tense, bursting ripeness that yearns for organizing and relieving insight. This is the point at which a dream becomes exceedingly helpful.

Certain progressive changes can generally be observed in dreams, regardless of the individual differences of life themes from person to person. Here, I agree with the authors (Anonymous, 1980) who reported that in guilt-ridden, inhibited neurotics, a certain pattern of development in dreams can be expected in the course of therapy. In the early phase, sexual and aggressive urges are severely constricted and distorted. They reported, for example, that sexual desire may be portrayed by a scene in which the man feels his penis will be seen and found wanting by an older woman, while anger may be expressed in hurt feelings or helpless frustration toward another person with power who is not gratifying the dreamer.

By the middle phase of therapy, given favorable developments, sex and aggression become more direct. Sexually explicit scenes with intense erotic feelings abound. Similarly, the aggressive urges are indiscriminately available. Murderous, mutilating scenes, with the dreamer as perpetrator, are shamelessly constructed. When therapy is reaching its conclusion and basic problems have been satisfactorily dealt with, the sexual themes remain rich and untrammeled. However, aggression has undergone another necessary transformation: the violent aggressiveness of middle phase dreams has been muted. Heated verbal confrontation, suffused with anger, has replaced destructive physical violence. I believe that when civility has replaced violence, the patient has achieved a nonrepressive transformation of aggression—which is our most urgent societal task.

Transformations of Dream Characters

The plasticity of dreams permits the observable change of a person while a dream is occurring. These transformations have at least two significant implications. One is that a meaning which has been shrouded by another meaning can now become visible, and the second is that, when such shifts occur, they indicate important changes may be occurring in the dreamer. The dreamer or some other person may be altered.

In the first instance, the dreamer has the awesome experience of seeing a person become someone else—the process of change is observed, and it becomes an unforgettable demonstration of the crucial linkage in the dreamer's mind between two other vitally important and conflict-laden people. Because of the vividness and power of the experience, I will report the following examples.

A man in his middle forties, on the eve of a separation between him and his wife, dreamed that he was gazing at his wife, and she was beautiful. As he watched, she became unattractive, and to his surprise, her face became his mother's face. His two chief complaints in this therapy had always been his mother's basic coldness and his wife's indifference to him. As this therapy evolved, he became increasingly aware of the interpenetrating meaning of these two women in his life. This understanding enabled him to handle the current problems with his wife in a more adult manner, instead of the hapless sentimentality with which he had previously been encumbered. Early in his therapy, he had cried a great deal and had hoped that, through his perseverence and fidelity, his wife would become loving and faithful. However, as he became aware that his yearnings toward his wife were heavily influenced by vain hopes for his mother's love, he was liberated from the painful neediness directed to these two women, neither of whom would or could meet his needs. Not only did the events of the dream convince him that his wife and his mother had the same unconscious meaning, but the active transformation of one face into another may also have reflected his increased active mastery of his life difficulties. This dream occurred as his divorce was becoming imminent. It consolidated his insight into the connection between his past and his present, and it symbolized his readiness to meet a momentous life change.

In the second dream, a 51-year-old female dreamer is standing in front of a thick oak door. She opens the door and sees her sick father, who looks awful. She asks him why he hadn't told her and her younger sister that he was still alive. He replied that he had his own life to lead. She feels hurt and begins to cry. Then he tells her that he has two more daughters, and she now sees his two little girls. She becomes furious with him, with a quality and intensity of anger that she had never felt before. As all this happens, her father's hair becomes blond, and he is her husband.

This woman had entered once-a-week psychotherapy approximately one year before the above dream. She wanted therapy because of intermittent inability to achieve orgasm. She knew, and her husband knew, that she was excessively nice and unable to express the underlying anger she felt to him, along with her love. The husband and wife also realized that this pattern of relating to important men derived from her experiences with a father who became fatally ill during the patient's puberty and died in her late adolescence. Circumstances had dictated that she become the anchor and caretaker of the family when her father was no longer able to fulfill these roles. She and I quickly established a friendly collaborative relationship in which I confronted her with her manifold altruistic traits as defenses against her unacceptable anger. She received my interpretations with good humor and intellectual acceptance. But she didn't feel it—until she had the dream.

On the basis of the dream, in which her brunette father turned into her blond husband, she could now "feel" her anger to her husband (who happens to have two children by a previous marriage), its roots in her earlier relationship, and its adverse effect upon her sexual function. An interesting element in her therapy was that she believed that she discerned in me some of the same personality traits that she possessed. When her loved ones pointed out her submerged anger, she would feel accused, but because she identified with me, she could accept such interpretations from me with more ease. So before the dream, she and I had already done considerable work on her presumptive anger stemming from adolescence. We agreed that her father's illness and death had stolen much of her youth and had propelled her into premature adulthood. The lesson of these events was that the luxury of expressing angry emotions was not for her. In the weeks before this dream, the patient had become somewhat more aware of the anger toward her father and more alert to a variety of frustrated feelings toward her husband. But these insights remained insecure, and the fundamental unity of father-husband anger was not yet experientially available to her until the dream, with its self-evident properties, consolidated her understanding of salient life problems in a much more powerful way than my interpretations alone could induce.

Therapists should always be alert to signs of change in a patient's perception and portrayal of himself or herself in dreams. Sometimes, patients report dreams in which the dreamer changes before our very eyes. A male patient once dreamed that he became a woman and was having sexual intercourse with a man. This dream helped make available more of his feminine identification. Another man dreamed of himself as himself, i.e., a typical urban type; then he finds that he is walking in a field like an old cemetery with old toppled gravestones or fallen timbers. He becomes a lithe and seasoned gunslinger whose enemies fire at him, so he skillfully hurls himself behind a stone or log and confidently fires his revolver at his foes. In this dream, an ordinarily unaggressive man seemed to be testing in wishful fantasy his newly developing skills in self-assertion. A change from passivity to activity occurs. A similar line of change is from withdrawal to engagement, from cringing to boldness, from prudishness to sexual exuberance. Also changes of affect may be noted: fear to confidence, guilt to acceptance, depression to well-being.

Change of Dreams from "Thin" to "Powerful"

Therapists who work with dreams must be capable of prolonged periods of patience and listening. Often patients report dreams during psychoanalysis or psychotherapy, but no insight results. This may be the case even when patients attempt diligently to work on their dreams. Yet neither patient nor therapist gleans useful understanding from these efforts. The therapy may be proceeding satisfactorily despite this deficit. I call the dreams of this phase "thin"; their value does not match the general quality of the therapy. Assuming that the problem does not arise from the therapist, the reason for the thinness is that the dream themes deal with conflicts which are beyond the current therapeutic capability of the patient. It may also be that the problem, or part of it, resides in the therapist, who has not yet become sufficiently attuned to the patient and therefore finds the patient's dream meanings impenetrable.

In one such situation, the patient had been in analysis for about two years. He reported dreams intermittently. I considered his dreams thin, because they were not particularly helpful. Important and complex life issues had been defined and modified to some extent in this period. Then he reported an unusual dream: he perceives the Hindu goddess Kali seated with her legs and knees bent, with a half-loaf of bread extending from her pubis, like an erect, partly amputated penis. This dream heralded a series of castration dreams revealing a complex, submerged fabric of interwoven themes of a phallic mother who was bitterly menacing, the dreamer's own castration feelings, and his associated masochistic identification which he cast in a feminine mode. The "feel" of this heraldic dream was firm and hard (pun intended). It could be "plugged" into the matrix of his associations, resulting in the emergence of valuable new meanings. Naturally, I considered this a "powerful" dream, in contrast to his previous thin ones. The time had now arrived for the therapist to abandon the previous stance of patient listening. It was now time for action.

Having dared to dream a damaged Kali, the patient could now move ahead in his dream life. An intense, even compulsive, talker, this man gave the impression most of the time of someone who was scurrying about in order to plug a leak in a dike, as though his very vigilant activity was necessary to prevent some catastrophe. Shortly after the Kali dream, he reported a dream upon which I pounced. The dream was:

> I have to shit. I do it in a chair with a hole in the seat. So the shit drops on the ground. How could I have gotten into this humiliating situation? I am worried about how I can dispose of the shit. Finally, I decide to spread it around. Then an older woman friend, the widow of a prominent psychoanalyst, calls to say that she had been pregnant but that she had gotten rid of the baby. I was very understanding, but to myself I wondered how she could have become pregnant at her age.

His associations led him to recall that he had been told by his mother that at age two he had played in his crib with feces and made a terrible mess. His mother told him that she had been very upset. He further associated to an incident of urinary incontinence one or two years later in nursery school. The teachers made him strip naked and sit on a stool in helpless shame before the entire class while his clothes dried.

We discussed this dream in terms of his anal urges to express, to share, to play, and to soil—and their counterpart phenomena. I talked of his anxiety associated with his anality and of the frantic compulsive defenses he employed, and how these phenomena reverberated into his character and the transference. He had previously disclosed both death wishes (and fears) to me as well as the fantasy of having anal sex with me. His sexual identity conflicts, although previously recognized, now become much more vivid and less disabling. For example, his sexual potency increased markedly. Previously, he had maintained a macho, conquering attitude. Now he could become aware, for the first time, of the pure joy of relating to a woman as a loved and loving equal.

Events such as these illustrate how psychological life is always in a state of flux and ever changing. The problem for therapists is that many of the manifestations seem to go nowhere—except to involution. On the other hand, directed change leads to development, strength, and productive change. The newly achieved directedness in this case appeared when the patient, through his now "powerful" dreams, came into possession of new liberating insights.

Longitudinal Transformations in Dreams

Some transformations occur over long periods of time. In the next case, the changes occurred over a period of ten years, but they were well worth waiting for.

The dreamer is a single woman in her middle thirties who has been in therapy with me for over ten years, with extended interruptions. The changes I describe have been of much importance in her life and are most graphic in her dreams.

In her early twenties, when she first came to see me, Ethel had recently completed college and had a tenuous hold on her newly obtained job in the field of child development. (Actually, she may have had a much more secure hold on the job than she imagined, but it was her terrified and outraged impression at this early time that her position was in jeopardy, and I had no way to confirm or refute her view.) She was socially quite isolated, dependent upon her parents, and still badly wounded by the recent violent death of her (nonconsanguineous) brother who, like her, was adopted. She was very anxious, depressed, and inhibited. Her typical dreams of this period can be examplified by this retrospective composite:

> The dreamer is in her bedroom. A male intruder approaches her. She is terrified, for his intentions are horrible. He begins to abuse her physically, culminating in hurling her about the room homicidally. She bounces off the walls with multiple fractures and awful soft tissue damage—even unto death.

At this time, her therapy sessions were filled with fears of unfair treatment and humiliation by authorities, dismal expectations of profound failure in love and work in the future, and a limited amount of whimsical, sexually tinged sadism toward the young men who happened to enter her orbit. Any time she felt closer and warmer to me, she would quickly follow with storms of rage and accusation in which she saw me as a polite version of the nocturnal attacker, although from my standpoint, she seemed more the attacker than I. Happier periods gradually became longer, and the frightened, rageful paroxysms slowly diminished in frequency. She did change—at a snail's pace.

Some five or six years later, her life had improved markedly. Her range of significant life involvements had expanded considerably. She enjoyed much respect in her career, and she was beginning a doctoral program. However, her social relations remained scant and shallow, and she acknowledged that in her recent two-year separation from me, she had been in psychological hibernation. Her key dream at this time occurred in two brief parts, as follows: "I am going down an aisle happily. Then I am walking furtively down a dark corridor, clutching my purse to my breast."

Ethel and I readily perceived that important movement was indeed occurring in her life. The dreams revealed her crucial feminine conflict over whether to become a confident woman with an open, legitimate sex life in marriage or its equivalent—as portrayed by "going down an aisle," or whether to remain severely constricted, frightened, and withdrawn—as in the second part of the dream. The vivid simplicity of the dream and its obvious meaning helped Ethel apply her cognitive skills to her life tasks, and the total effect was very encouraging to a young woman who needed all the encouragement she could get. Without the crystal-clear message of the dream, she probably would have been unable to realize how strong and effective her growth tendencies and accomplishments had become. This is an excellent example of the nodal clarifying and direction-pointing value of dreams. Although danger is suggested in the second part of the dream, the violence of Ethel's dreams had diminished greatly.

In response to Ethel's associations (as well as to my associations), I constructed interpretations that asserted the psychological points made in the above paragraph. In our work, my interpretations tended to be made both emphatically and discursively, with a great emphasis on repetition and using a firm, raised voice. This was my antidote to her tense, laconic, semi-whispered verbalizations.

My emphasis on her sexual dilemma, and my vote in favor of the positive side (going down the aisle), correlated with Ethel's entrance into her first serious and extended relationship with a man. It is a tribute to her growing hardiness that she undertook this relationship despite some realistic obstacles that might have daunted even a hardy veteran of the war between the sexes.

Now fortified by her success, particularly the stability of her love relationship, Ethel's defenses melted still more. The culmination of this warming phase was a dream some two years later. "I am doing a sexual dance for you, removing one layer of filmy silk after another, as you recline on pillows, getting excited. I am extremely aroused sexually."

Here, she is frankly erotic, gaining pleasure, and assuming active responsibility, and she is not drenched with guilt. My main point is not to prove that dreams constitute the crucial surface and mirror of therapeutic change. Doubtless, a good deal of Ethel's psychological growth could have occurred without the conspicuous role of dream interpretation in my work with her. Without the dreams, however, the therapy would have been more of a benign, amorphous drift toward maturity. With the dreams, the therapy became a fascinating and creative chronicle of a young woman's journey to self-discovery and self-transformation. I have no doubt that the dreamwork, which provided such vivid and graphic representation, sharpened our conscious perceptions, expanded our cognitive comprehension, and facilitated experiential learning.

Dreams in Therapeutic Impasse

A more recent dream of Ethel's illustrates the particular value of dreams in the working out of a therapeutic impasse.

A serious block occurred later in the therapy when Ethel was trying to complete the requirements for her doctorate. She became anxious, hypochondriacal, depressed, and neglectful of her studies. The therapeutic discussions indicated that once more she was misconstruing constructive activity as destructive because in her childhood she had so feared the violence of her brother's behavior that she concluded the only way to be good and safe was to be passive and compliant. But this, of course, meant that she would also have to be ineffective and unhappy. In the face of the current challenge, she had regressed to her traditional defense. For several weeks, my interpretations of all this were not helpful. I finally proposed that perhaps ten years of therapy was excessive for her and me and that perhaps she would find a new female therapist more helpful. Ethel's response to this was expressed in the following dream: "I am in a boat, not pulling my oar. The captain, an older man, firmly ordered me to do my job or be left behind. Frightened, I comply."

My approach to the blocked therapy may have left a little to be desired, but that is not the issue of the moment. Her dream provided the necessary data: she was shirking her therapeutic duty out of fear, but a superordinate motive was to continue with me and to go forward. She was validating my expectations of a high level of performance. Her therapy quickly resumed its course toward the appropriate goals.

Key Dreams

Key dreams possess a nodal, pivotal quality. A dream of mine may illustrate this point. A number of years ago I dreamed that a black man had invaded my home, intent on wreaking mayhem. Although terrified, I dutifully stood in the doorway, expecting to be killed. However, because I stood up to him, we became friends, and the dream ended as we walked down the corridor, arm in arm, in animated and amiable conversation. This dream dramatized my ongoing efforts to recognize and integrate my own aggression. This simple and rather obvious dream has remained in my active consciousness and has helped in opening many doors of insight in me and in my patients. Hence, I call it a key dream.

Dreams should not be approached with ritualistic formulas. Flexibility and informality are necessary. With regard to the key dream mentioned in the preceding paragraph, I had two separate uses in mind. First was the immense value for me of a particular dream which reinforced my conviction that similar benefits are possible for others if they too can become conscious of their key dreams. Also in this category is my use of the dream specifically when I am reminded of it at a particular time with a patient. I am then alerted that some similar matter may be ongoing in the therapeutic situation, and my analytic attention is correspondingly alerted and directed. In such instances, I consciously employ my dream while retaining its privacy by not mentioning this aspect of my ongoing experience to the patient. In the second category of use, I elect to talk about the dream with the patient, but only if I am confident that I am doing so in a resonant therapeutic manner. Some patients are encouraged to learn that the therapist too has problems. A dream such as this one can effectively convey to the patient the message that the therapist has also had to struggle in life. However, I do recommend caution and restraint in the deliberate disclosure of personal matters.

Another key dream contributed crucially to the ushering in of a later important phase in Ethel's very long therapy. I will report the entire session as I have reconstructed it from my detailed notes.

The patient entered my office, on time, brisk, and smiling.

Ethel: This week has been very interesting and satisfying. I went to a nuclear freeze party in mid-week. I was so different. I didn't feel shy. It was as though I really belonged there. An older man, I guess he's about fifty, was obviously attracted to me. I wasn't particularly attracted to him, but I felt flirtatious, and we had fun flirting with one another all evening. It was a very fancy Hollywood event, and lots of superstars were there, but I didn't feel out of place or shy, the way I used to. And even though I went with my mother, I didn't feel like the little girl. It was a new sensation, as though we were friends and equals.

Therapist: Well, you've sure come a long way.

Ethel: I had this really interesting and important dream:

"It's Saturday, not a workday. I, you, and two of your male friends are having fun. Although I feel like a woman, I nevertheless feel like one of the guys. There's a general atmosphere of easy camaraderie. I think we are playing basketball. I felt wonderful."

I awoke with a glow. I realized it's the first dream I've ever had of being a close friend of yours but without being sexual. It was a very powerful experience.

Therapist: It sounds as though you are reclaiming your friendly feelings toward men.

Ethel: Oh yeah. Something else that's connected is that I let myself have thoughts of seducing Bill's father (Bill is her lover). Actually, I'm being much more generous toward Bill's parents than I ever could be in the past. I actually cooked a meal for them and enjoyed it. And I realize having that fantasy about his father wasn't so terrible.

Therapist: You are feeling more and more like a woman and less and less like a child.

Ethel: I really think the "cure" here will be my increasing ability to relate to you with natural, warm, intense sexual feelings, to express them, to accept them as good. You know, I used to think it was wrong to feel that way, because it meant I was being bad, I wasn't working. I thought I had to find a terrible traumatic memory which would explain everything and then I would be perfect and cured.

Therapist: You are certainly much freer. I also think that you no longer need to be so restrained and allusive and paradoxical. No more secrets or tricks. And as you become more available and transparent in our relationship, you are inevitably discovering parts of yourself which you have hitherto sequestered.

Ethel: Do you remember when we started years ago, I was so afraid of Mrs. P. She was the boss and the terrifying authority. Well, she's retired now, but she still comes around, and she's still a pain in the ass, correcting and criticizing everything. She came in this week. I actually volunteered to assist her. For instance, she criticized my driving. I just laughed and told her it's my car and I'm the driver, and I'm doing it my way. And Mrs. P. just shut up and accepted it. I know it's very important and creative to focus on our relationship. You are the most emotionally available man I know; only now, I'm beginning to realize and appreciate it. Now I'm eager, even excited, about coming to see you. It's fun, just like in the dream. That dream is so striking and unusual; it really puts together the powerful things that are going on here. The dream is about me knowing that I have a right to enjoy my life and being who I am. Funny, I never previously felt I could do that.

Therapist: Are things also changing with you and Bill?

Ethel: Oh yes! I'm being so much more assertive and expressive with him. And he's responding with a lot more warmth to me. By the way, I'd like to come in for a third appointment next week. I hope you have a free hour. Maybe having fun with you and the other two guys referred to my wish for three sessions.

Therapist: Sure, I do have time to see you three times next week.

(End of session)

I call this dream of Ethel's a key dream because it is a very intense experience for her which clearly states her newly achieved feelings of liberation and equality. She is rapidly relinquishing her depressed, inferior feelings and is becoming self-confident and self-assertive. The dream dramatizes these gains in terms of her relationship with me, but the discussion stimulated by the dream includes virtually all the significant problematic areas of her current life.

Dream Interpretation and Dream Experience

Therapists should bear in mind that dreams are substantial human events, as emphasized by such authors as Ullman (1979) and Delaney (1979). To assume that dreams are mere records of psychological events is to ignore the growth and development of the dreamer as dreamer.

A dream of mine illustrates the point. Many years ago, I dreamed of a beautiful peacock with marvelous, glittering plumage. I could not recall ever having had such a colorful, pleasing, and obviously symbolic sort of dream. I felt surprise and enjoyment, but I did not understand the dream. When I discussed the dream with someone who knew me and who also knew about dreams, he rather dryly noted that "nothing struts like a peacock." I had not expected this response, and my feathers were a bit ruffled. However, I did have some reason to be proud. I have always believed in art, but I have always doubted my artistic capabilities, and I have always known that I could not draw. Yet, this dream proved to me that, at least in my mind, I am able to construct a most beautiful and pleasurable picture. This *experience* has encouraged me to continue having "artistic" dreams. Had I been influenced only by the *interpretation* made by my acquaintance, this stimulation might not have occurred.

The distinction between dream experience and dream interpretation can be a useful one. Experience and interpretation are obviously not absolutely separable. For instance, my response to the dream experience, in that I became more confident of my artistic gift, gradually became an interpretation, a significant contribution to my self-definition. This powerfully illustrated what skillful clinicians have always known, namely, that the best interpretations require the available experience of the patient as well as the therapist. Theodor Reik (1935) emphasized that insight should come as a surprise to both analysand and analyst. But he also emphasized the deep collaborative spirit of the therapeutic encounter, likening it to a duet.

The therapist is not a police detective or sniper waiting in concealment to discover the patient's fatal flaw and then leaping interpretively upon the unsuspecting patient. Such interpretations are often incorrect and poorly timed, since they usually focus on some emotion, such as anger, of which the patient is still fearful. So some more available and acceptable issue should be noted and the emphasis on aggression delayed until a later day. A shocking interpretation of a dream, proffered by a therapist who needs to exercise power over the dreamer, usually has an antitherapeutic effect. It discourages patients from creating and sharing those rich metaphors that we call dreams. So a clinician imposes a double bind on a patient by indicating a therapeutic interest in dreams but at the same time responding to the dreams with intellectualized and unempathic interpretations that disrupt the process of therapeutic emergence.

My peacock dream and my own understanding of it, both experiential and interpretive, was a powerful event in my progress toward creative living. The same is probably true of most dreamers. For instance, the gentleman who dreamed of Kali and the broken bread-penis was similarly affected. The dream had a shattering effect upon a deeply ingrained set of conflicts and defenses. He continues to refer to that dream with awe and pride. Not the least of his satisfactions is his newly found certainty that he can recreate and employ rich symbolism in an unselfconscious way.

New Psychoanalytic Dimensions of Dreams

Although prepsychoanalytical artists such as Dostoyevski recorded the revelatory potentials of dreams, it was Freud who made a major conceptual issue of dreams for modern consciousness. He averred that every dream expresses a disguised, unconscious childhood wish which was repressed because it conflicted with the moral standards of the person. The task of the therapist then became unraveling the repressions and thus freeing the person from the encumbrance of those unconscious wishes in adult life.

I have been an ambivalent Freudian since adolescence, when I first read *Moses and Monotheism* (1939). Since I was always socially conscious, the fact that Freud situated the instinctual unconscious in the position of motivational primacy bedeviled me perennially. This dilemma over the intrapsychic and the social made it even more difficult for me to accept Jungian notions about the collective unconsciousness and universal symbols, which seemed to make a human being even less of a socially derived creature.

Several decades of analytic experience has only enhanced and refined my appreciation of the ambiguity of this field. I am obsessed with the immeasurable complexity of each psychotherapeutic moment. This means that, while I rely upon my psychiatric and psychoanalytic systematic knowledge, I also appreciate the vast uncertainty in my work. So instead of possessing a neat and satisfying "understanding" of the psychological nature of dreams and their interpretations, I make every dream interpretation with caution and humility—but also with pleasure. In this spirit, my interest in the nature of therapeutic action causes me to think that every interpretation is the result of a passionate, complex, and largely obscure or unconscious transaction between the therapist and the patient. While the formal characteristics of an interpretation are systematic, clinical, and conventional (on the part of the therapist), I believe that the subtext is considerably different.

Kohut (1977), shortly before his death in 1982, redirected the emphasis of psychoanalysis and psychotherapy to the empathic introspective aspects of the therapeutic process. And he placed the self in the center of the psychotherapeutic field. I have attempted to explore some of the possibilities and problems of his work for both psychotherapists and social theorists (1981). Kohut helped open the door to the necessity of understanding the ongoing idiosyncratic, unconscious events within the therapist as he or she works with the patient. The intersubjective process goes on during the analysis of dreams—perhaps especially at such times. After all, dreams are formulations of the sensitive, intimate interior of the dreamer. So would they not then resonate with the same zone of the therapist? This concept renders dream interpretation more powerful. Yet it may sometimes be more hazardous because twisted sensitivity in a therapist may be worse than none at all.

The contributions of Roy Schafer (1983) and Merton Gill (1982) seem convergent with the notion I have just proposed. Schafer believes that the analyst brings his or her own "narrative structure" to the analysis, and this significantly influences the verbal and attitudinal behavior of the analysand. Gill suggests that transference not only replicates an old aspect of life but includes an element that is interpersonal and created by the patient and therapist.

My approach to dreams has a Freudian origin but has evolved into an intersubjective orientation. I regard the psychotherapeutic dialogue as essential for both the occurrence and understanding of dreams in psychotherapy. My approach to dreams has much in common with the other authors' dream theories and techniques in this book, yet I recognize significant differences among us.

Delaney encourages the dreamer to describe concretely all the dream images and thereby to generate his or her own interpretations. Delaney withholds her own hypotheses unless the dreamer is blocked in achieving these interpretations. Craig and Walsh emphasize the manifest dream, thus attending to the actuality and meaning of the dream experience in an atheoretical way. They regard the dream as another way of being in the world. Ullman works exclusively in an experiential group context. He obtains relatively few associations from the dreamer and accords exclusive interpretive privileges to the dreamer. Greenberg and Pearlman operate from a psychoanalytic perspective and attribute, as does Kramer, exceptional revelatory value to the manifest dream. Beebe utilizes traditional Jungian methods by interpreting universal symbols, and he imparts knowledge to the dreamer about the origins of these symbols in human culture and religion.

The study of psychotherapy and the interpretation of dreams is still in an emerging state. It is richly endowed by the work of earlier thinkers, but new concepts, current and future, continue to transform therapy and therapists, as well as add texture and sophistication. Dreams are one of the great gateways to a more human consciousness.

References

Anonymous. (1980). A Collaborative Account of A Psychoanalysis Through Dreams. In *The Dream in Clinical Practice*, ed. J. Natterson. New York: Jason Aronson, pp. 58–84.

Breger, L. (1980). The Manifest Dream and Its Latent Meaning. In *The Dream in Clinical Practice*, ed. J. Natterson. New York: Jason Aronson, pp. 3–27.

Cartwright, R. (1979). The Nature and Function of Repetitive Dreams: A Survey and Speculation. *Psychiatry* 42: 131–37.

Cartwright, R., Tipton, L., and Wickland, J. (1980). Focusing on Dreams. A Preparation for Psychotherapy. *Archives of General Psychiatry* 37: 275–77.

Delaney, G. (1979). *Living Your Dreams*. San Francisco: Harper and Row.

Freud, S. (1900). The Interpretation of Dreams. In *Standard Edition*, vols 4,5. London: Hogarth Press, 1953–1958.

———. (1939). Moses and Monotheism. In *Standard Edition*, vol 23;: 2–132. London: Hogarth Press, 1964.

Gill, M. (1982). *Analysis of Transference: vol 1. Theory and Technique*. New York: International Universities Press.

Gitelson, M. (1952). The Emotional Position of the Analyst in the Psychoanalytic Situation. *International Journal of Psychoanalysis* 33: 1–10.

Kohut, H. (1977). *The Restoration of the Self.* New York: International Universities Press.

Natterson, J. (1975). Extra-analytic Transference: A Two-Way Tide. *Psychoanalytic Forum* 5: 263–80.

Natterson, J. (1981). The Significance of Kohut. *Humanities in Society* 4(2–3): 221–43.

Rangell, L. (1987). Historical Perspectives and Current Status of the Interpretation of Dreams in Clinical Work. In *The Interpretation of Dreams in Clinical Work,* ed. A. Rothstein. New York: International Universities Press, pp. 3–24.

Reik, T. (1935). *Surprise and the Psychoanalyst.* London: G. Routledge and Sons.

Rycroft, C. (1979). *The Innocence of Dreams.* New York: Pantheon Books.

Schafer, R. (1983). *The Psychoanalytic Attitude.* New York: Basic Books.

Spanjaard, J. (1969). The Manifest Dream and its Significance for the Interpretation of Dreams. *International Journal of Psycho-Analysis* 50: 221–35.

Ullman, M. (1979). Experiential Dream Group. In *Handbook of Dreams,* ed. B. Wolman. New York: Van Nostrand Reinhold, pp. 406–23.

3

John Beebe ━━━━━━━━━━━━━━━━

A Jungian Approach to Working with Dreams

Jung's Search for Meaning

It is instructive, in trying to identify the special nature of Jung's approach to the dream, to read again the introduction to his first major statement of his own position, *Psychology of the Unconscious* (*Wandlungen und Symbole der Libido*, 1912) in its ambitious 1916 American edition. This was the work in which Jung, emphasizing Freud the mythmaker at the expense of Freud the biological observer, drove a wedge within psychoanalysis that led to schism and the formation of his own "Zurich" school of analytical psychology. Here, in Beatrice Hinkle's spirited rendering, is how Jung begins this fateful work, which remains the key to understanding Jung's approach to all spontaneous fantasy, including dreams:

> Any one who can read Freud's "Interpretation of the Dream" without scientific rebellion at the newness and apparently unjustified daring of its analytical presentation, and without moral indignation at the astonishing nudity of the dream interpretation, and who can allow this unusual array of facts to influence his mind calmly and without prejudice, will surely be deeply impressed by that place where Freud calls to mind the fact that an individual psychologic conflict, namely, the Incest Phantasy, is the essential root of that powerful ancient dramatic material, the Oedipus legend. The impression made by this simple reference may be likened to that wholly peculiar feeling which arises in us if, for example, in the noise and tumult of a modern street we should come across an ancient relic—the Corinthian capital of a walled-in column, or a fragment of inscription. Just a moment ago we were given over to the noisy ephemeral life of the present, when something very far away and strange appears to us, which turns our attention to things of another order; a glimpse away from the

incoherent multiplicity of the present to a higher coherence in history. Very likely it would suddenly occur to us that on this spot where we now run busily to and fro a similar life and activity prevailed two thousand years ago in somewhat other forms; similar passions moved mankind, and man was likewise convinced of the uniqueness of his existence. I would liken the impression which the first acquaintance with the monuments of antiquity so easily leaves behind to that impression which Freud's reference to the Oedipus legend makes—for while we are still engaged with the confusing impressions of the variability of the Individual Soul, suddenly there is opened a revelation of the simple greatness of the Oedipus tragedy—that never extinguished light of the Grecian theater. (Jung, 1916b, pp. 3–4)

It is clear from this passage that the interesting thing for Jung about Freud's mythologizing move in naming an early sexual fantasy "Oedipal" is not the underlining it gives to the centrality of this motif in infantile psychological existence but rather the move itself to a poetic rather than biological basis of mind. Near the end of his life, Jung speaks in his autobiography of the dreams that appeared while he was working on this book, dreams which for him

presaged the forthcoming break with Freud. One of the most significant had its scene in a mountainous region on the Swiss-Austrian border. It was toward evening, and I saw an elderly man in the uniform of an Imperial Austrian customs official. He walked past, somewhat stooped, without paying any attention to me. His expression was peevish, rather melancholic and vexed. There were other persons present, and someone informed me that the old man was not really there, but was the ghost of a customs official who had died years ago. "He is one of those who couldn't die properly." That was the first part of the dream. . . .

After a hiatus came a second and far more remarkable part. I was in an Italian city, and it was around noon, between twelve and one o'clock. A fierce sun was beating down upon the narrow streets. The city was built on hills and reminded me of a particular part of Basel, the Kohlenberg. The little streets which lead down into the valley, the Birsigtal, that runs through the city, are partly flights of steps. In the dream, one such stairway descended to Barfüsserplatz. The city was Basel, and yet it was also an Italian city, something like Bergamo. It was summertime; the blazing sun stood at the zenith, and everything was bathed in an intense light. A crowd came streaming toward me, and I knew that the shops were closing and people were on their way home to dinner. In the midst of this stream of people walked a knight in full armor. He mounted the steps toward me. He wore a helmet of the kind that is called a basinet, with eye slits, and a chain armor. Over this was a white tunic into which was woven, front and back, a large red cross.

One can easily imagine how I felt: suddenly to see in a modern city, during the noonday rush hour, a crusader coming toward me. What struck me as particularly odd was that none of the many persons walking about seemed to notice him. No one turned his head or gazed after him. It was as though he were completely invisible to everyone but me. I asked myself what this apparition meant, and then it was as if someone answered me—but there was no one there to speak: "Yes, this is a regular apparition. The knight always passed by here between twelve and one o'clock, and has been doing so for a very long time [for centuries, I gathered] and everyone knows about it." (Jung, 1963, pp. 163–65)

There is a striking correspondence between Jung's unstated feeling "suddenly to see in a modern city, during the noonday rush hour, a crusader coming toward me" and his evocation at the beginning of the book he was writing at the time he had this dream of "that wholly peculiar feeling which arises in us if, for example, in the noise and tumult of a modern street we should come across an ancient relic." It is quite clear that it is the feeling for the transcendence of the past that, for Jung, is the important thing. This emphasis defines his standpoint to the dream and marks his important difference from, on the one hand, Freudian approaches to the dream (in which the past is traumatic and neurotic, not transcendentally therapeutic) and, on the other, existential approaches to the dream (in which the present reality and context, not the historical seductions, provide the effective key to meaning).

Although one will find in Jung much that is Freudian and much that is existential (and his own thought has deepened both traditions, usually without their acknowledgments), one cannot really understand what Jungians try to do with dreams if one does not grasp the profound acceptance of the wish for transcendence that informs Jung's approach to the dream and led him to find in the dream what he did. That this approach seemed wish-fulfilling and avoidant to psychotherapists of other schools was the price Jung had to pay for pursuing his instinct for the transcendent, but it is important to stress that Jung was taking seriously the feelings of his own dreams in so doing, and following the hints they gave him as to what was important and what not so important. Eventually, the inherent energy of the images drove him to turn to amplificatory material beyond the dream itself and beyond even the dreamer's own associations in order to help the dream symbols achieve the transcendent effect. In his own view, Jung was merely doing justice to the symbols. We will see in this chapter how this approach leads subtly beyond what interpreters of other schools might feel safe in attributing to a dream's meaning, yet how the leap to a wider meaning can sometimes "open up" a dream.

Jung describes his work with the dream in which the figure of the customs official is followed by the figure of the knight:

> I set about analyzing this dream. In connection with "customs" I at once thought of the word "censorship." In connection with "border" I thought of the border between consciousness and the unconscious on the one hand, and between Freud's views and mine on the other. The extremely rigorous customs examination at the border seemed to me an allusion to analysis. At a border suitcases are opened and examined for contraband. In the course of this examination, unconscious assumptions are discovered.
>
> As for the old customs official, his work had obviously brought him so little that was pleasurable and satisfactory that he took a sour view of the world. I could not refuse to see the analogy with Freud.
>
> At that time Freud had lost much of his authority for me. But he still meant to me a superior personality, upon whom I projected the father, and at the time of the dream this projection was still far from eliminated. . . . I had told myself, "Freud is far wiser and more experienced than you. For the present you must simply listen to what he says and learn from him." And then to my surprise, I found myself dreaming of him as a peevish official of the Imperial Austrian monarchy, as a defunct and still walking ghost of a customs inspector . . . the dream recommended a rather more critical attitude toward Freud. I was distinctly shocked by it, although the final sentence of the [first part of the] dream seemed to me an allusion to Freud's potential immortality. . . .
>
> The knight and the customs official were contrasting figures. The customs official was shadowy, someone who "still couldn't die properly"—a fading apparition. The knight, on the other hand, was full of life and completely real. The second part of the dream was numinous in the extreme, whereas the scene on the border had been prosaic and not in itself impressive; I had been struck only by my reflections upon it.
>
> In the period following . . . I did a great deal of thinking about the mysterious figure of the knight. But it was only much later, after I had been meditating on the dream for a long time, that I was able to get some idea of its meaning. Even in the dream, I knew that the knight belonged

to the twelfth century. That was the period when alchemy was beginning and also the quest for the Holy Grail. The stories of the Grail had been of the greatest importance to me ever since I read them, at the age of fifteen, for the first time. I had an inkling that a great secret still lay hidden behind those stories. Therefore it seemed quite natural to me that the dream should conjure up the world of the Knights of the Grail and their quest—for that was, in the deepest sense, my own world, which had scarcely anything to do with Freud's. My whole being was seeking for something still unknown which might confer meaning upon the banality of life. (Jung, 1963, pp. 163–65)

In her book *The Myth of Meaning in the Work of C. G. Jung*, Aniela Jaffe, who transcribed these autobiographical memories, states what has become the quintessentially Jungian position: "The experience of meaning depends on the awareness of a transcendental or spiritual reality that complements the empirical reality of life and together with it forms a whole" (1970, p. 21). A favorite Jungian name for this experience is *numinous*, taken from Rudolf Otto's *The Idea of the Holy* (1958) in which he chose this word, coined from the Latin *numen* (which originally referred to the nod of a god in response to a supplicant's question) to suggest the quality of deeply felt religious awe. It is akin to the state that is often, in common speech, called wonder. It really is not possible to examine Jungian dream interpretation without realizing that the Jungian interpreter is always on the lookout for what is new, unknown, numinous, or wonderful about the dream. There is a deliberate reaching for the part of the dream that has this special effect, and there is an expectation that the dream exists to provide it.

All of the special ideas Jung brought to the understanding of dreams must be subsumed under this one big idea, that the unconscious exists to enlarge consciousness, and that it does its work by means of symbolic suggestion. Jung saw images as symbols whose content is not fully known—perhaps cannot ever be fully known—which exist to fascinate consciousness so that it will flow along new potential channels of experiencing. He founded his entire approach to the dream on this readily experienceable daily mystery.

Personifications of the Unconscious

Of the early depth psychologists, Jung therefore became the one most willing to trust dreams as the basis for establishing relations with the unconscious. Early on (Jung, 1916a) came his important discovery that the dream shows (in image form) personifications of the unconscious complexes—the very complexes he had been painstakingly trying to demonstrate through the pattern of the words that elicited unusual reactions in the word association test. He found that the emotional clusters that he could infer from the patterns in high-yield words were matched by the dream images of the subjects who reacted to those words, and so it became evident to him that the dream depicted charged emotional events in an individual's unconscious. From this point on, he became interested in dreams as the central tool for uncovering unconscious life. His willingness to learn from dreams must have unleashed a responsive chord in his dreams themselves, for they soon rewarded his interest with a series of fascinating images that became the basis of his psychology. It was as if he let them tell him what human psychology is.

Later, after publishing *Wandlungen und Symbole der Libido*, Jung experimented with a procedure he called active imagination. This involved him in a direct inner dialogue with specific figures who had appeared in his dreams. His earliest intimation of such figures was, in fact, an imagined descent into the unconscious itself, which is described in his autobiography (Jung, 1963, 170–99). There he saw, in a landscape suggestive of another world and the feeling of being "in the land of the dead," an old man with a white beard and a beautiful young girl. As Jung expressed his first contact with these figures:

> I summoned up my courage and approached them as though they were real people, and listened attentively to what they told me. The old man explained that he was Elijah . . . the girl called herself Salome! She was blind. What a strange couple: Salome and Elijah. But Elijah assured me that he and Salome had belonged together from all eternity, which completely astounded me. . . . They had a black serpent living with them which displayed an unmistakable fondness for me. I stuck to Elijah because he seemed to be the most reasonable of the three, and to have a clear intelligence. Of Salome I was distinctly suspicious. Elijah and I had a long conversation which, however, I did not understand. (Jung, 1963, p. 181)

Out of such experiences, Jung's special psychology of the collective unconscious was developed, and he often brought his sense that the unconscious was peopled with specific archetypal figures to his later understanding of dreams. It is important not simply to pick up his later ideas about what is "in" the unconscious and in the process forget the empirical attitude with which he learned about these supposed contents. Jung met his archetypes experientially and phenomenologically;

only later did he decide what to call them and what they meant, and even then, as much as possible, he let them tell him who they were and what their nature and business was. His own description of the process of his ruminations is characteristic:

> Naturally I tried to find a plausible explanation for the appearance of Biblical figures in my fantasy by reminding myself that my father had been a clergyman. But that really explained nothing at all. For what did the old man signify? Why were they together? Only many years later, when I knew a great deal more than I knew then, did the connection between the old man and the young girl appear perfectly natural to me.
>
> In such dream wanderings one frequently encounters an old man who is accompanied by a young girl, and examples of such couples are to be found in many mythic tales. Thus, according to Gnostic tradition, Simon Magus went about with a young girl whom he had picked up in a brothel. Her name was Helen, and she was regarded as the reincarnation of the Trojan Helen. Klingsor and Kundry, Lao-tzu and the dancing girl, likewise belong to this category.
>
> I have mentioned that there was a third figure in my fantasy besides Elijah and Salome: the large black snake. In myths the snake is a frequent counterpart of the hero. There are numerous accounts of their affinity. For example, the hero has eyes like a snake, or after his death he is changed into a snake and revered as such, or the snake is his mother, etc. In my fantasy, therefore, the presence of the snake was an indication of a hero-myth.
>
> Salome is an anima figure. She is blind because she does not see the meaning of things. Elijah is the figure of the wise old prophet and represents the factor of intelligence and knowledge; Salome, the erotic element. One might say that the two figures are personifications of Logos and Eros. But such a definition would be excessively intellectual. It was more meaningful to let the figures be what they were for me at the time—namely, events and experiences. (Jung, 1963, pp. 181–82)

Jung tried to bring precisely this attitude to the exploration of the fantasy lives of his patients, as opened up to him through their accounts of their dreams. He tried to enter the dream of the patient and let it tell him, on its own terms, what it meant, supplementing what it could directly tell him with comparisons from analogous fantasy material he had studied.

Since dreams were Jung's given, he considered it a methodological error to dismantle them. He did not, like Freud, want to present a systematic theory of the way dreams are constructed. Rather, he took the dream as a modern critic might a difficult Shakespearean text, as a composition to be accepted on its own terms until its ambiguity, irony, humor, and beauty yield up the effect that is its only secret—its power to fascinate, delight, and transform consciousness. This power was for Jung the dream's own mystery—in the ancient sense of mystery as initiatory experience, a rite of vision with a purpose, offering meaning and perspective. Jung sought to make interpretive statements that would enhance the dream's mystery, not to mystify but to lead the patient through the threshold of significant attitude change. Out of respect for the initiatory power of the dream, Jung did not try to use analysis to explain the mystery itself, and those in search of an explanation of dreams and dreaming will find in Jung instead an attitude of respect for the dream's autonomy.

The Intelligence of the Background

One can, however, find in Jung's many writings and seminars on the dream (Jung, 1916, 1974, and 1984) four fundamental ways of regarding the dream, ways which offer at least access to the "peculiar intelligence of the background" (Jung, 1970) that he claimed to find in the dream. These four ways can be listed as Jung's basic assertions about the dream, and they are the underpinnings of his entire approach to dream interpretation.

1. A dream compensates the position or attitude of consciousness.
2. A dream reveals the actual situation in the unconscious at the time of the dream.
3. A dream carries a message from the unconscious to the conscious. Frequently it has a point, purpose, or punch line.
4. A dream depicts the interactions of psychological complexes.

These assertions about the dream carry, in turn, a number of underlying assumptions, which are basic to Jungian psychology in general and to Jungian dream interpretation in particular. I would like to explore a few of these tenets of Jung's thought.

The first assumption is about *attitudes*. Where Freud's dream psychology seems to center on the way the psyche handles impulses, Jung's focus is on the way attitudes are handled. For Jung every conscious thought or feeling involves an attitude, a stand taken toward a human situation. Conscious adaptation to the situations that make up life demands such attitudinal stances, but the prejudices of the individual and of the culture that shapes the individual's stance may lead to attitudes which are not truly adaptive to all the contingencies the individual must eventually face. Jung felt that the unconscious functions in a compensatory way to critique the attitudes by which the individual lives. Dreams perform this function by showing the individual what the unconscious feels about the standpoint taken by consciousness.

Jung's vision of the unconscious could be compared with an ecologist offering an environmental impact study to a developer, who is like the ego at risk of injuring the inner environment if its attitudes are developed in defiance of the needs of the total psyche. For Jung, the unconscious reacts in terms of the needs of the total inner environment, whereas the ego, the center of conscious life, is governed by "egoistic" considerations—immediate anxieties, wants, and fears.

A second assumption is that there really are *two centers* of any individual's psychological life—an *ego*, which is the center of conscious life, and a *self*, which is the center in the unconscious, considering the needs of the psyche as a whole. Presumably dreams emanate from the self and carry the self's point of view. The self is the great poet within who knows the best way to put the matter, and interpretation must not violate the self's great poetry. Beyond the poetic aptness, the self has a serious ethical purpose, and working with dreams involves learning not only to appreciate but to honor the self. The dream is sometimes quite clear about the damage a particular point of view may cause if it is allowed to continue to govern the life of the individual. Jungian dream interpretation means taking the inner environment seriously, recognizing the sensitivity of the psyche to one-sided, prejudice-ridden attitudes. The self, in Jung's view, based on long experience with many dreams over time in the lives of many dreamers, not excluding himself (Jung, 1963), is striving for a standpoint that takes all sides of human nature seriously.

A third Jungian assumption is the *reality of the psyche*. The dream comes from a living source and reflects a living reality. A dream is therefore more than a diagram of the unconscious and not a defensive structure erected against the force of raw unconscious energy. The dream's images *are* that raw energy, and what we see in them is what unconsciously really is there. Not only does this experience not stand for something else too terrible to be faced; it is really getting lived, existing not literally but concretely, in the life of the psyche. The existential sense of a dream's reality is part of many dreams, and Jung gives this sense of reality ontological priority in his approach to the dream. Since what is depicted is what is actually going on in the unconscious, and since the symbols are alive, filled with psychological energy, it does not surprise a Jungian analyst that a seemingly distant image will suddenly become a living affect in the consulting room when the dream is discussed.

A fourth assumption is that unconscious life is *purposive*. For Jung, dreams have something to say: they make a point. A Jungian dream interpretation is incomplete if it can't find this point. Sometimes it is possible to restate a dream to the dreamer in one sentence in such a way that its point comes across like the punch line of a joke. Other times, the punch line is nonverbal, delivered as the feeling some dreams leave, the thought that one wakes up to. (*This is all wrong!* or *This feels good!*) In getting to the purpose of the dream, which often involves the experience of its compensatory function vis-à-vis waking consciousness, it is important to study the feelings of the dream ego. This dream ego—the unconscious representative of the dreamer—is not the waking ego but rather a representative of the self (Beebe, 1979). Although the dream ego may enact a neurotic attitude dictated to it by the conscious position of the dreamer, it will signal through its affects how the self really feels about being put in this position.

Yet the purposiveness of the unconscious is not limited to compensation. Entirely new attitudes may emerge out of the unconscious, or old attitudes may be brought to rest there, not as prospects to be lived but as healthy repressions. The psyche that dreams mirror to us is both the mother of emerging outlooks and the burial ground of former behavioral patterns (Hillman, 1979). The dream may reflect what is coming up from one's depths or what is being phased out of active ego-life. In the latter case, contemplation of action (for instance, a compulsion to drink) enables emotion, at last, to belong to the sphere of psyche rather than behavior (as in an anxiety-producing dream about drinking, which often correlates with recovery from alcoholism).

Jung became convinced of the purposiveness of the unconscious after long study of dream series in many dreamers. Usually Jungian dream interpretation is governed by a tacit belief that the dream being interpreted is doing something for the dreamer—telling something new, exploding a preconception, paving the way for a new attitude, bringing an old attitude into perspective. The Jungian dream interpreter's "moves" are guided by this assumption.

A fifth assumption (and the last I will explore here) is that the images in the dreams reflect psychological structures within the unconscious, structures that Jung called "complexes." A complex is a cluster of affects and ideas grouped around a central unconscious image. The mother complex and father complex involve a central mother or father imago, and even the ego is a complex, centered around the unconscious image of the hero—a supreme coper. When persons appear in dreams, the usual Jungian move is to see them as complexes. The personification may come quite close to the central unconscious imago, or the person may reflect some peripheral part of the complex, some single attribute of the essential complex. Often architectural units such as apartments are used to represent complexes: as the dream ego moves through the apartment one can imagine the self exploring one of the complexes that has been interfering with conscious functioning (Sandner and Beebe, 1982). When persons interact in a dream, a relation between complexes is often being depicted; one is observing an internal object relation, a relation between parts of the personality.

The assumptions Jung brings to the dream are all part of what a contemporary Jungian analyst, Joseph Henderson (1984), has called the *psychological attitude,* an attitude emerging in our time in which respect for the psyche is the paramount feature. The psychological attitude is grounded in the psyche itself, and may be distinguished from the scientific attitude and from earlier traditional attitudes like the religious, the aesthetic, the philosophic, and the social, in the primary emphasis it gives to the data of the psyche as a basis for meaningful communication. Jung's work with dreams has been a prime mover in the development of this new cultural standpoint.

Seen from the vantage of an attitude of respect for the psyche, Jung's four specific ideas about the dream—that it compensates the attitude of consciousness, that it reveals the actual situation in the unconscious, that it carries a message to the conscious mind, and that it depicts the interactions of psychological complexes—seem almost like natural conclusions. They become in a circular fashion guidelines to enforce the interpreter's respect for the dream. If the dream is considered to deliver an opinion from another standpoint that can correct the onesidedness of the dreamer's ego position, if it can reveal the actual situation in the dreamer's unconscious after he or she has been worried or upset, if it has an important message to deliver, if it can show exactly which complexes are responsible for the present conflict, then one has to take the dream seriously. James Hillman (1967) has spoken of the existentialist term "befriending the dream" as a way to define the subtle attitude toward the unconscious that Jungian dream interpretation tries to foster.

Unfortunately, Jungian dream interpretation is sometimes confused with the method of *amplification* that Jung developed to pursue the ramifications of certain dream images. Amplification means introducing an image to its cultural context; for example, a bathtub in a dream may reverberate with the symbolism of alchemical transformation, where deeply transformative processes of basic elements took place in a bath. A baseball diamond can become a modern mandala (since a run around the bases is a circumambulation of four points). In psychotherapy, interpretations based on amplification can enhance the meaningfulness of the image at the risk of slipping the dream into an ongoing Jungian context, where a subtext of the enterprise is teaching the client Jungian psychology. Such tutoring loses the true Jungian spirit of letting the dream speak for itself and threatens that the mysterious autonomy of the psyche will be lost in favor of chasing down therapy-based associations to Jungian ideas.

Exploring an AIDS Patient's Dream

Yet, with a background of ongoing Jungian therapy, considerably more depth of exploration is possible. To illustrate what Jungian analysis sometimes makes possible, I asked a patient of mine who had already mentioned to me the possibility that some day I might want to present some of his material, if we could discuss one of his recent dreams for use in this chapter. The dream he brought was dreamed a couple of weeks before I made this request; it was a dream he had forgotten to bring to our previous session. It seemed right to both of us that this particular dream would become the one so emphasized here.

The dreamer was a 48-year-old man whom I had been seeing for psychotherapy since 1972—thirteen years at the time of his dream. At the time of his entrance into treatment, he was struggling with the emotional consequences of much split-off rage at a sociopathic homosexual partner. My patient was himself a high-minded, unusually nurturant person with a long pattern of being bullied by others, and our first work involved connecting him with his own self-worth and with a number of dream indications to him that he needed to take better care of himself. He was successful in taking this advice from his unconscious, and he settled into a much less stormy relationship with another partner.

Some years after the conclusion of this first work, my patient called upon me again to explore with him the anxiety generated by a long-term candida infection. Candida (a yeast) is one of the infections which, when it appears in an otherwise healthy male, suggest immune system suppression, and our worst fears were confirmed when the patient developed Pneumocystis pneumonia, one of the AIDS-related opportunistic infections. After his release from the hospital, where he had recovered from the bout of pneumonia, the patient resumed analytic work with me to see if we could help his psyche make sense of, and even potentially resist, the much sensationalized life-threatening illness that he had contracted.

At this point in the treatment, I saw new opportunities to support the patient in expressions of anger, a still incomplete part of our previous work. He had always had difficulty connecting affectively with his sense of violation, even though he could intellectually appreciate it in the images of his dreams. I had been told of studies which suggest that cancer patients without manifest rage often have a poorer prognosis than those who express irritation readily.

A recent dream had indicated that he might be setting limits on the "good" part of himself. Its last scene was: "I am alone on the bed with a little baby lying on her back looking up at me. I believe it is my younger sister, Cathy. I begin to pinch her breasts. I am rather horrified at what I am doing and begin to pinch even harder." I felt that this dream indicated that he was getting hold, in anger, of the part of himself that had let him be bullied—a passive femininity not mature enough to nurture him, which he now hated. Associations about the real-life sister revealed her to be self-effacing and dangerously deferential, exactly like this part of himself. Her emotional stance, like his, did not seem to include a working sense of evil. I felt the dream had used her to point out a style of emotional expression (what Jung would call an anima) that was still immature, and vulnerable because it did not contain enough trickster meanness. I concluded that the dream ego persisted in punishing this figure even though it felt bad about doing so, because the self had decided it was time to direct some malice toward this excessively passive anima.

I thought this dream might herald a shift in my patient toward a willingness to externalize at least some of his frustrated aggression. Perhaps the self wanted to introduce to the anima the palpable reality of evil so that she would adopt a less open, more self-protective stance.

The anima interpretation had rather far-reaching implications, since the feminine side of a man, his inner "sister," represents much of his unconscious affective life and particularly his spontaneous feeling-reactions in situations. Timely anima expressions of negativity actually protect the psyche: this baby girl was too helpless and passive, which made me think not only of this man's at times excessive patience but also of his lack of immunity at the biological level.

He and I were somewhat naïvely hoping to promote an improvement in his immune system through our work, since we both knew of

Simonton and colleagues' (1978) well-publicized work on the healing properties of imagery with cancer patients. He was cautious, as it was not clear to him what the self really wanted at this point in his existence, and he was loath to manipulate himself out of a death whose time might truly have come. I was more willing to be heroic. In situations of lesser magnitude, I had had clinical experience of the anima as a truly psychosomatic entity; severe migraine headaches had, in my personal analysis, been accompanied by dreams involving overstimulated anima figures, whose subsequently improved circumstances had correlated with my reduced frequency of headaches. I was therefore willing to entertain a more than metaphoric connection between my patient's too-vulnerable anima figure and the current status of his immune system, which was far from capable of defending itself against the form-shifting, trickster virus that appears to cause AIDS. I dared hope that a shift in the overall level of his emotional response (symbolized at present by the little girl) could be achieved, and I believed that it might possibly correlate with a remission from his immunosuppressed condition.

My patient was in fact to die, but the dream we recorded for use in this chapter belongs to a particularly intense piece of analytic work, where the analysis had come to seem to both participants literally like a matter of life and death. The patient had much familiarity with me as an analyst, had read widely in Jung, and was quite skilled at interpreting his own dreams. All this psychological knowledge, however, gave way to the exigencies of a dream image that occurred at exactly this time. He felt challenged by this image, and my task was to help him find a way to hear what the self was trying to convey to him now.

He had typed the dream in duplicate: he recorded his dreams on a word processor, and this was the printout:

> I looked down at the top of my right thigh. There were round formations about the size of buttons on the surface. It almost looked as if soft-drink bottle caps had been pressed into the skin and released, producing the button effect. I thought of Kaposi's.

Kaposi's, as was well-known to both my patient and me, is the malignant sarcoma that is another opportunistic AIDS infection. Even before we began to speak to each other about the dream, there was a worried sense between us that the dream might be literally precognitive, indicating a new bad turn in his illness. From the standpoint of our shared effort at hope, the dream felt, initially to me at least and I think also to him, as a defeat. Nevertheless, we were committed to follow the self's own view of his course, even if it went against our ego wishes, and we had to honor the dream. Here is the transcript of our session:

Subject: This is one of those dreams that is really kind of an impression. It's visual. I see it visually. It's one of the short ones.

Interviewer: And this came before our last session and you forgot to bring it in.

S.:   Right. And I had not typed it into the file system, and I remembered it again when I got home and typed it up then.

I.:   Why don't I read it to you?[1]

S.:   Okay.

I.:   "I looked down at the top of my right thigh. There were round formations about the size of buttons on the surface. It almost looked as if soft-drink bottle caps had been pressed into the skin and released, producing the button effect. I thought of Kaposi's." Now were the bottle caps pressed down as if from the side they were pressed down onto the top of a bottle, in other words, the sharp end?

S.:   Yes, right, to make the impression, the circular impression, as if like a cookie cutter, something of that nature.

I.:   But small?

S.:   Maybe about the size of a nickel, the largest.

I.:   Well, it's certainly a worrisome thought. You have had the pneumocystis, but no Kaposi's.

S.:   Right.

I.:   In the dream, were you terrified or worried or upset?

S.:   No, I wouldn't say there was a strong emotion. I wasn't terrified, and yet I didn't feel it was Kaposi's at the time either. But I did think I might be warned of it.

I.:   So in the dream you didn't really feel that it was?

S.:   No.

I.:   Is there a feeling that went with the dream?

S.:   Not very much. It was really a kind of simple statement, and I suppose I didn't react to it until a bit later when I really recalled it.

I.:   And then?

S.:   Then I began to think of it as a warning dream like the dream when I had to go back to St. Mary's and have surgery again, or it might be a preparatory dream.

I.:   Did that dream, in fact, come true? The dream about St. Mary's?

S.:   Yeah.

I.:   So you thought it was preparing.

S.:   I thought it might be. It might be making a statement.

I.:   The dream is pure perception, and yet, in the dream is the thought there may not be, even though the thought crosses your mind. And also there is an inner feeling that this doesn't really look like what you've heard Kaposi's looks like.

S.:   I don't really know what Kaposi's looks like. I remember reading something quite some time back about raised, round, button-like lesions or sores, but I don't know whether that was actually referring to Kaposi's or what at the time. It's been a couple of years.

I.:   Now this dream is two weeks old today. The date was December 16th, and today is December 31st.

S.:   Yes, on or about the 16th. I don't have a specific date.

I.:   What about the top of your right thigh in reality? Is that an area that means anything to you?

S.:   I don't think there's anything offhand except that it would be very conspicuous.

I.:   I get the feeling that this is a brand of some kind.

S.:   It is kind of like that.

I.:   Where are cows branded?

S.:   Yeah, right on the thigh, or certainly within this joint.

I.:   Very similar areas.

S.:   Uh huh.

I.:   And now we get into soft-drink bottle caps. What does that get into for you?

S.:   It would certainly have to be self-branded or by hand. It's certainly not coming internally, or from an internal source.

I.:   Yes, that's right. I think we're not dealing with some organic, natural substance. I think we're dealing with something synthetic. Made for mass consumption.

S.:   That's kind of what I'm feeling, too, in this confusion I was talking about when I came in is that sense of being branded, in a way. There is a feeling of being branded. Okay, what do I do now? I'm branded.

I.:   Branded how?

S.:   Well, as an AIDS patient or as an AIDS victim. And I will be the rest of my life.

I.:   And interestingly, with the form of AIDS that you don't really have, so you've got a kind of collective projection on you that you have thus and so. I think it's very interesting that the form that is branded is the skin form. What's skin? To me it means persona.

S.:   Yeah, absolutely.

I.:   The surface. How you appear to other people and that, so the persona is altered, and you are stamped with a cookie cutter of collective projections as a certain kind of person, and not far from leprosy.

S.:   Right. Like I used to think in terms of individuation being very isolated. Certainly being one of the 649 AIDS cases is far more isolating than that ever was, or however many there are in the city at the time.

I.:   There are only about 850 Jungian analysts in the world.[2]

S.:   Yeah, right.

I.:   But I see the difference. This is isolating without any prestige, exactly. Although there is some kind of fascination.

S.:   A little perverse prestige there.

I.:   A kind of fascination attached to this illness.

S.:   Uh huh. I would say that's very definite about persona.

I.:   So if there's a threat in this dream or a warning in the dream, it's really a threat to your individuality. Even in the dream, there is a hidden sense that this is not really Kaposi's, but it's something else. And that comes through as we interpret it that there's something else. The real damage this could be doing to you right now is this thoughtless branding. Can we get even more specificity on soft drink?

S.:   Well, I don't know if there's any point, but I do remember thinking after the soft-drink bottle cap that I had to recall what types of materials would make the kind of impression that was left on the leg. And I kind of realized you hardly ever see soft-drink bottle caps anymore. It's mostly the pull-top cans.

I.:   That's interesting.

S.:   So it's a little bit as if only a very few of the esoteric soft-drink bottlers use caps anymore. That's almost an out-of-date form of bottling.

I.:   That's interesting: Cap—Kaposi's.

S.:   That's true.

I.:   But I like your idea better of the fact that it isn't as common anymore. Didn't kids once collect bottle caps?

S.:   Yes. There used to be different things imprinted on the insides, and sometimes under the cork.

I.:   What would be imprinted underneath?

S.:   I can't remember. There were a lot of things when I was a child, but each bottling company would have its own contest. They would have the letters under there, or photographs of sports figures.

I.: Okay, well this still touches, to me, the idea of adolescence. And also your childhood and adolescence. And were you the target of projections then, brands then, were you called things as a child?

S.: I'm sure.

I.: Do you remember? How were you treated as a child?

S.: Are you speaking of a particular type of projection? I'm not sure of what you mean.

I.: If these are the messages for kids, and maybe ones that kids trade and pass around to each other, and if bottle caps are being punched onto your skin, I wonder if this whole sense of stigmatization you're experiencing now is a result of your having been diagnosed with AIDS, which makes you the target of collective projections and echoes back in your psyche to earlier experiences of having been the butt of collective name-calling or rejections. I don't know enough about this part of your childhood. I remember things I was called as a child.

S.: Yeah. It doesn't strike me right off.

I.: Were you a popular child or an unpopular child?

S.: Well, I was always, you know, a rather popular child. Energetic and busy and into things until that situation happened in high school.

I.: What was that?

S.: That was where I was branded as gay or homosexual, I mean.

I.: And what grade was it?

S.: It was probably about the tenth grade. Anyway, I was really humiliated. What had happened there had been there was a group of boys who played together, and somebody got some dirty books, and we had a circle jerk-off. I guess to assuage their feelings of guilt, they picked one person to proclaim as being gay, homosexual, and that was me. And that just destroyed me as far as school was concerned, being branded. And so from then on, I became totally introverted and didn't have anything to do with school activities.

I.: Well, that really speaks to the bottle caps, as if a group of people with their bottles all put the lid on you.

S.: Um hmm.

I.: The lid had come off all their bottles. They were letting their homosexuality, or just some of their sexuality, out.

S.: Right. At that point, it was just really experimenting with sexuality at the beginning.

I.: Wouldn't that be like opening a bottle?

S.: Yes.

I.: An adolescent bottle . . . if you think of the bottle as a container. Soul juice and a little bit of soft drink comes out. I mean, it's not really whiskey yet . . . it's just . . .

S.: No, but its's like carbonated and it has the inner propulsion to ejaculate the material that's in the bottle.

I.: Exactly. And when it's all over, then the caps are all placed on you as the scapegoat. And this has disastrous effects on your socialization, and hurts your feelings terribly, and really was probably something that changed your life.

S.: Well, it did, it totally changed it, because I was very outgoing and very social, and that all just totally changed. I even left the city as soon as I was able to leave. So it's like having to give up your home, where you were born. I didn't feel then that I could even stay in the same town, my hometown. So that's really like being dispossessed from whatever you were born to. I mean, to leave is one thing, but to be unable to stay is another.

I.: I would also have to say that that would be the kind of event that creates the pattern of anonymous sex, which is supposed to be at least partially responsible for this condition. That one dare not be open about one's sexuality with others again. That if one wants to experiment with one's sexuality, they're going to do that only in a very sequestered sector of society, not in the mainstream. This is a powerful dream.

S.: It is.

I.: I would have to say that I would not have expected . . .

S.: Such a tiny little thing. But images like that can just have so much in them. But I think you're so right about the branding.

I.: Is there anything else you would like to say about this dream?

S.: That's about all I can recall. I can't recall anything associated with it. It was just really the visual impression of it there on the leg, on the top of the thigh.

I.: And now that we've talked about it in this way, I would just be interested to know where you are now in terms of your feeling state around this. I'm having feelings of outrage. I mean, I'm impressed by what we've done.

S.: Well, it fits in so beautifully with what I've been learning from the Simonton books about what beliefs or emotional thoughts . . . let me think of the exact way to say, but it is as if going back and finding that these patterns of perceiving myself have brought about this type of branding that I've accepted for years, or tried to deal with. Maybe I haven't confronted them yet. But the ideas in this dream fit so well with the Simonton idea of setting up conditions where the type of psychogenic illness can come down. It's just really being part of a structure, a psychogenic structure that would just really help something of that nature materialize. And this really kind of unfolds, helps me unfold, helps me to see that process that would produce a branding.

I.: And how do you then understand the cancer itself that would develop under those conditions?

S.: Well I don't know if I could safely say . . .

I.: Could you relate it to other's projections on you?

S.: Well, I think that something like that would be something that would happen as a child, what happened to me. It could produce a lot of anger, a lot of stress that puts one in a position in life where you have to live with an enormous amount of stress, and of course, stress is a huge factor in bringing about these things, but a stress that you can never deal with.

I.: Since the button/cap image is a circular image, I can't help thinking about the self. But I think of it in terms of false self, or at least other people's collective self-images being impressed on you, as you said, baseball heroes on the side of caps. In other words, these self-images of adolescent boys are being stamped on you in some way.

S.: And also I believe now I have an idea of like it being shut up so it can't come out like the bottle cap holds it in. Buttons, referring to buttons, buttons close things rather than open. I mean, you can use a button to open, but they're used to close things.

I.: The heart of your message was that you have to hide your homosexuality. That after you moved to another city—I know your history—you actually married a woman.

S.: Um hmmm.

I.: And at least for some period of time tried very hard not to . . . . It had the effect of driving your homosexuality in. It didn't mean that it emerged into a full-blown homosexuality after that. It was a very long and painful coming out process later on. It never quite completely came out of shadow.

S.: No.

I.: Even after you had settled down and had a lover and were stable in a relationship.

S.: Well, in fact, this illness brought it more out of the shadow than it's ever been, certainly as far as family is concerned. My sisters and my aunts and the rest of my family still living, they never knew from me, but they had their ideas.

I.: And now you've become extremely close to your daughter who is being very supportive.

S.: Um hmmm.

I.: A good friend and an ally, and who helped you connect with the Simonton materials.

S.: Yes.

I.: So we're looking at some kind of macho trip laid on you. What does branding mean? Branding makes the animal belong to the branders, isn't that right?

S.: Right.

I.: So it's as if your self, if you think of your self as your body, your total being, was branded with these collective self images that presumably you had to be submissive to. An adolescent boy idea of what you ought to be to be a man, so that's in there, too. And as you're telling, it did a great deal of damage to the unfolding of your own personality.

S.: Yes.

I.: I've worked on the idea that when people engage in anonymous sex in adult life, aside from the pleasuring aspect, there might be some attempt to redeem some early experience. Your parent's promiscuity or some earlier experience that still somehow if I can repeat it often enough that maybe one can bring something good out of it, to maybe transform what had been traumatic into something good. And when you describe this traumatic experience from your childhood, I can't help thinking that you've repeated that circle jerking in whatever sex club or back room experience you've had. There's been some repetition or maybe an attempt to master it.

S.: Yeah, well it certainly seems like that, almost a fixation, and it does develop a fixation, that if you're not aware of what's happening then it goes into unconscious patterns, and it certainly would lead into something like that. You'd have to want to seek to work it out, but the consciousness is not necessarily going along with the physical inclinations so that it is repeated over and over. But the soft-drink bottle caps certainly were in their heyday at the time that my branding took place. I was wondering myself why, why does this image come to me, and then I realized that it was almost an archaic image as far as a teenager of today. They wouldn't think of bottle caps.

I.: This would have been the late 1940s?

S.:   Well, it was the early 1950s.

I.:   Early 1950s, right in the midst of the McCarthy era, which I remember, too, was a very crew cut . . .

S.:   It was a vicious time.

I.:   Yeah, vicious.

S.:   I don't know if the world is still that vicious. I think I'm still hiding
from that McCarthy time trying to keep from coming out, because
of the attitude that prevailed at that time.

I.:   Very intimidating.

S.:   Particularly growing up in the South. It was like they didn't hesitate to lynch people. And certainly if they couldn't do it physically, there were lots of other ways. So it was really for protection
that I fled. It's hard to go back now and see if the event was real or
imagined.

I.:   Some of your difficulties in manifesting on the material plane
could be traced back to just plain fear.

S.:   Yeah, of not wanting to stand out, be noticed.

I.:   I feel complete with this dream. It's an amazingly . . .

S.:   I didn't realize quite how powerful it was.

I.:   A powerful image.

S.:   I've learned so much.

I.:   I thank you for it. In a way, I'm glad to get the record down. Do
you see what I mean? I'm almost glad to have this on public record.

S.:   Uh huh.

I.:   Given what was done to you on public record.

S.:   Uh huh. Yeah, it feels good, it feels good after having talked about
it because I really am seeing from the Simonton books, and I
haven't really gotten into the visualization because I think it's
more important, that my mind is trying to clear of certain preconceived ideas, and I'm just going along reading every morning as
much as . . . until I feel as if I've taken in as much as I can assim-
ilate. I'm just sort of letting the process evolve itself.

The Trickster and the Mystery

As this session suggests, the mystery of dream interpretation
ought to reside in the dream itself, not the language or idiom with
which we approach it. With this patient, a few Jungian terms did pass
from my lips, because I knew he would be familiar with them, and I
would not have hesitated to use more if they had been needed. But the
point was to connect him with his own imagery. My knowledge of

dream symbolism—which enabled me to identify the bottle-cap imprints as aspects of a false self intruding upon his persona—was really only accessible to me in the hour because I had taken the first step of accepting this man's inner material. For both of us, this session was a turning point in our work. His angry denunciation of the society in which he had grown up marked the session with a decisive engagement with affect that had eluded us in earlier treatment. This was the anima shift I had looked for. It saved the quality, if not the fact of his life.

The dream can accomplish shifts like this because it is itself shifty. All dreams, and all dream interpretation, can be amplified in terms of the trickster archetype, the mythologem of sly mischieviousness. To say dreams come from the self is not to imply that they are the voice of a kindly Christian god. Homer came closer to the truth when, at the beginning of the second book of the *Iliad*, he had Zeus send a false dream to Agamemnon, urging an untimely attack. The dream state is a great trickster, like Homer's Zeus, and I want to end this chapter by pointing up the *slyness* of the dream.

Freud emphasized this trickster aspect in his dream theory, demonstrating all the ways a dream can disguise and juggle affect (Richman, 1975). I have noticed that dreamwork sometimes backfires with patients who already have too much of the trickster active within them: manic-depressive, sociopathic, and certain borderline patients. These patients can misuse sincere efforts at dream interpretation. Their dreams may be employed in a deviously defensive way, often hysterically or antisocially, as a license for destructive enactments of the dream solution, taken literally and not symbolically. With patients who are in the grip of the trickster (Sandner and Beebe, 1982), one must therefore be cautious with dream interpretation. Yet even they can sometimes be helped by a dream that speaks to them alone, that no one else has to interpret for them. One recalls how in the fairy tale Rumpelstiltskin's power was destroyed when his name was rightly called.

But usually, the trickster is the dream's great healer. It reflects the part of the self that can shift the ground on familiar sets of thought to introduce a really new perspective on a seemingly open-and-shut situation. To this patient fearing the development of Kaposi's sarcoma, the dream brought alarming news of *another* malignancy blighting his persona—the psychosocial malignancy of the internalized prejudice against homosexuality. The dream's sick visual pun released his resentment.

Jung often spoke of dream interpretation as hermeneutics, identifying its practice with the cult of the trickster god Hermes. Jung's own dream interpretations were often abstrusely hermetic, leading to confusions and terminology I have tried to skirt in this chapter. But there is one complexity Jung introduced which must not be avoided. It is that in addition to the craft of Jungian dream interpretation there is an art, which lies in catching hold of the paradoxical, outrageous level of the dream. It is this trickster level which shifts the emphasis of one's concern as one dreams—a grasp of it takes the dreamer beyond appreciation of the compensatory effort of the unconscious to the threshold of genuine personality change.

Notes

1. This is a method I often use with my patients. It helps them hear the dream more objectively and gets me closer to it.

2. The actual number was closer to 1,200 at the time of this dream.

References

Beebe, J. (1979). Review of J. Hillman's *The Dream and the Underworld. The San Francisco Jung Institute Library Journal* 1(1): 11–13.

Cohen, D. B. (1974). To Sleep, Perchance to Recall a Dream: Repression Is Not the Demon Who Conceals and Hoards Our Forgotten Dreams. *Psychology Today* May: 7:50–54.

Henderson, J. (1984). *Cultural Attitudes in Psychological Perspective.* Toronto: Inner City Books.

Hillman, J. (1967). *Insearch.* New York: Charles Scribners.

———. (1979). *The Dream and the Underworld.* New York: Harper and Row.

Jaffe, A. (1970). *The Myth of Meaning in the Work of C. G. Jung,* London: Hodder and Stoughton, p. 21.

Jung, C. G. (1916a) [1973]. Association, Dream, and Hysterical Symptom. In *Experimental Researches*, translated by Leopold Stein and Diana Riviere, vol. 2 of *The Collected Works of C. G. Jung*, edited by William McGuire. Princeton, N.J.: Princeton University Press, 1953–1992 pp. 353–407.

————. (1916b). *Psychology of the Unconscious*. New York: Dodd, Mead.

————. (1963). *Memories, Dreams, Reflections*. New York: Pantheon.

————. (1970). Fragments From a Talk with Students (Notes recorded by Marian Bayes, Zurich, May, 1958). *Spring* 1970, pp. 177–81.

————. (1974). *Dreams*. Princeton, N.J.: Princeton University Press.

————. (1984). *Dream Analysis*. Princeton, N.J.: Princeton University Press.

Otto, R. (1958). *The Idea of the Holy*. New York: Oxford.

Richman, D. (1975). Personal communication.

Sandner, D., and Beebe, J. (1982). Psychopathology and Analysis. In *Jungian Analysis*, ed. M. Stein. La Salle, Ill.: Open Court, pp. 294–334.

Simonton, O. C., Matthews-Simonton, S., and Creighton, J. (1978). *Getting Well Again*. New York: Tarcher.

4

P. Erik Craig *and* **Stephen J. Walsh** ▬▬▬▬▬

Phenomenological Challenges for the Clinical Use of Dreams

Throughout history human beings have been fascinated by the enigma of dreaming. For many centuries, the mysterious event of dreaming was believed to be the product of an alien mind, a prophetic message spoken in the unintelligible language of deities and devils. Despite even ancient venerable efforts by Aristotle and Artemidorus, for example, to challenge these unscientific views, superstition, sorcery, and divination still dominated the popular perception of dreams through the beginning of this century.

When Freud (1900) (1901), first introduced a scientific approach to the interpretation of dreams, he painstakingly sought to demonstrate that dreaming was indeed the product of an alien mind, a revolutionary "internal" master which Freud called the unconscious. He was convinced, therefore, that it was impossible to understand a dream without first knowing a good deal about the very dreamer whose unconscious had constructed the dream in the first place. His technique was simple. "Look here," he would say to the dreamer. "Why not lie down here, close your eyes and relax. I'll sit over here behind you so you won't have to be concerned with me at all. As I mention each of the elements of your dream, you just tell me whatever comes to your mind. And please don't be harsh with yourself. You needn't worry if your thoughts seem silly, embarrassing, trivial, or offensive. We won't concern ourselves with such judgments here. Simply relax and take up the attitude of a fascinated, objective witness of your own stream of consciousness. All you have to do is say whatever passes through your mind with complete equanimity, as though you were looking through the window of a passenger coach while traveling through the countryside."

These simple, respectful instructions, describing what is known as the psychoanalytic technique of free association, formed the basis of our first scientific method for analyzing dreams and offered the interpreter a thoroughgoing acquaintance with the experiences and thoughts of the dreamer. Several major systematic methods for dream inquiry have appeared since that time, all of them having one conviction in common, that the proper study of dreams must be grounded in the dreamer's own experience and thought. These methods have made it possible for persons of all walks of life to systematically recover their dreaming experience and to use it for self-knowledge and personal or professional development.

Philosophical Foundations

We are indebted to Freud for his insight that even the most bizarre and unintelligible human experiences, such as neurotic symptoms, everyday slips of the tongue, and dreams, are structured in an intelligible and meaningful fashion. Nevertheless, although he provided a radical methodological breakthrough for the investigation of such enigmatic psychological phenomena as dreams, his theoretical assumptions often betrayed the integrity of the very phenomena he sought to understand. Freud made the assumption with dreams, for example, that they were intended to deceive the dreamer and that the manifest dream could *not* be trusted to be a fair and faithful portrait of how things stood for the dreamer. He even said, on one occasion, that once "the patient has told us a dream, we decide to concern ourselves as little as possible with what we have heard, with the manifest dream" (1933, p. 10).

The Phenomenological Attitude

The phenomenological approach presented in this chapter takes exception to this theoretically induced suspicion of the integrity of the manifest dream. As an approach to philosophy and science, phenomenology begins with the simple, straightforward appeal "to return to the things themselves." Characterized by a rigorous effort to relinquish unnecessary assumptions and presuppositions, phenomenology aspires to examine phenomena exactly as they present themselves in conscious experience. Therefore, in contrast to Freud's skepticism about the manifest content of dreams, phenomenological investigators maintain an abiding faith in the value and meaning of the dream precisely as it is given in the conscious memory of the dreamer.

Paraphrasing the founder of phenomenology, Edmund Husserl (1962), we might say that, with respect to dreams, we are invited to look at dreams afresh, to learn to see what stands before our eyes, to ask ourselves what is the meaning of the dream itself, as the very specific concrete human experience it is. Phenomenology therefore asks, why not let the dream be just what it is? Why not let it speak for itself? Following such an approach we are encouraged to insist that our understanding of the dream includes nothing that does not actually appear in the dream itself. Further, we are also encouraged to be suspicious of theoretical conjectures about entities that do not appear in our dream as such and, therefore, about the unconscious intents of those same purely hypothetical entities. For example, according to phenomenologists, the fact that we are so often baffled by our dreams upon waking is no reason to accuse our so-called unconscious mind nor, certainly, our dreams themselves of duplicity. After all, are we not, while dreaming, usually quite capable of understanding the immediate meaningfulness of our situations regardless of how extraordinary these situations may seem to us upon awakening? Would it not be closer to the manifest facts of experience, therefore, to suggest that the reason we are bewildered by our dreams is not because we are deceitful while dreaming but because we do not see plainly while fully awake?

A number of psychologists, psychiatrists, and psychoanalysts have adopted a phenomenological approach to the investigation of human existence. These investigators, known as existentialists, are concerned with understanding human existence as it is actually lived on a day-to-day basis by the individual. Many of these existentialists have shown a particular interest in dreaming since it is one of the most prevalent and primordial of our common, everyday (or should we say every night?) existence. In the existential-phenomenological approach to understanding dreams (Binswanger, 1963; Boss, 1958 and 1977; Craig, 1987a, 1987b, 1988a, 1988b, and 1990; Stern, 1972 and 1977), we find a gentle art, a hunger for the obvious, and a commitment to "reading" the straightforward "poetry of dreams" with courtesy and respect. As Paul Stern (1972) wrote, "What is needed more than anything else to understand the gesturing of the dream is an almost childlike incorruptible simplicity which is not taken in by contrived complexities and is able to see, in the midst of them—the obvious" (p. 43). What clearly distinguishes this sort of dream analysis is its faith in the power and potential of the manifest.

Sharon's Dream. For example, a middle-aged woman, whom we shall call Sharon, dreamed one night of being at home on her porch in a heavy snowfall. As she turned to go inside, someone called out her name. "Is that you, Mother?" Sharon asked, aware that her mother had just recently passed away.

"Yes," the voice responded. As Sharon turned around, her mother emerged from the shadows. The two women then embraced and said how much they loved one another. However, when Sharon invited her mother to come inside for tea, she declined. Sharon repeated her invitation once more, but again, her mother declined: "No, I really do need to go. But I love you and I'm all right. Everything will be just fine." With these words, Sharon's mother "dissolved" into the snowfall and disappeared without a trace.

Contrary to the rather tender mood of the dream itself, upon waking, Sharon felt suddenly anxious, particularly with the thought that her dream or her deceased mother might be "trying to tell her something." This anxiety persisted for Sharon despite the fact that while dreaming there was no evidence of any cause for alarm. In this case, Sharon's attitude reflects the common prejudices that dreaming always points to something beyond itself to something hidden and basically *other* than what the dream itself suggests. Countering this common assumption phenomenologists ask why look *behind* the dream for its meaning? Why attribute a given instance of dreaming with anything *other* than what it appears within the dream as such? Why not let the dream speak for itself?

If we pause with this dream of Sharon's, for example, we see simply that the dreamer and her mother had visited. They had met at Sharon's home, in the midst of heavy snowfall, the very kind of New England weather of which, Sharon herself said, she and her mother were both especially fond. In this very same mutually satisfying atmosphere the two women had felt and expressed their love for one another. Again, Sharon was quick to say that this was precisely how she and her mother had felt toward one another during the last few years of her mother's life. There is no evidence here that during Sharon's dreaming her mother was *trying* to tell her anything. On the contrary, in the dream itself Sharon's mother *actually had told her*, directly, that she loved her, that she could not stay and that everything would be fine. While dreaming, Sharon had experienced the warmth and affection that she had known with her mother while she was still alive. She had permitted her mother to appear as a tangible, meaningful presence in her world. How stark is the contrast between this *reality* and the sense of *unreality* that accompanied her mother's physical death! Why not, therefore, accept this moment for what was: a vivid, intensified experience of Sharon's relationship with her mother, including her mother's sudden, gentle disappearance?

If this dream were shared in a clinical context, the dreamer's immediate experience while dreaming would form the basis for inquiry. "But so what?" it might be asked. "What's new in this?" Again, taking a phenomenological attitude, we are encouraged to look to the dream itself for what is "new" and not assume that there is some deceitful or hidden purpose or message trying to break through. What, then, do we actually witness with this dream? We see that Sharon was open to the possibility of her mother actually saying several things: first, that she was, in fact, the very person she appeared to be, Sharon's mother; second, that her love for Sharon was still extant despite the fact that she had undergone such a revolutionary event as her very own death; third, that she could not continue their relationship in the same manner they had both enjoyed in the past; and finally, that despite these radical changes "everything will be just fine." Although, while dreaming, Sharon *was* open to hearing her mother insist on the necessity for her departure, Sharon could only consider this possibility while at the same time resisting it. A therapist might therefore ask if Sharon's relationship to her mother was not only good but if it was almost *too* good and, in some way, keeping Sharon from letting go and moving on with her life alone. A woman of Sharon's age and intelligence could obviously do many things with an evening such as this one in her dream. Why would she insist on having tea with her mother when her mother was so ready to leave? And finally, what might it mean that, upon waking, Sharon felt so anxious about the significance of being snowed in without her mother?

The above questions are all fully in keeping with Sharon's own experience while dreaming and do not presuppose something hidden or other than what is revealed in Sharon's dream per se. They exemplify the phenomenological invitation to set aside our theoretical assumptions and *return to the things themselves*. In the arena of dream interpretation this may be understood as an invitation to return to the dream itself, to the manifest dream, to that vital, concrete episode of being-in-the-world as which the dreamer existed while dreaming. In heeding the phenomenological maxim to *the dream itself*, we devote our whole attention to *the dream as given*. By tarrying in that world with all its fullness, we not only come to appreciate the manifest dream's inherent value as a human experience but also remain surprisingly faithful to the dreamer's existence as a whole, that is, to an existence which entails being sound asleep and dreaming as well as being fully awake and aware.

The Primacy of the Manifest

In offering such an alternative to understanding dreams, we might anticipate some questions from a thoughtful inquirer. For example, since phenomenology suggests that dreams reveal nothing other than what is manifest, why should we be concerned with them at all? Or in other words, what is so special about dreams if they reveal only what stands plainly in front of our eyes?

These questions rest on the assumption that the meaningfulness of phenomena is entirely exhausted with the single act of perception, that perceiving the obvious is tantamount to understanding it. Clearly, however, there is a difference between that which is manifest and already known and that which is *manifesting itself but is as yet unacknowledged* or unappreciated. Our final questions about Sharon's dream, for example, illustrate the importance of considering not only the initial, casual appearance of things but also the meaningfulness of these same apparent things after they have been given some thought. Our existence as human beings is relentlessly opening up before us in such a way that what is obvious or manifest constantly expands, exposes, and enriches *itself*. In other words, our attitudes, perspectives, and circumspections are remarkably fluid, and what is entirely "lost" to us in one moment is extremely apparent in the next; what is obscure from one vantage point or in one situation may be surprisingly obvious from another. Phenomenologists, like other analytically oriented investigators, are particularly concerned with this "as-yet-undisclosed meaningfulness" of things. However, contrary to other kinds of investigators, phenomenologists insist that such hidden meaningfulness be found *in the things themselves* rather than in *our* theories, assumptions, prejudices, or hunches about these things. In a sentence, phenomenological thinkers are concerned not only with what is *immediately manifest* but also with what *may eventually make itself manifest* through continued direct and thoughtful observation.

Dreaming and Possibility. How does this relate specifically to the understanding of dreams as a unique domain of self-realization, a safe and sacred arena for the manifestation of human possibility? Our experience with dreams consistently reveals that while dreaming we are inevitably concerned with three kinds of existential possibilities. First, we are concerned with those possibilities of our lives that we openly acknowledge on a daily basis while fully awake. Second, we are concerned with those possibilities that we acknowledge in our waking lives but which, at the same time, we choose to ignore. Third, we are concerned with possibilities that help constitute our waking existence but that, because of our own inexperience, fear, or prejudice, we do not recognize at all.

Penny's Dream. Perhaps an example will help. Let us warn you, however, instead of picking some especially exotic dream story, we have chosen what seems to be a relatively unexceptional dream, and we have done so just in order to demonstrate the richness of the mundane.

> Penny, a senior in college, dreamed one night of doing her laundry and putting her clothes in the dryer. In her dream, her friend Claire walks into the laundry room dressed in a new suit. Claire stops Penny from proceeding with her laundry and asks if Penny isn't going to clean out the dryer first. Penny doesn't understand this at all, but when Claire hands her a half a cup of water to throw in the dryer and tells her to turn it on, Penny does so. As she watches the water tumbling about, Penny sees all kinds of lint and tiny bugs in it. Just then her dog comes in and jumps up and down in front of the dryer. Penny says, "No, you can't go in the dryer," and then wakes up.

This is an example of one of those ordinary kinds of dreams that, at first glance, seems nearly entirely commonplace in itself but leaves one a bit bewildered about its relation to waking life. It is also typical of the initial reports of such dreams that, as in this instance, there is little or no emotionality on the part of the dreamer: even upon waking, the experience apparently stirs no particular anxiety or desire. It is the very kind of dream a dreamer is likely to dismiss as trivial and meaningless. However, in this instance, when we invited Penny to describe her dream in greater detail, to fill us in on who these dream characters were, what they were like, and how she felt throughout the dream, she had quite a lot to say. Eventually, the following understanding of her dream emerged.[1]

Already Recognized Possibilities. Penny immediately recognized in the dream the great sense of pleasure she took in doing laundry. Laundry was, in fact, her favorite chore, and she described the sensual delights she experienced in doing her wash. She added that she tended to be "pretty compulsive" and mentioned a couple of recent instances when she became annoyed or angry that her laundering had not gone well. She said she was disgusted with "other people's lint and filth" at the laundromat and tended to be frightened at the sight of bugs. She was impressed that her entire existence while dreaming was consumed by this enjoyable but trivial task.

Penny also acknowledged that Claire, her friend, was even more perfectionistic than she. Penny felt inferior to her in various intellectual pursuits, especially in the sciences, such as biology. They were both applying for jobs following graduation, but Penny was certain Claire would receive an offer before she did. It didn't surprise her, therefore, that her friend was taking the initiative in the dream, wearing a new suit and looking successful.

Finally, Penny took it as a natural thing for the dog, which she loved and missed while she was away at college, to be in the laundry room with her. She remembered, with much warmth, giving baths to this same dog when he was a puppy.

Before going on now, you may have noticed that it was only as a *descriptive context* for this dream was gathered that the dreamer openly acknowledged affective possibilities like pleasure, delight, anger, disgust, fear, inferiority, love, and warmth. Each of these moods were embedded in Penny's dreamed and waking relationships to the phenomena that appeared to her while dreaming. This is frequently the case with dreams: until one gathers some kind of context for the initial dream report, the emotions and moods and their subsequent implications for understanding the dream may be entirely omitted.

Recognized But Ignored Possibilities. While Penny already openly acknowledged the above-noted possibilities in her waking relationships to these dreamed phenomena, as she continued to think on her experience, she became aware of some incongruities. For example, she was surprised that her friend had been so abrupt with her in the dream since, in waking, Penny perceived Claire as "very soft-spoken," as "a marshmallow who wouldn't say boo!" She added that she remembered, while dreaming, that she felt annoyed with Claire for telling her to clean the dryer since, normally, Penny would have taken the initiative to do so on her own. She wondered, on reflection, why she hadn't "questioned" Claire but almost automatically complied with her friend's commands even when she, Penny, might have suggested more appropriate and effective ways to clean the dryer. These thoughts suddenly reminded Penny of her mother, whom she described as "stern but soft" and "harsh but helpful." She recalled various instances when she had disagreed with her mother but still had gone along with her requests.

In addition, Penny said that while dreaming she hadn't been surprised that her dog had wanted to jump into the dryer. Once awake, however, she wondered why he wanted to do such a thing. She was then reminded that when her dog comes in the house, he jumps up and down as he did in the dream. She said that she gets "really bothered" when his paws are all wet and he gets her dirty though she doesn't "get mad."

Before examining her dream, Penny had tended to think of herself as a mature and independent person. Although, in waking life, she *had* experienced a recurrent sense of inferiority, *had* occasionally felt guilty about her acquiescent inclinations, and *had* had some doubts about her own readiness for independent adult existence, she also tended to ignore these experiences as important features of her own existence. While dreaming, however, she became open to the possibility that she was not nearly as confident, independent, and assertive as she preferred to think she was. Although in rebuking her dog she did reveal her capacities for being assertive, confident, and firm, she carried out these capacities only in relation to a pet who would not speak back and whose attachment could never be questioned.

This dream, then, enabled Penny to acknowledge a hidden or very private sense of vulnerability, acquiescence, and dependency that she had previously recognized but ignored. Such openness to one's own particular reality, to one's own sense of existential encumbrance, is the very basis for developing more mature and authentic possibilities for being-in-the-world. In keeping with this idea it is important to note that Penny's dream did *end* with an act of self-assertion. It is also promising that Penny indicated her openness to the possibility of maturation when she recognized, in Claire, the presence of a malleable, fainthearted soul who had blossomed "overnight" into a person of confidence and command. True, Penny did not yet perceive these possibilities as authentically her own, but she was open to acknowledging their meaningfulness and, furthermore, as quite nearby, that is, in the presence of her own roommate who was also right there with her in the very same space.

Unacknowledged Possibilities. With these last considerations we can see how certain possibilities which an individual may successfully ignore in waking may appear quite explicitly while dreaming, even though these possibilities may be embodied in the presence of other phenomena, persons, animals, or objects. Penny's dreamed experience of Claire's confidence and strength reveals Penny's own fundamental openness to these possibilities. One reading of this aspect of her dream might be to suggest that Penny's compliance with her friend's assertive behavior may indicate her readiness to recognize both her own still dependent demeanor as well as her imminent ripeness for complying with these same kinds of assertive capacities in her own self.

Considering Penny's dream from this perspective, we can now say that one obvious feature of Penny's existence while dreaming was the absence of *human* passion—of a spontaneous, energetic, and emotional human relationship. During her dream Penny was open to the possibility of passionate physical response only as a nuisance and as a feature of animal existence, that is, when her dog was jumping in the air at the end of the dream. It is encouraging that Penny was open to the appearance of this spontaneous vitality in a familiar setting and that it was not so foreign that it could only appear in strange or surreal surroundings. It is also interesting that, while dreaming, Penny was open to the appearance of an animal's desire to go someplace where there was dirt and lint, bugs and filth. While dreaming, then, Penny was open to the possibility of impassioned relating but only as something which was not her own, which was animal-like and leading to what was, for her, filthy.

No wonder this dreamer's immediate response was prohibition, for we see from the very beginning of the dream that Penny could only perceive dirt as something almost unnatural and outside herself, as something to eradicate. And yet, is not dirt as much a part of a full human existence as cleanliness? Do we not all constantly shed dead skin and hair and provide a living sanctuary for whole armies of bacteria? Do we not all sweat, defecate, and constantly both produce and evacuate wastes in myriad ways? Indeed do not the very heights of sexual intimacy, unless we insist on only the most prophylactic and missionary-like of possibilities, require a liberal exchange of secretions and sweat? How has it happened, then, that while dreaming, Penny was open to dirt only as something alien to herself, indeed alien to what is human, and as something that she must eradicate and avoid? Since the meaningfulness of dirt and filth is something to which Penny is so aversive while awake (to the point of trying to exclude its presence from her life entirely), it may be worth inquiring how she feels about this now that she is wide awake; that is, how she feels about expending so much energy on remaining fresh and clean and pure. If her response indicated any openness to reconsidering this aspect of her life, we might ask if she is aware, now that she is awake, of any ways in which her absorption in eradicating dirt from her life gets in the way of her own enjoyment and pleasure, her own development as a woman, or the realization of the full range of her own possibilities as a person.

As you have followed this account, you may have formulated a number of other personal impressions or "interpretations." In keeping with a phenomenological attitude, you should ask if your impressions are respectful of the dreamer's experience with the dream precisely as it appears or if you have drawn on personal or theoretical beliefs that do not appear with the dreamer's experience as such. In keeping with the phenomenological attitude, we hope to have shown, thus far, how the dream itself manifests the particular possibilities that constitute the dreamer's existence. These possibilities include those fully recognized while awake, those recognized but ignored, and those that remain as yet unrecognized as one's own, as alien to one's own manner of being-in-the-world.

Undreamed Possibilities. Before moving on to the more methodological aspects of the phenomenological approach, we would be remiss not to mention another kind of possibility suggested by our dreams: possibilities that do not appear at all. For example, if you recall, our dreamer was struck by the fact that her entire existence while dreaming was taken up by a trivial but pleasurable task, that is, consumed by a concern with cleanliness. Consider then, something of the vast array of pleasurable possibilities that do not appear at all. For example, there are such pleasures as taking a walk in the woods, attending a concert, dancing, making love, taking a trip, and dining in a gourmet restaurant. Possibilities such as these, which do not appear, reveal ways in which the dreamer was not at all open while dreaming, which may, in turn, mirror existential possibilities to which an individual is also closed while awake. For example, we see that while dreaming Penny had been open to relating with another human being but only in a manner attuned to competitiveness—to dominance and submission, control and compliance. It is important to note that there are no words of encouragement, tenderness, or support; no exchange of friendship or affection; no burst of surprise or appreciation; no feeling of warmth or love. Indeed, Penny's friend joins her in a new suit, as if prepared for only the most business-like modes of relating.

Might we not profitably inquire just how Penny feels about this and what thoughts she has about how these particular *missing possibilities* in her dream may correspond to these same features of her waking life? Could it be that her dream bears a strikingly accurate resemblance to how Penny experiences her most important relationships in waking, that tenderness is assumed and never spoken, leaving her privately unable to entertain it openly as an important feature of her existence? Or could it be that Penny's dream contrasts with her waking experience of being fawned, flattered, and favored, leaving her feeling guilty and unworthy of such excessive affection? In either case, it is clear that our understanding of the meaning of the missing possibilities in Penny's dream will depend entirely on *her* response to our inquiry. If, phenomenologically, we are not justified in assuming we know the meaning of what actually appears in a dream, we are surely not justified in assuming we know the meaning of what never appears! Nevertheless, those meaningful aspects of being human that do not appear at all in a dream may help us understand what does appear. And the dreamer's response to these missing features of human existence is likely to shed light not only on her particular existential predicament but also on her possibilities for future growth.

We will come back to this dream before we are through, but for now, we hope mainly to have illustrated how dwelling with the manifest content of the dream as such can reveal structures and struggles that constitute the dreamer's very own manner of being-in-the-world. We also hope to have shown how the phenomenological dream analyst seeks to remain as faithful as possible to the experience of the dreamer while, at the same time, not ignoring the significance of that which may be initially latent or hidden from the dreamer.

Methodological Foundations

Now that we have considered some underlying philosophical perspectives for a phenomenological approach to dreams, we are faced with the problem of how, in practice, to carry out the analysis of dreams. While exposing the technical aspects of phenomenological dream analysis, we will compare and contrast this approach with other major analytic traditions and also examine specific conceptual and clinical grounds for the particular attitudes and methods being presented. Although several brief examples of this kind of dream analysis will be offered as we go along, we will close with one more extensive illustration of the existential-phenomenological use of dreams in the clinical situation.

In the following we describe in some detail a phenomenological approach to the analysis of dreams, focusing especially on two critical phases: (1) the gathering of data or a context for understanding dreams and (2) the manner of interpreting this dream-related data. In the model presented here, these two phases are called explication and elucidation, respectively.

Explication: Disclosing the Dream Itself

Almost all contemporary dream investigators recognize the validity of Freud's original conviction that a "correct" interpretation of a dream was utterly dependent upon the context of personal and biographical data provided by the dreamer. As noted above, Freud's method for gathering this context of dream-related data was known as free association. Following Freud's lead, analysts of various theoretical persuasions have since developed several different methods for this opening phase of dream analysis. All of these methods for gathering data have one essential effect, that is, to provide a fuller, richer, more individualized basis for the analysis of dreams.

Phenomenological dream analysts agree that a complete understanding of the dream is impossible without the presence and participation of the dreamer. They, too, have developed their own methods for gathering information relevant to the dream and what distinguishes their methods in particular is their emphasis on obtaining a rich and accurate description of the manifest dream. Naturally, this concern with the manifest dream is bound to lead to some noticeable differences in what is required of the dreamer and, later on, in how the analyst or therapist then makes sense of (i.e., interprets) what has been said. In order to provide a concrete sense of this phase of analyzing dreams, we will begin by describing how a phenomenological psychotherapist recently responded to a dream in the course of psychotherapy.

Lilly's Dream. The dreamer, Lilly, as we shall call her, happened to have been a 45-year-old female patient who, despite her seemingly relentless anxiety, managed to take quite good care of herself and her family. This lively and intelligent, though manifestly hysterical, individual reported one week, nine months into her therapy, that she dreamed her therapist and she were having an affair. The therapist was initially struck by the suggestive nature of this announcement but also realized that he had no idea whatsoever about what had actually occurred to Lilly while dreaming. He had no knowledge at all of what Lilly saw and heard or how she felt during her dream. Therefore, setting aside, for the moment, the seemingly provocative nature of her report, he simply asked, "How did that happen to come about?"

"I was away alone for a weekend, and I met you at a bar. . . . We had some drinks and then went to my room. We were in my room kissing and holding each other when I began to wake up and hear my son calling me to get up. I wanted to stay asleep and see what would happen, but he kept calling me. So I got up." The therapist, convinced of the significance of the particulars of Lilly's dream as such, then asked about the location of this dreamed rendezvous: "Where did all this happen, and how did we happen to be away at the same place for the weekend?"

Lilly then mentioned another dream from the same night, the night preceding her session. In this earlier dream, she had been asking her mother who her real father was (she was conceived out of wedlock and the identity of her biological father had been kept secret). The mother refused to answer Lilly's question but kept saying, "It's not important. Roy will take care of you." Lilly had no idea who Roy was and felt immediately puzzled, but before she could ask anything her mother started to walk away, and the next thing she knew she was at a resort for the weekend. She said she had apparently gone away without her family and then said, "I met you in the lounge. Later on we went to my room where you were holding me, just holding me very gently." Lilly then made a gesture with her hands and arms imitating the position of an adult holding a child.

The therapist noted to himself a number of interesting features in Lilly's experience: that it was the first time she had ever reported a dream involving her deceased mother; that she seemed to have hardly any anxiety in or about this encounter; that the name Roy was nearly identical to his own last name, Royce; that in being away on her own Lilly had done something she had never previously attempted in waking or dreaming; and that the event she interpreted as "having an affair" had been disclosed more specifically as, "We were in my room kissing and holding each other," and still more explicitly as, "You were holding me, just holding me very gently." While many possibilities occurred to the therapist regarding the potential significance of these dreamt experiences, he was still convinced that neither he nor Lilly had dwelt sufficiently long with the dream itself. He therefore suspended his own conjectures about these dreamed events and simply inquired, "How did we happen to get from the lounge into your room? What was it like there?" Lilly answered roughly as follows:

> Like I said, it was some kind of hotel or resort where I'd gone away. I was in the lounge and about to order a drink when I looked up and saw you. You said "Hello," very warmly and then asked me if I knew you would be there. I said, "No, I didn't." Then you asked me if I would like some wine. I said, "Sure," and you ordered us a bottle. We drank a couple of glasses together and then you said, "It's getting late, why don't I take you to your room?" And then in the room you just held me. You were very gentle and patient and just holding me. It was so nice. Then I was frustrated when my son woke me up. I wanted to go back to my dream.

Again, the therapist noticed some interesting new features in the dream experience. In particular he noted that he had been the one to initiate all the action in the dream while Lilly compliantly responded. This behavior sharply contradicted Lilly's waking tendency to be the one in charge and in control. The therapist also observed to himself that Lilly had dreamed that she and he had gone to her room only after having had a couple of glasses of wine which *he* had offered. Even with these descriptions, the therapist sensed that Lilly still had not finished recounting her dream. So again he inquired, "What was your room like anyway? And how did I happen to end up holding you like this?"

> Oh, it was just an ordinary room. It was nice and spacious. It had some large paintings on the walls and a couple of lounge chairs just like these (gesturing to chairs in which she and her therapist were seated). When we came into my room you asked me if I wanted to talk for a while. I said I'd like that and we sat down in the chairs which were very close together and facing in the same direction. You asked me if I wanted another glass of wine. I said, "Yes," but when I leaned over towards you I lost my balance and fell on you. Then I leaned up and kissed you. It was so nice. You just held me while we talked. You were so gentle. We didn't do anything sexual. You were just holding me patiently. It was nice and comfortable. I felt safe and warm being with you. You were like you are here. I could tell you anything. I was really upset about waking up. I wanted to stay there longer. I wanted to see what would happen. I even tried to go back to sleep but I couldn't.

Again the therapist was struck by a number of the details in Lilly's report: that she had dreamt that he had continued to offer her wine; that she had "lost her balance" and "fell" on him but consequently had taken some initiative in the dream by leaning up and kissing him.

Conceptual and Technical Reflections. This brief vignette illustrates the particularity of dreamed experience that is often overlooked in the initial mention of a dream. Quite often, the dream is presented as already interpreted, as in this case with the comment, "we were having an affair." The foremost phenomenological strategy, therefore, is consistently to invite the dreamer to return to the palpable event of the dream itself, again and again, encouraging the individual to recall and relive the dream itself precisely as it was experienced while dreaming. This process of recounting the dream enables the dreamer and the therapist to review together the events precisely as they are presented in the memory of the dreamer. This therapeutic encounter emboldens the dreamer to reconsider those particular existential possibilities that appeared in the dream. The therapist also benefits from this opportunity to extend and enrich his or her own acquaintance with the dream and with the dreamer, helping to insure that the eventual understanding of the dream and of the dreamer will be grounded, as much as possible, in the dreamed phenomena themselves and not in various theories, hunches, or fantasies about them. Such descriptions enable both the dreamer and the listener to "while away" some time in the dreamer's world, to tarry long enough to gather an accurate picture of these events in the dreamer's life. During this phase of the analysis of a dream, the therapist is best advised to concentrate on listening and to avoid interpretation altogether.

This heightened familiarity with the dream and the dreamer was the identical objective sought by both Freud and Jung with their methods of free association and *amplification*, respectively. A phenomenological therapist simply goes about this task in a different manner, using a method designated by the Swiss existential analyst, Medard Boss, as *explication*. Boss describes this method for gathering data as one that involves "letting the subject supplement his first sketchy remarks with more detailed statements . . . so that the dreamer may give . . . an increasingly refined account of the dream sequence" (Boss, 1977, p. 32).

As is clear, from the foregoing example, that explication requires one to pay considerable attention to the manifest dream per se. While Freud and Jung both recognized the importance of beginning with the concrete elements of the manifest dream, their methods of free association and amplification often drew dreamers far afield from the original event of the dream. To be sure, one might make good clinical use of these meanderings but do they permit one to understand the dreamer's existence while dreaming?

Jung (1960) himself was wary of this shortcoming and criticized Freud's use of free association for its tendency to leave too much room for analysts to introduce their own "preconceived opinion" (p. 285). Jung's own method, amplification, therefore emphasized a manner of "taking up the context," which "consists in making sure that every shade of meaning which each salient feature of the dream has for the dreamer is determined by the associations of the dreamer himself" (pp. 285–86). Jung's associational method, called amplification, discouraged *free* association by requiring the dreamer to return to the original dream element before offering any new associations. While this method remained closer to the elements of the original dream, revealing a variety of the dreamer's perceptions of and experiences with the *kinds* of phenomena appearing in the dream (hotel rooms or kisses, for example), it often lost sight of the meaningfulness of the *particular* phenomena (the particular hotel room, the particular kiss) that appear in a given dream. So despite his intent to remain more faithful to the dream itself, Jung's method also could lead him astray from the original dreamed phenomena.

In contrast to such associational methods for gathering a context, a phenomenological approach insists on a direct acquaintance with the dreamed phenomena themselves as the most reliable ground for understanding the meaningfulness of the dreamer's existence while dreaming. In keeping with this requirement, therefore, Boss (1977) described the phenomenological method of explication as one of "opening and revealing the meanings and frames of reference that belong *directly* to concrete elements of the dreaming world or to the way the dreamer conducts himself toward these elements" (p. 32, emphasis added).

Although various associations, including day residue as well as recent and childhood memories may occur in the process of explication (as they did in our example), no deliberate effort is made to obtain these traditional sources of associational material. Therefore, Boss (1977) emphatically states that the premier concern of this procedure is to get "a full account of just what kinds of things can reveal themselves to the dreaming person, as well as an equally complete description of the ways he has of responding to them" (p. 38). "The aim," Boss writes, "is to make visible the dreaming subject's whole being-in-the-world: the particular way of being open (or limited) that characterized—and was—his *Da-sein*[2] for the duration of the dreaming" (p. 32).

A quick review of the particular therapeutic interaction described above reveals that the therapist confined himself to three activities—listening, observing, and questioning. Using a phenomenological approach, the initial phase in the therapeutic use of dreams simply requires the dreamer to tell everything he or she knows and is willing to share of his or her dream experience. During this phase of the inquiry, dream therapists are encouraged to make every effort to keep themselves out of the arena of the dream so that the dreamers *themselves* might recall and relive their own dreams with minimal interference. The memory of the dream becomes a kind of playground to which dreamers return to "hang out" and, in the process, notice those particular existential possibilities to which they found themselves originally open while dreaming. In other words, the therapist's initial challenge is to provide a safe time and space for remembering and reliving the dream, much as sleep itself provided the time and space for the occurrence of the dream in the first place.[3] What this waking therapeutic situation adds to the original sleeping situation is the person of the therapist, an alert and concerned human presence offering genuine attention and a desire for understanding.

Clinical Reflections. In Lilly's dream above, we saw how the therapist repeatedly invited Lilly back into the world of her dream. He did not worry about wasting time with repetition for what was of value was worth repeating, and as it turns out, there was almost always something new. With each new review, Lilly's recall of the particularity of her own dream life was enhanced. Likewise, the therapist was given an increasingly detailed account of the dreamer's situation while dreaming and, in this case, of the nature of her particular relationship to him. Through her repeated visits to the world of the dream, Lilly recovered an experience of warmth, gentleness, and security in relation to her therapist. Her dream affair actually revealed not a free, fully adult sexual liaison but rather a dependent *child-like* relationship centered on acceptance, protection, and safety.

While explicating her dream, Lilly was emboldened to recognize the possibility of experiencing from her therapist a quality of concern she had not known in her own childhood. Meanwhile, the therapist was alerted to the possibilities of Lilly's misinterpretation of the nature of this concern. After all, the dream had been set in the unambiguously *adult* situations of a lounge and hotel room in which the therapist was brought face-to-face with the possibility of his own contribution to the sexualization of the therapeutic relationship. Could it be that he had behaved in a covertly seductive manner with this patient? After all, in the dream, it was *he who had offered the wine* to Lilly and then also offered to take her to her room. The therapist was thus challenged to reflect honestly not only on Lilly's perceptions and desires in relation to him but also on his unexamined attitudes and behaviors in relation to her. Appropriately, the discussion that followed this dream did indeed lead not only to a clarification of the boundaries of the clinical relationship but also to the patient's first report of previously undisclosed experiences of incest in her childhood.

A Classical Illustration and Summary. A hypothetical example may offer an even clearer, more systematic (albeit less realistic) overview of this phase of the analysis of dreams as carried out by a phenomenological analyst. Let us suppose that a woman dreams that, while enjoying a leisurely walk in the forest, she suddenly slips and falls down a bank to the edge of a stream from which a large green snake slithers toward her legs. She wakes up in terror.

Remember, our first concern is to learn as much as possible about the dreamer's existence while dreaming. Inviting the dreamer to *explicate* the dream, we might inquire about *the setting and the mood* in which the dreamer found herself while on her leisurely walk. We might ask about the *time* of day, the weather (*atmosphere*) or the location and nature of the forest. We might also wonder about the *events* of the dream, for example, just how it happened that the dreamer suddenly slipped and fell down the bank. We might ask about the *space* of the dream and what it was (e.g., persons, animals, or objects) that the dreamer was open to perceiving as integral features in this dreamed space. Hopefully, we would take nothing for granted, permit ourselves no assumptions since, for example, though there are innumerable forest banks down which a dreamer may tumble, our dreamer slipped and fell down this bank alone. Streams, of course, come in many varieties, and we would want to be sure we were "seeing" this stream, as much as possible, just as it appeared to the dreamer. How different, for example, is the shallow, clear, fast-running stream from the stream that is deep, slow, and murky with shores lined with dense brush, mud, and slime. Naturally, we would want to hear more about the snake, its texture and size, the shape of its head, and so one. We might also inquire about the details of the snake's behavior and any awareness or intent which the dreamer may have imagined it as having. Finally, we would most certainly want to hear about the dreamer's *mood* as she fell down and encountered the snake.

These are only a few of the kinds of features of dreamed experience we may invite the dreamer to describe. The therapist's primary task throughout this phase of the analysis is to facilitate a rich and accurate description of the dream itself. This done, however, how are we to make sense of this interesting report? What does it mean?" Now we shall turn to the second major aspect of the analysis of dreams, interpretation.

Elucidation: Understanding the Dream Itself

Although the initial phase of dream analysis, gathering a dreamer-generated context of dream-related data, is by far the most important component of the analysis of dreams, it is with this second phase, that of interpretation, that the entire enterprise of dream analysis is usually identified. In philosophy, literature, theology, and the human sciences, the art and science of interpretation is called *hermeneutics*, deriving its name from Hermes, the messenger of the gods. Hermeneutics therefore may refer to one's *overall approach to interpretation* in general or to one's *specific interpretation of particular phenomena.* With respect to dreams, both meanings are relevant.

Conceptual and Historical Perspectives. In his *Interpretation of Dreams* (1900) Sigmund Freud noted that, prior to 1900, dream interpretation was approached in one of two ways. The first of these, which Freud designated as "symbolic" (p. 97), emphasized interpreting the dream en masse, as a whole. The second, which Freud called "decoding" (p. 97), approached the dream in detail by taking up each of the separate elements of the dream and translating their meaning according to some predetermined code. While the first approach was more intuitive and relied on the effectiveness of the interpreter, the second tended to be more mechanical and relied heavily on the effectiveness of the code.

As a humanist, Freud was sympathetic with both of these methods, in the sense that they both avowed a commitment to the essential meaningfulness of dreams. Furthermore, he consistently maintained this sympathy despite the fact that it defied the so-called scientific consensus of the day that dreams were froth, the mere by-product of somatic events. On the other hand, as a scientist himself, Freud disputed the validity of popular, mystical, or superstitious approaches which lacked any objective theoretical, methodological, or scientific foundation. Freud therefore set out to correct this deficiency by introducing the first modern scientific approach to interpreting dreams. As noted at the beginning of this chapter, Freud's method of free association emphasized the expression of the dreamer's own uncensored, spontaneous thoughts in relation to each of the elements of the dream. The method provided a new and expanded framework for interpreting dreams, a framework established, not by intuitive prowess or cryptological sophistication but rather by the dreamer's own life. Freud's method began with a consideration en detail, through the dreamer's concrete associations to each element and then moved toward a consideration en masse, using an understanding of symbols to synthesize the meaning of the dream as a whole.

But, it may be asked, what was Freud's approach to interpreting the wealth of data gathered from the dreamer? In other words, what was Freud's hermeneutic attitude toward the data? It takes little study of Freud's works on dreams to realize that he actually had two strikingly different, and in many ways contradictory, approaches to interpretation, two entirely different hermeneutics in the analysis of dreams. Freud himself openly discussed the necessity and justification for this dual approach in his first book on dreams (1900, pp. 350–53). While, on the one hand, Freud realized that he was the first modern scientist to introduce *experientially based,* life-historical grounds for understanding dreams, he also felt compelled to maintain, simultaneously, *theoretically based,* symbolic grounds for interpreting the so-called latent content of dreams.

Freud championed this second, more theoretically grounded hermeneutic specifically in order to surpass the dreamer's resistances to certain thoughts arising in relation to the dream. Consistently, Freud found that despite the dreamer's good intentions, his or her associations to the dream would contain gaps which, according to Freud, required some kind of translation through the "interpreter's knowledge of symbols" (p. 353). Thus, while Freud began with a scientific, experiential, and even somewhat phenomenologically based approach to understanding dreams, an approach profoundly grounded in the dreamer's own subjective stream of consciousness, Freud's particular view of psychic life inevitably induced him to revert at times to a method of interpretation quite similar to that of ancient cryptologists. While it was true that Freud justified his "symbolic code" on the grounds that it was derived from so-called clinical evidence and not superstition, his own symbolic translations still relied on the effectiveness of his code, leaving him vulnerable to the same problems as his prescientific predecessors.[4]

Freud's own dualistic approach to the interpretation of dreams has had a profound impact on the various hermeneutic traditions that have sprung up in the wake of his investigations. Regardless of the theoretical orientation espoused and the purported importance placed on the contextual data provided by the dreamer, one repeatedly observes analysts violating their own clinical principle of gathering such data and, instead, rushing headlong into clever symbolic interpretations. Unfortunately, even phenomenologists who profess to eschew the use of symbolism may be found taking up this questionable activity. While it can be granted that there are times when, as a therapist, one must find a way to understand the dream without the benefit of any further dreamer-generated data (as, for example, when a person reports a dream on the way out the door at the end of a session), it is our opinion that the practice of arbitrary, symbolic interpretation is still far too common among experienced analysts of all persuasions.

A common phenomenological criticism of modern approaches to dream interpretation, therefore, is that they are too often too quick to leave the dreamer in the dust of theoretical speculation. It is, unfortunately, not at all uncommon for dreamers to have their dreams systematically dismantled and replaced with an interpreter's favorite set of theoretical icons, icons which not only fail to inspire the dreamer's own interest and belief but also fail to illuminate, for the dreamers themselves, the particular meaningfulness of that which so dramatically impressed itself upon them while dreaming.

Thus, phenomenological dream investigators are skeptical about interpretive and analytic methods that denigrate a dreamer's report of his or her own experience by considering it incapable of standing on its own as a reliable index of just how things stand for that individual while dreaming. Despite the fact that these less respectful methods may have occasionally demonstrated themselves to be effective therapeutic tools, it is not at all clear that a more gentle approach cannot achieve the same ends and at much less of cost to the authority and integrity of the dreamer. The contention of phenomenological dream analysts is not so much with interpretation as such—indeed, even our very use of language is in itself already an interpretation—but rather with the fact that in our interpretive fervor we stray too far from the manifest significations of the dream itself as well as from the implication of these direct significations for the life of the person who dreamed.

Phenomenological Perspectives and Methods. When carefully following their own principles, then, phenomenological dream analysts employ a radically different kind of hermeneutic or approach to interpretation. In fact, the phenomenological hermeneutic is so different we hesitate to even call it interpretation at all but rather prefer to use the term *elucidation,* that is, literally, "drawing light from" dreamed phenomena so their significance is revealed *on their own terms.* The challenge is to discern the meaningfulness of the dream precisely as that meaning is given in the dreamer's dreamed experience per se. In other words, the phenomenological task is simply to receive or intuit the meaning *already there* in the dream phenomena themselves. Analysts using a phenomenological approach to interpretation are often asked if they are not expected to contribute something beyond what the dreamer already knows, and if so, how can this be done without referring to theoretical concepts or symbols or to anything beyond the dream itself? The following sections lay out some basic features of this approach to the interpretation of dreams.

Listening. Anyone who listens carefully to others as they describe personal experience, whether it be waking or dreaming experiences, realizes that much of what is said is entirely taken for granted, that is, never thoughtfully examined. Careful listeners, therefore, learn to attend not only to what an individual openly acknowledges but also to what he or she ignores or even blatantly dismisses. In other words, the careful listener makes it his or her business to hear not only *what is said and recognized* as such, but also *what is said but unrecognized* as such, as well as *what is never even spoken at all*. This is nothing new, of course, to anyone trained in the art of interviewing or interested in the dynamics of human speech and communication. Nevertheless, in listening to dreams, it is worth remembering that individuals often say things that they themselves are not quite ready to hear! One of the therapist's most important tasks is to help dreamers discover what it is that they are afraid of hearing themselves say. The challenge is to return to the dreamer not just those features of the dream that are already appreciated and tolerable but also those aspects that are still somehow unacceptable, troublesome, or vexatious. Naturally, this must *not* be done in a way that increases the dreamer's fear about what they themselves are saying but, rather, in a way that "detoxifies" the psychologically acidic content such that the dreamer's openness to his or her own existential situation is palpably increased. The greatest obstacles to these objectives are: (1) the tendency of therapists themselves to take too much for granted; (2) the threat of misinterpretation due to the therapist's own resistance to recognizing painful or threatening features of the dream; and (3) the temptation to translate the meaning of the dream in terms of personal assumptions and theories instead of in terms of the dreamer's own experience of his or her own existence. To assist in overcoming these difficulties, phenomenologically oriented dream analysts use a method called phenomenological epoche or phenomenological reduction.

Phenomenological Epoche. More commonly referred to in English as "bracketing," phenomenological epoche involves the systematic suspension of belief and requires a dream analyst continually to set aside any thoughts, beliefs, assumptions, concepts, or theories that do not actually appear manifestly in the dreamer's description of the dream as such. Epoche may be thought of as disciplined naïveté, a deliberate, systematic skepticism with reference to assumptions, presuppositions, concepts, or hypotheses that do not show themselves directly in the dreamed phenomena per se as well as an equally trenchant and thoroughgoing questioning of anything that is left unexplored or appears to be taken for granted.

For example, let us imagine that we are listening to a woman who tells us the dream of the snake described above. As we listen to the dream, we may recall Freud's conviction, first declared in *The Interpre-*

tation of Dreams, that snakes are "the most important symbols of the male organ" (1900, p. 357). We recognize immediately, however, that there is no male organ in this dream and that to suggest that this reptile is not a snake at all but rather a symbolic façade for a penis is a matter of purely theoretical inference and conjecture. Indeed, no male, not to mention male organ, appears anywhere in the dream. The dreamer herself is the only human being present. Therefore, invoking the phenomenological epoche, we suspend our theoretical belief that this snake is a phallic symbol and return to consider this dreamed snake itself.

Now, however, we may suddenly recall Jung's suggestion that a snake may be a symbol of good or evil (1956, p. 374), of instincts (1956, p. 396), of the unconscious (1956, p. 374), of wisdom (1959, p. 234), or of healing (1953, p. 144). Another quick review of the dream reveals no concern with morality, no unconscious biological drives, no reference to wisdom or healing in the dream itself, so once again, we suspend these theoretical beliefs and return to the particular snake of this dream.

As we continue to listen to the dreamer's description of her dream, we may recall a dream we ourselves once had about falling into a pit of slimy, black serpents. We may even recall waking with feelings of horror and disgust. However, *in spite of the similar elements* of snakes, fallings, abrupt awakenings, and anxious feelings, we recognize that this person's dreamed snake, the setting in which it appears, the dreamer's response, and indeed the person of the dreamer herself are only a few of the ways in which *this dreamer's existence while dreaming was indisputably unlike our own.* So once more, we overcome the temptation to form preconceived interpretations of this woman's dream, this time by *bracketing out our own personal experience,* by suspending our recollection of our own dream along with all of the feelings and beliefs associated with it. Again, we return to this particular person's encounter with this particular large green snake.

Now, listening afresh, we may suddenly remember a dream that this very woman had shared with us some months previously, about seeing a long black snake hanging from a tree across the street from her apartment. However, guided by the maxim to return to the things themselves, we suspend our memory of even this snake. For although this earlier black snake appeared to the dreamer, it was a different snake, in a different setting, and at a different time in the life of the dreamer. Once again, invoking the phenomenological epoche, we avoid superimposing our understanding of even this same individual's previous dream upon this one, utterly unique, dreamed event in her life. If we want to understand the special significance of this woman's existence while dreaming *this* dream, we must allow this one dreamed snake to appear precisely and only as the particular snake it was. *We must allow this dreamed snake maximal freedom to address us in and on its very own terms.* In short, we permit *this* dreamer, on *this* occasion, to describe *this* dream of *this* snake appearing in this sequence of events in *this* setting in exactly *this* way. It is precisely for this reason that we always begin with the process of explication, as described above, inviting the dreamer to give us an increasingly rich and accurate description of the dream, just as it was given to her in her memory.

It takes little reflection to see that the effect of employing both explication and phenomenological epoche is to bring the listening therapist or dream analyst repeatedly back to the dream itself. A phenomenological approach is one that does not brook the introduction of anything which does not inhere in the experience of the dream as such. Dream analysts employing description and epoche are drawn, again and again, back into the dreamer's experience of the dream itself.

Elucidation: Reading Dreams Phenomenologically

At this point it may still be asked, "How are we to make sense of the dream itself without referring to symbolic or theoretical hypotheses?" Sigmund Freud wrote: " 'Interpreting' a dream implies assigning a 'meaning' to it— that is, replacing it by something which fits into the chain of our mental acts as a link having a validity and importance equal to the rest" (1900, p. 96). Although phenomenologists may concur with Freud's view that dreams are meaningful and that this dreamed meaningfulness has a validity and importance equal to the meaningfulness of waking thought, they are deeply suspicious of his procedure of *assigning* a meaning to the dream which *replaces* the dream itself. Phenomenologically seen, dreams address and reveal themselves to us with their own "meaning-fullness" already intact: there is no justification for replacing these *given meanings* with other *assigned meanings*. The phenomenological challenge is to discern the meaningfulness already lying there in the dream as such, to allow the dream "to reveal itself *from itself* and not from our ideas or assumptions about it" (Craig, 1990, p. 70).

Phenomenologically speaking, every being that appears to us (whether it be an object or an animal or another human being or an event, or whether it appears in waking or dreaming) always refers us to more than one kind of meaning. Dreams especially, like poetry refer both *to themselves* and *to something more*. For Freud, that something *more*, that as yet concealed meaning, was actually something *else:* a wish which, once uncovered, replaced the dream in the so-called chain of conscious mental acts. For phenomenologists, the something more is *not something else* but *literally something more of the thing itself.* In other words, with the appearance of any given phenomenon, a car for example, we are referred not only to its own *particular being* (i.e., the way the particular car strikes us, casually, prereflectively, as if at first glance in everyday life) but also to its *being-ness* (i.e., its formal or essential structure, its "car-ness," i.e., that constellation of constitutive characteristics that make it precisely a car and not something else). If, for example, you are standing on a street corner and happen to be watching when a 1957 Chevy convertible passes, then in that moment you are addressed by a particular entity, this automobile of such and such a color, condition, and rate of speed. You may or may not have a personal response to this car, for example, of admiration, jealousy, or nostalgia. Whatever is contained in this encounter, the initial sense of meaningfulness occurs in the manner of causal, ordinary, everyday experience that focuses, for the most part, on this *particular being,* this *particular* Chevrolet convertible. However, if your thoughts happen to dwell on this passing convertible a bit longer, as they might on a poem, for instance, then you may begin to apprehend a whole different kind of meaning, that is, the *being-ness* of that particular vehicle, the *meaning-full* structure of this thing that allowed it to appear as the very thing it is. In considering the being-ness of this 1957 Chevy convertible you might consider the fact that this car is a machine, a product of human technology as well as a means of transportation, a way to get about in the world. You might then also realize that this is not *any* means of transportation but a means for private travel, i.e., unlike train, a bus, or taxi cab, this vehicle is to be driven by oneself, a family member, friend, or chauffeur. Certainly, this means of mobility is not like a plan or ship and even less like a horse or a camel. In other words, this automobile refers you not only to itself as the particular automobile that it is, but also to "automobile-ness." In this case, it also refers you not only to its own vintage but also to "vintage-ness," to "1957-ness"; and more, it refers you not only to its own particular convertible top but to "convertible-ness."

Now obviously this same twofold nature of meaningfulness inheres in dreamed phenomena fully as much as it does in waking phenomena. Here, therefore, is an example of the elucidation of a dreamt phenomenon using the hypothetical instance of a woman who dreams of falling down a bank to a stream "from which a large, green snake slithers toward her legs." This snake initially calls our dreamer's attention to itself as a particular being, a snake that slithers toward the legs of the dreamer and leaves her in a mood of terror. Already this particular snake means something to this dreamer, at least in an everyday, prereflective sense, or she could never perceive and respond to it in the first place. However, by virtue of this snake's being the *kind* of thing it is—a snake—it also may refer her to certain meanings that inhere in its particular being-*ness*, that is, its "*snakeness.*"

Likewise, this dreamed snake refers us, as listeners to the dream, both to its particular being (as a common, "everyday" snake) and to its being-ness (its snake-ness). We know, for instance, that this very same snake discloses something of the nature of all living things and, in particular, of animal things. More specifically, it discloses not only something of the nature of all living things, *living-thing-ness* (e.g., that which is born, undergoes a process of maturation, and dies), but also something of the nature of so-called primitive living things such as reptiles and amphibians, *primitive-ness* (e.g., an ancient existence carried out close to earth, water, and grass). Furthermore, in being the very snake *this* snake is, it also alludes to that which evokes terror and from which the dreamer escapes only by waking. Also, in being the specific snake it is, *this* snake refers to that which is encountered by accident, which approaches the dreamer beyond her volition and control. It is worth underscoring, however, that this snake refers to these latter possibilities simply and only because it *does* frighten her, it *does* approach her in the midst of an accident and *is* beyond her control.

This method of *elucidating* the dream,[5] of allowing the meaningfulness of dreamed phenomena to disclose itself directly, is the means by which phenomenologically oriented investigators may apprehend the so-called deeper or hidden meaning of the dream without having to rely on predetermined theoretical or symbolic solutions. In philosophical parlance, these two kinds of meaning are called *ontic* (referring to the immediately apprehended, prereflective, everyday meaning of a *particular being*) and *ontologic* (referring to the reflectively perceived formal structure of beings, their *being-ness*). All phenomena appearing in a dream address us, whether we choose to think about it or not, in both of these ways. The French hermeneutic philosopher Paul Ricoeur (1979) describes this *twofold characteristic of meaning* in terms of a "*split reference*" which contains, first of all, an "*ordinary reference*" (the everyday, prereflective, or ontic meaning of the dream just as we experienced it) and, secondly, a "*second-order reference,*" the ontological significance which "constitutes the primordial reference to the extent that it suggests, reveals, unconceals—or whatever you say—the deep structures of reality" (p. 151).

Ricoeur writes that what is required to apprehend these two aspects of the meaningfulness of phenomena is what Bedell Stanford calls "steroscopic vision" or the "ability to entertain two different points of view at the same time" (p. 152). This suggests that an analyst listens not only for the dream's ordinary (ontic) references, the *immediately manifest references* of the dream that are casually apprehended just as the dreamed existence was lived, but also for its "deeper," "hidden," or "primordial" (ontologic) references—the *eventually manifest references* of the dream apprehended only upon thoughtful reflection regarding the formal structure of the dreamed phenomena. In other words, the phenomenologically oriented dream analysts do seek to apprehend both the obvious significance (i.e., its ontic, ordinary, or so-called everyday meaning) and the so-called hidden significance (i.e., its ontologic, primordial, or formal meaning) of dreams. Both kinds of significance appear manifestly with the dream. On the one hand, the obvious, ontic, or ordinary significance appears *immediately* with the experience and description of the dream itself. On the other hand, the hidden, ontologic, or primordial significance appears only *eventually*, once the dreamed phenomena have been thoughtfully reconsidered. Both kinds of meaning or significance, however, oblige one to remain faithful to the dreamed phenomena precisely as they have presented themselves to the dreamer.

At this point it is of paramount importance to emphasize that, in the process of elucidating the dream, an analyst make every effort not to impose his or her own understanding, however phenomenological it may be, on the dreamer. There is a common temptation, especially among experienced analysts, to inject their own ontologic meanings onto the dream, meanings not shared by the dreamer. For example, when we elucidated the dreamed snake a while ago, we mentioned its "primitivity." How do we know that for *this dreamer* the snake refers to primitivity? The fact that the scientific study and classification of snakes suggests this fundamental characteristic of "snake-ness" does not justify the conclusion that the appearance of this snake has the same significance *for the dreamer*. Therefore, in "interpreting" the dream, it is the dreamer who is given the primary responsibility for perceiving and articulating (i.e., elucidating) the meaningfulness of the dream and each of its images (in this case, the snake) for himself or herself. The dreamer's elucidation of his or her own dream actually turns out to be a much easier and more natural process than one might imagine. It simply requires that the dream analyst invite the dreamer to define and describe each of the phenomena of the dream, not only as the generic entities they are but also as these generic entities appear specifically, uniquely in the flesh and bones of the dream itself. No one has done a better job at articulating how to invite dreamers themselves to elucidate their own dreams than Gayle Delaney (1988, 1991), an American dream psychologist who has developed and refined a descriptive (i.e., phenomenological) approach to working with dreams that is similar in spirit to the approach of Medard Boss and that has the advantage of being able to be quickly and easily taught and learned.

Dream as Allusion

One major problem remains in our discussion of existential-phenomenological challenges in the clinical use of dreams and that is the problem of how an individual's dreaming is related to his or her waking. As noted at the beginning of this chapter, perhaps the most commonly held scientific view of the problem is simply that there is no meaningful relationship between dreaming and waking, that dreams are nothing but cognitive froth which does not even deserve the time it takes to recall it. Also, as noted earlier, Freud was the first modern scientific figure to effectively dispute this view, and in his *Interpretation of Dreams* (1900) he set out to prove that "every dream . . . has a meaning . . . which can be inserted at an assignable point in the mental activities of waking life" (p. 1). Since the publication of Freud's first work on dreams, the number of scientific figures who have come to accept the possibility that there is a demonstrable relationship between dreaming and waking has steadily grown. Today, there are actually at least three different schools of thought on the matter: first, that dreams are continuous with waking; second, that they are oppositional to waking; and third, that dreams are complementary to waking. Regardless of which of these three views of the dreaming-waking relationship a particular therapist may take, however, virtually every dynamically oriented therapist in the world believes that there is *some* important relationship between these two different kinds of human capacities.

Rather than argumentatively hypothesize about which of these points of view may be true, Medard Boss, the existential analyst, simply observes that dreaming and waking are "but two different modes of carrying to fulfillment the one and the same historical existence" (1977, p. 190). Furthermore, Boss disputes any specific attribution of purposefulness in the formation of dreams. For example, according to Boss, there is no reliable evidence that dreams in general are produced either with the intent of concealing something from the dreamer, as Freud maintained, or with the intent of revealing something to the dreamer, as Jung believed. For Boss and most of his existential colleagues, dreaming simply appears as nothing other than a historical episode in the life of the one who dreams. Although this certainly suggests an important relation between the dreaming and waking existence of the individual, Boss suggests that the precise nature of this relationship with respect to any given dream can only be discovered through careful analysis.

Nevertheless, a few more points should be made before going on to offer a specific example of the phenomenological use of dreams in psychotherapy. As noted earlier, anything that appears to us, whether in waking or in dreaming, has a double reference, that is, first, to the *particular being* of the thing itself (this particular snake in the dream) and, second, to the *being-ness* of the thing itself or the *kind* of being the particular being is (the "snake-ness" of the dreamed snake). Thus, to begin with, every dreamed entity refers an awakened dreamer to *all* such *kinds* of things in his or her existence, whether those kinds of things are recognized only in dreaming or in waking as well. Thus, every phenomena appearing in a dream always *alludes* not only to itself as the *particular* entity it is (we could call this its *primary allusion*) but also to the very specific *kind* of entity it is (we could call this its *secondary allusion*). As it turns out, however, both the primary and secondary allusions of a dream seem, inevitably, to have a great deal in common with certain meaningful features of the dreamer's waking life. Indeed, clinical evidence repeatedly discloses that the various phenomena of an individual's dreaming are generally found to be *homologous* with certain corresponding features of that same individual's waking. But should this come as any surprise since "a person's waking and dreaming 'belong' to the same individual, are both modes of a singular human existence" (Craig, 1987a, pp. 128–29)? This is, in fact, what gives dreams their renowned therapeutic significance: that dreaming and waking, as two different modes of the same historical existence, are "manifestly homologous with one another, that is, they appear as constituted by corresponding structures, forms and meanings and as lived out in corresponding relationships and proportions" (p. 129).

Perhaps a brief example will help. If you will recall the dream, reported above, about Penny doing her laundry, you may also recall that at the end of the dream she described her dog jumping up and down and wanting to get in the dryer, something which Penny refused. It so happened that toward the end of her discussion of her dream, Penny's therapist repeated some of her own words with reference to the dog: "So there you were with this little fellow that you 'love.' You like it when he's all 'cute and clean,' but sometimes, when he's delighted to see you, 'his paws are all wet' and you 'get annoyed' because you end up 'feeling dirty.' And now here he is 'jumping up and down wanting to get into this dryer' and you have 'no idea why he would ever want to do such a thing' so you just flat out tell him no, you won't let him do it. Does this remind you of anything or anyone in your waking life?

Penny (blushing but recovering quickly): "Yes, of course, my boy-friend Shawn. Sometimes we have such great times together, but lately he has wanted to be a lot more involved sexually than I feel comfortable with. We've actually had some pretty intense arguments about it lately, but I keep holding my ground."

This brief exchange led to a number of prolonged conversations over the ensuing weeks focusing on Penny's feelings and on her familial and fundamentalist upbringing with reference to sexual values and be-haviors. Clearly, the homologous relationship between Penny's dream-ing and waking was the key to opening the door to a frank discussion of this vital arena of her existence. Although the main purpose for coming back to this dream here is to illustrate the significance of the homolo-gous relationship between dreaming and waking, this brief exchange also reveals the manner and value of helping dreamers to discover this relationship for themselves.

To summarize now, dreams may be found to allude not only to the particular entities that appear in the dream as such (*primary allusions*) as well as to the deeper structures of meaning that constitute those entities as the kinds of entities they are (*secondary allusions*), but also to specific, corresponding and homologous features of the dreamer's waking life (*tertiary allusions*). In any case, a phenomenological perspective suggests that these allusions may be taken in remarkably straightforward manner and that one need not be concerned at all with being duped or deluded as Freud's theory of dream distortion, for example, would suggest.

This claim may raise a few eyebrows given the frequently bewil-dering or even plainly bizarre and fantastic nature of dreams. In fact, our dream examples thus far have been admittedly rather ordinary, con-taining little of the farcical, burlesque imagery with which dreams are so frequently (albeit unjustifiably) identified. Freud himself, though, would have categorized the above sample dreams as being largely "in-telligible" because of their initially unclear relation to waking life, slightly "bewildering" (Freud, 1901, p. 642). However, as we hope to now show, dreams that initially appear as utterly *un*intelligible, as "dis-connected, confused and meaningless" (p. 642), and which seem to us to be wholesale nonsense also soon reveal themselves phenomenologi-cally as remarkably straightforward allusions to intelligible meanings. Indeed, it is our conviction that even the most ludicrous dreams even-tually reveal themselves as pellucid bearers of meaning through phe-nomenological analysis.

The Existential Use of Dreams in Therapy

Having focused on the philosophical and methodological foundations for *making sense* of dreams phenomenologically, we can now consider the problem of *making use* of this phenomenological understanding
in the therapeutic situation. Every day, psychotherapists and psychoanalysts of every theoretical persuasion encounter persons who are suffering and are in need of immediate assistance, often in the form of an
increment in self-understanding. The following vignette, involving a
so-called bizarre and unintelligible dream, will show how the above
methods and perspectives may be employed in the clinical interview.

We will begin by reporting a dialogue between the therapist and
his patients and then later discuss its significance with respect to the
clinical use of dreams.

Ted's Dream. A 25-year-old graduate student in social work,
whom we shall call Ted, dreamed of being chased by a hideous monster.
Hoping to escape, Ted climbed up a tower, and when he found no
where else to hide, he crawled inside an opening in one of the stan-
chions. He watched with relief as the monster passed him by on the way
up the tower, but a moment later the monster started back down. Ted
leaned back inside the stanchion and squinted his eyes closed. On its
way down, the monster noticed Ted's face in the opening and, reaching
in with a massive index finger, opened Ted's eyes. Ted awoke terrified.

When his therapist asked what this monster was like Ted responded: "He looked like Spiderman from the newspaper cartoon
strips, but he was huge, maybe twenty feet tall. The feeling of the dream
reminds me of my dreams as a kid where a gorilla-like space monster
used to chase me. It's odd that when this monster found me all he did
was open my eyes, actually quite softly."

"What do you make of that?" Ted's therapist asked.

"It's like he was trying to get me to look at him. Something monstrous and huge and red just trying to make me look at it. . . . What
came to my mind just now was my feelings about Judy (Ted's old girlfriend who had recently left him for another man). I feel like I'm constantly pursued by my feelings for her. Some days I wake up in the
morning crying and don't get anything done all day. Other days I feel so
angry I could strangle her. I know that's a terrible thing to say, and she
has a right to do whatever she wants. I keep trying to understand all
of this, but it doesn't seem to do any good. I just can't seem to stop
the hurt. I miss her so much at night that I still keep wishing she'll

come back. I even imagine I hear her car. . . . Sometimes I feel like I'm going crazy. Do you think that's what this monster means, I'm afraid of going crazy?''

The therapist noticed that Ted had suddenly switched from simply describing the dream to describing his waking life and then to trying to interpret the dream symbolically in relation to his waking life. The therapist therefore responded: "It's hard to know just yet what the monster means to you. Why not, for now, just let it be the monster it was in the dream. We'll have plenty of time to sort through what it has to do with your waking life as we go on. Tell me more about this monster and where you were in the dream.''

"It began with my just walking in a field somewhere, a big open field on top of some hill, a wide open grassy field like some of the hills out in Harvard and Bolton where Judy and I used to live. But the monster was tall and had a red suit or red skin and, though I didn't actually see it, I imagined its face was really ugly, something that was so awful it would just kill you to look at it. That's odd, because Spiderman in the cartoons doesn't look that ugly. His face is covered with a mask, and he's actually a nice guy. But in the dream I didn't think this was Spiderman—it just looked something like him—strange and alien.''

As the therapist listened to these descriptions he noted a second reference to Ted's relationship with Judy. Though it would be tempting to pursue this connection further, the therapist felt he still did not have an accurate picture of Ted's concrete existence while dreaming. He therefore asked how the monster happened to be chasing him and what it was that Ted imagined the monster wanted. Again, Ted was quick to respond.

"I don't know what it wanted. It just suddenly came out of nowhere and was after me. I don't remember anyone else being in the dream, but even if there were I had the feeling the monster was after *me*. There was something about *me* it wanted. Why me? I hadn't done anything wrong and was minding my own business except for the fact that I was walking in somebody else's field.''

"Somebody else's field?" Ted's therapist inquired.

"Well, yeh. We used to go for walks in farmers' fields when I went to U Mass and Judy and I always took the dogs for a walk in fields like this. There were sometimes no-trespassing signs around, but we never paid much attention to them. I never thought the farmers particularly cared either, but there was always a little discomfort about it in the back of my mind, and once, in college, one farmer got mad as hell and chased us off his land. Come to think of it, when I was at U Mass we used to go climb town watertowers just to get away from studies. Some of us even had a party on top of one of them and that was definitely off-bounds."

At this point Ted was coming up with a number of associations to the dream which, though potentially important, also threatened to turn the whole focus into a consideration of Ted's waking life. While this might lead in some fruitful directions, Ted's therapist felt it important to learn the significance for Ted of his having dreamed this dream and then having brought it up in therapy. The therapist, therefore, pulled in the associative reins a bit and brought Ted back to the dream itself by asking, "And was that how you felt in this dream, that you were somehow off-bounds?"

Ted replied, "Well not exactly. In a way it felt fine being there, like nothing was wrong, but in another way, I felt I wasn't really supposed to be there. In any case, I don't know why the monster was trying to get ahold of me. Maybe to kidnap me, torture me, kill me, I don't know. But it seems funny now that all it did was just open my eyes!"

The therapist now felt sufficiently familiar with Ted's dreamed existence to begin to elucidate its meaning more fully. He had been struck by a number of Ted's comments, for example, that the entire dream took place in an open, elevated, and apparently enjoyable space but also a space in which Ted felt his behavior was acceptable in one moment and unacceptable in another. Within this field of his existence, Ted was suddenly accosted by something which he saw as monstrous, ugly, and alien to him, something which wanted to get ahold of him and provoked such anxiety that Ted could only run from it and hide. The presence of this entity was so awful to look at that even the sight of it could mean the end of Ted's existence. Since, at this point, the therapist was unsure which aspects of his dream Ted was ready to explore in greater detail, he simply gave a condensed thematic summary of the dream as a whole.

"So there you were, walking along perfectly content in your world when all of a sudden something monstrous comes out of nowhere and threatens your entire existence. You're terrified by this thing and do everything you can to get away from it. In the end it gets you in a spot where there's no way to avoid it, but to your surprise, all it does is open your eyes."

"When you put it like that," Ted responded immediately, "it really does remind me of my feelings toward Judy. I had always felt so good about living with her. I was really shocked when she told me that she and John (one of Ted's own friends) were in love and having an affair. I was crushed and furious and let them both know it, but afterward I tried to figure out how it happened. The more I thought about it the more I realized things hadn't been going all that well with us, and she and John really do have a lot more in common. But all this thinking never seems to do me much good. Inevitably, I just get jealous and hurt again. At times, I've gotten really angry, like I could lose control. Of course, I never would *really*, but I've had some terrible fantasies."

With a bit of encouragement from his therapist, Ted went on to describe one of his sadistic fantasies of physically mutilating his former girlfriend and then interrupts himself to say how awful and guilty he feels talking about these fantasies.

Ted's therapist countered quickly, "Makes you feel like a real monster, I'll bet!"

"Exactly! I don't recognize myself at all. I'm not a violent kind of person or at least I've never thought I was."

"So all this feeling and aggression seems pretty alien to you, maybe not even human."

"Yeh, I've always tried to be a nice guy, kind and friendly and have prided myself in not being a typical macho type. I was always taught to turn the other cheek, and the fact that I can't seem to do that now makes me think something's wrong with me, like I could go crazy. I'm also afraid that if I show Judy how much I sometimes hate her, she'll think I'm a bastard. That will just prove she did the right thing to leave me, and she'll never come back."

"You're afraid *she'll* see you as a bastard?"

"Yeh. Ha, big deal. I guess *I'm* the one who's afraid to be a bastard. It's as if I'm afraid to be really angry, the kind of guy who could be nasty and violent. On the other hand, I also feel like a coward sometimes, like a real wimp, for not standing up for myself. What an ugly mess! Ha, that's funny, just like I imagined the monster's face, so ugly and disgusting it would kill me to see it."

"So the possibility that you could be really aggressive, openly mean and nasty, is so repugnant to you that you can't even look at it. But what do you make of the fact that while dreaming you were actually open to the possibility of being in such an intense relationship with this kind of beast and, in the end, even having your eyes opened to it?"

"It's not like I had a choice. The monster did it to me."

"Well, perhaps, the therapist said, unconvinced by Ted's proclaimed helplessness. "But it's interesting that you didn't wake up *before* the monster opened your eyes. You must have been open to seeing him open your eyes, or you would have awakened before he actually did so.

You weren't so open, of course, that you could leave your eyes open and look him straight in the face. But still, don't you think it's interesting you were open to dreaming precisely long enough to feel him push your eyes open? Is it possible that you are just beginning to entertain the idea of really looking at this possibility for aggressive behavior? Could it be that you are even coming very close to perceiving the power and extent of your *own* aggressive feelings? In fact, if this is so, why not consider the possibility that such feelings are not at all necessarily alien, inhuman characteristics but, rather, that they may even be legitimate and worthwhile capacities of human beings?"

"I'll tell you why not, because people wouldn't like me like that."

"*People?*"

Well, *I* wouldn't like *myself.* Aggressive people have always seemed very foreign to me. They really bother me, and I just don't think I could live with myself if I were like that.

Therapist: Maybe you just never met anyone who appreciated your anger or enjoyed seeing you when you were mean. But is there anything really so wrong about getting a bit nasty, especially if you think it's called for? Is there any reason why *you* have to be so perfect? Don't jilted lovers everywhere get pretty nasty under these circumstances? Why not, for a change, be a little easier on yourself and let yourself be an ordinary fellow for a change? Are you afraid you might actually enjoy getting a little down and dirty?"

Ted replied (with a hint of a smile suddenly crossing his face), "You know, just as you said that I suddenly remembered the time when I was a kid and I really yelled at my father and called him all kinds of filthy names right to his face. Of course, I got the shit kicked out of me afterward, but still, it felt great to stand up to my old man like that. It's funny, I haven't thought about that for years."

At this point Ted seemed to have experienced a concrete shift in his own feelings and self-perceptions. Following this recognition, he began to muse further about his own narcissistic needs to keep up an appearance of kindness and stoic integrity, an image of a person who is slow to anger and who is so together that even the most painful and insulting blows to his feelings and pride are endured with resolve, understanding, and equanimity. Although it was still some time before Ted could freely express his genuine anger and rage, his own capacity for "brutishness," as he called it one day, and although it was even longer before he could integrate these new possibilities with his long standing image of himself as a nice guy, with this dreamwork he had at least begun to travel more honestly in those directions.

Discussion. At this point readers may be wondering how this dreamwork is any different from the standard symbolic interpretations of Jungian analysts who suggest that each element in the dream represents an aspect of the dreamer's personality. Such a view would suggest that this dreamed monster symbolized the dreamer's own undeveloped aggressivity. While it must be acknowledged that the *outcome* of various approaches to dream analysis may be, as in this particular case, quite similar, the *process* of phenomenological approach emphasizes the discovery of this meaning entirely within the framework of the dreamer's experience as such. In other words, an existential phenomenological approach to dream analysis offers a systematic method for understanding dreams on the basis of the dreamer's own experience and not on the basis of predetermined theoretical formulations. The fact that different approaches to the same phenomena may lead to compatible conclusions simply confirms the phenomenologists' faith in the power and persistence of the phenomena themselves!

Nevertheless, while these phenomenological perspectives and methods may not always make a great difference with respect to the outcome of an analysis, the difference for dreamers is enormous. With the phenomenological approach, dreamers are assured that the final authority is with themselves and not with the founder of the analyst's theoretical system. The dream belongs to the dreamer who is not only a full and equal partner in the collaborative inquiry but also the final arbiter. This is especially important in the therapeutic situation where we are required to remain attuned to the patient's experience of his or her own existence. In the example above, for instance, only the dreamer himself could tell us which of his own particular possibilities for being seemed so monstrous that he felt compelled to flee them, lest they consume and destroy his existence as he had known it. The above vignette demonstrates how the meaning of the dream and of its relation to waking, though initially obscure and hidden, may be made manifest through simple direct procedures of description (*explication*) and phenomenological interpretation (*elucidation*).

On the So-Called Problem of Dream Distortion. From this perspective the problem of the *unintelligibility* of dreams is *not that dreams are themselves deceptive*, as Freud suggested, but rather that those who listen to dreams fail to see the essential meaningfulness of dreams precisely as it is given in the dreams themselves. The obscurity of dreams is not a product of unconscious distortion and censorship but rather of a conscious failure to perceive accurately and deeply what stands before our eyes. In the graduate student's "monster dream" the dreamer simply failed "to see" the obvious, that he was running and hiding from something which he perceived as monstrous, ugly, and alien to his own human existence. He was trying to rise above or hide from these possibilities which he perceived as so distasteful that he could not even bear to look at them. In fact, it is this very kind of limited freedom in relation to the full range of one's own authentic possibilities for being-in-the-world that constitutes psychopathology in the existential-phenomenological understanding of the term. In other words, psychopathology is essentially a failure of freedom, an individual's inability to perceive and carry out a complete and well-balanced range of human possibilities for being-in-the-world. Whenever an individual places an inordinate emphasis on any given set of human possibilities (e.g., in Ted's case, being kind, understanding, or loving) there is a danger that these possibilities, however positive they may be, will exclude other equally valuable, equally human possibilities, (e.g., being assertive, aggressive, or angry).

On the Focus of Interpretation. At this point we should also make a comment on the problem of the focus of interpretation. Over the last century, two basic perspectives have developed for the *interpretation* of dreams. The first of these suggests that each of the elements in the dream refer to the "objects" of the dreamer's feelings or perceptions. Freud's approach to the interpretation of dreams relied almost entirely on this view, considering the dream to be about the objects of the dreamer's desires (wishes) or fears. This kind of interpretation has come to be called *object-level*, or *objective*, interpretation. One of Carl Jung's most significant contributions to the science of dream interpretation was to point out that dreams often refer not to persons or objects in the dreamer's world but rather to features of the dreamer's personality. According to this view, every element of the dream represents some unrealized feature of the subject's own personality. This kind of interpretation, therefore, is called *subject-level*, or *subjective*, interpretation.

Existential analysts take issue with these one-sided approaches since, according to these existentialists, our human existence does not appear as one which is split off from one's world but rather shows itself as one of being-in-the-world, that is, of being constituted *as* a world. Existentialists thus dispute the Cartesian subject-object dualism and propose that human existence is properly understood only as a "worldly" existence, a being-at-one-with-one's-world. Thus, for existentialists every dream must, of necessity, present us with both levels of significance, even if, practically, the initial primary focus of any given reading tends to emphasize one view or the other. For example, even though Penny's dream had a rather tidy object-level significance (her dog reminded her of her boyfriend), further exploration might easily have disclosed ways in which she herself (subject-level significance) has unrealized potentials similar to those embodied in her dreamed dog (for example, her unrealized possibilities for wanting to have a good time getting into places she once considered filthy). With Ted's dream we had an excellent example of a subject-level perspective (the monster reminded him of his own ugly and frightening possibilities for anger and aggression). Yet further exploration with Ted might have revealed considerable similarity between this Spiderman-monster (a good man turned evil) and his male friend who had an affair with and then "stole" his girlfriend and lover. Deciding which way to focus one's initial reading of a dream is one of the most valuable skills an analyst can master. But, again, the most important basis for making this choice is to be found in the experience and words of the dreamer and not in one's favorite psychological theory.

Summarizing This Phenomenological Perspective

Medard Boss suggests that the problem of the clinical use of dreams may be solved by discovering the response to two basic questions (1977, pp. 19–27). The first question is *to what phenomena is a person's existence open while dreaming?* (Boss, 1977, p. 26). This includes all dreamed objects, events, animals, persons, behaviors, and moods. It also includes the temporal and spatial contexts of the dream as well as the dreamer him or herself. Finally it includes all of the ways in which the dreamer responds to the phenomena which appear in the dream. A full answer to this question also reveals certain phenomena and ways of existing to which the dreamer was *not* open while dreaming, for this, too, is an indication of just how things stood for the dreamer during the time of the dream.

The second question that must be asked in order to make adequate sense and use of the dream in the therapeutic situation is: *Now that the dreamer is awake, how is it that he or she is able to recognize meaningful features appearing in the dream which correspond to meaningful features in his or her waking life?* (ibid, p. 27). Again, we are interested in knowing the dreamer's response to this question with reference to all the phenomena mentioned above, including his or her dreamed responses to these phenomena.

Simply answering these two questions in relation to a patient's dream enables the clinician to determine not only the meaning of the dream itself but also its implication for waking life. They enable a therapist both *to make sense* and *to make use* of the dream in the therapeutic situation. Boss's two questions thus offer ready access to primary, secondary, and tertiary allusions of the dream.

We hope this brief introduction to these more systemic aspects of the existential-phenomenological approach to understanding dreams will be useful to dream analysts and psychotherapists who seek to ground their work increasingly in the authority of the dreams themselves and to proceed with increasing respect for the integrity and responsibility of the dreamer. We would like now briefly to explore some more recent American applications of the kind of European approach we have been discussing. Although these applications use a somewhat modified philosophical terminology, they nevertheless adhere to the basic tenets and spirit of the phenomenological approach.

American Applications of Existential-Phenomenology to the Clinical Use of Dreams

The existential-phenomenological perspective brings to the clinical understanding and use of dreams three additional considerations. These include: mindfulness of the existential givens of human existence, particularly their role in suffering and emotional and physical illness; the centrality of immediate inner experience in our lives, i.e., the primacy of subjectivity; and the importance of understanding processes of presence, i.e., the ways in which the flow of immediate subjective experience is accessed and expressed, and the ways in which it is warded off from full awareness. A clear appreciation of these emphases in the existential tradition can be of enormous assistance in understanding and working with dreams and the dreamer in a helpful manner.

Existential Givens of Being Human

Yalom (1980) and other writers have listed several of the inescapable facts of human existence especially relevant to clinical work with distressed patients. These include death (inevitable for all and in conflict with the wish to continue living), freedom/responsibility (we are inescapably free and bear ultimate responsibility for creating and shaping our lives, our identities, and our experience of the world), isolation (each of us is separated from all others by an unbridgeable gap even in the most intimate relations, and this may conflict with the desire for union and protection), and meaninglessness (in a universe with no certain meaning, we must personally create or discover a sense of meaning and purpose around which to structure goals and realize values). A person's experience of these facts of existence may include painful and conflicting thoughts and emotions, with symptoms and maladaptive behavior and character patterns resulting from a failure to confront directly and work through these feelings and givens of human life. Others in the existential tradition have emphasized such givens of human life as our embodiedness; contingency (vulnerability to chance); our essential relatedness to world and others; the intentionality of consciousness; the existence of unique meanings to be discovered; and issues of choice, personal authenticity, and self-realization; and the actualization of potentials within each person. We believe that dreams as lived experience can be openings to information and experience highly relevant to these existential concerns. Dreams can illuminate previously out-of-awareness feelings, thoughts, insights, and imagery flowing from personal confrontation with the givens of human life. They can thereby enhance fuller living in accord with those givens.

A family physician in his late thirties reported the following dream during a period of moderate anxiety and somatic concerns:

"I'm walking in a beautiful primeval forest, enjoying the lush undergrowth and ancient trees. But I feel uneasy, a bit anxious, and concerned about my mild back pain. I'm admiring the large condors high in the trees looking down, and I wonder with a slight chill where the animal is that is dying and which they will scavenge and recycle. I think about that being the way of nature. I look again at the condors. Slowly a feeling of fear fills me, growing almost to terror. Suddenly I realize it is I for whom they are waiting. I will inevitably die and be recycled. I scream and cry out for help. Then I awaken, with my heart pounding."

This vivid confrontation with his own mortality led to clarification of the ways this doctor warded off full awareness of his own inevitable death. He eventually was able to let go of some compulsive behaviors and distracting somatic concerns related to his fear and awareness of death, increasing his capacity to enjoy life and to immerse himself more fully in it by going ahead with some commitments in his work and love life. He no longer believed that he had endless time to make choices or that he would have a special exemption from inevitable aging and death. With the help of this dream he also became more able to empathize with ill patients and to discuss their fears of death more honestly and directly.

A 30-year-old secretary with moderate depressive episodes and a pattern of prematurely clinging to inappropriate male partners had the following short dream on the anniversary of her mother's death sixteen years earlier:

"I'm with my mother again, but she is needing to leave. I'm sad, and I try to cling to her, to get her to stay. She turns to me and says, 'Karen, I need to go but I will remain always with you.' My mother disappears, but I'm left with a feeling of her continuing presence and love and of her strength."

Explication of this dream, with questions evoking a sense of the substantial lovingness of Karen's relationship with her mother, as well as her vivid description of her mother's qualities of will, toughness, and warmth led to Karen's being able to acknowledge consciously these qualities in herself. She was able to confront and work through the fact of her loss and separateness from her mother, while revaluing the loving relatedness they had had for many years. With this came an understanding of how Karen's mother remains with her in the qualities with which Karen had identified and incorporated as her own. Acknowledging her own power, freedom, and responsibility, she was able eventually to move more autonomously out of a constricting overly dependent relationship, and a year later she married a more consciously chosen and appropriate partner. Confronting the existential issues of death, separateness, and self-responsibility in this dream led to more freedom and to healthier choices in Karen's love life and later on in her career.

An opening of awareness through dreams to issues and feelings concerned with his existential embodiedness was depicted vividly in three dreams of a middle-aged attorney:

"I'm standing in ancient Rome in a crowd watching a parade. Emperor Nero is being carried aloft on a reclining couch eating grapes. I know that I'm obliged to bow down before him, and I resent having to do that. Then the dream ends."

"Who is this Emperor Nero in your dream?"

"He's a Roman tyrant. He has no control over his appetites. He ate and drank a lot."

"Can you describe what he looks like?"

"He's lying down. He's fat and sort of grotesque."

"Does he remind you of anything?"

"Um! My wife says I've gotten fat lately. She thinks I'm eating and drinking too much."

"Oh?"

"I've been worried that I'm not getting the exercise I used to. I work hard, come home from the office, have a couple of drinks and just lie down until supper."

"What have you felt about that?"

"I'm angry at myself. I feel I can't do much about it."

"Is that a little bit like the feeling in the dream?"

"I'm angry for having to bow down for Emperor Nero. I feel sort of helpless there too! It's like I have to pay tribute to a powerful glutton."

Further questions and explication led to the dreamer's beginning to assume responsibility for the mode of existence in waking life depicted by the figure of Emperor Nero in his dream. He was in fact sedentary and overweight and had been drinking significant quantities of alcohol for several months in response to increased stress at work. An earlier dream had depicted a scruffy-bearded overweight alcoholic, in need of treatment but still uncooperative, in bed with him and his wife. A later dream was more effective in gaining the attention of our attorney, depicting the sedentary and sinister Peter Lorre stating directly in his classic ominous film style, "I'm going to kill you!" In explicating this dream, the man reminded himself that Peter Lorre had died of heart disease and that he himself had a family history of this as well as an elevated serum cholesterol. This led to his drastically altering his diet and lifestyle to lower his own heart disease risk factors, with no recurrence subsequently of similar kinds of dreams. We believe dreams open our awareness to more of what we know and experience about our bodies, thoughts, beliefs, feelings, social forces with which we are engaged, and other givens of our existence. Bonime (1980) has illustrated the role of dreams in clarifying existential difficulties in responsibility-taking and free choice in some depressed patients. Yalom (1980) notes that dreams often contain anxiety related to the existential issues of isolation and death. We believe dreams may also contain useful experiential awarenesses that can be brought forward into waking relations, personal authenticity, and the realization of useful and pleasurable potentials otherwise unattended to.

A middle-level executive in his late forties sought help for feelings of anxiety and depression after losing a job with a large corporation on which he had depended for twelve years. Early in his work with the therapist he presented the following dream.

"I'm in a hot stuffy room with a group of people who are unfriendly. They were once like family but they've become tense and unfriendly. They're focused on papers in front of them, and they don't seem to care much about each other. The room has low ceilings and it's very crowded. I'm suddenly pushed out of the room in an impersonal way. I'm scared and protest but to no avail. Then I find myself in a large, calm open space outside the boxy room and inside a large cool hall. I'm relieved to be outside that hot room. The large open hall is Beard Hall at my old undergraduate campus. I start down the wide staircase toward the ground floor. I encounter Lou, one of the guys at my old job. He wants me to engage him, but I decide to move on past him to the ground floor of Beard Hall. A voice says, 'You did the right thing not to stop for that guy.' I move easily down the stairs with a feeling of relief and excitement. Then the dream ends."

"Tell me about Beard Hall."

"It's a wonderful place. That's where I took all my Humanities courses. Literature and history and philosophy. Those were always more fun than the business courses I took in order to be able to get a job. Whenever I visit my old campus I always go to Beard Hall. It's like a great cathedral to me. The architecture of the place is wonderful too."

"Who is Lou, the guy you encounter on the stairs?"

"Oh, he's a guy who'll always be with the corporation. Can't do much else. He's real dependent, and he's kind of power-oriented. He's wedged his way into the structure of the place so they could never get rid of him. I think he doesn't have much fun though."

"You pass up his invitation to engage you."

"Yeah. He's headed for the hot stuffy room, and I don't want to go back there even though they threw me out against my will at the time. Taking my job away from me was a impersonal matter too, just like being tossed out of the room in the dream. The chief simply had another guy he liked and wanted in the company, so he made room for him by getting rid of me. I was the vulnerable one. In the dream though, I'm really liking my new environment. It's free and open, and it feels like there are exciting possibilities. There's a sense that when I get to the ground floor I can move in any direction I want to go."

This dream was a rich one, and a turning point for this man. In waking life he was just beginning to experience the possibility of new directions for his career and relief that he no longer worked in a place that had become uncomfortable for him during the past two or three years. His old friends had moved on, and a new management structure, with a philosophy with which he deeply disagreed, was in place. The work atmosphere had become "stuffy and hot and unfriendly." In the dream he passes up the possibility (embodied in Lou) of his returning to a like place to remain destructively dependent, in favor of moving on to take up new possibilities in the context of the historically enriching Beard Hall. He's moving in the direction of the ground floor, with a feeling of increased groundedness of his being, accompanied by excitement, pleasure, and expectation. The full explication of this dream and its meanings required, of course, a good bit more dialogue and exploration than can be included here.

This executive later went into business for himself, with work and leisure activities much more consistent with the humanities interests he had carried forward but to which he had attended less during his years with the corporation.

The Primacy of Subjectivity

Bugental (1978) has reminded us of the crucial importance of refocusing our awareness on our own homeland, the inner world of subjective experience. He believes that an adequate objectivity must include human subjectivity. Our culture has taught us to be suspicious and guilty about living from our center out, but we can work with this in ourselves and those who come to us for assistance. Internal wholeness and making choices from an inner sensing of our own unique needs and wants are worthy goals of the therapeutic process and enhance the sense of richness, integrity, and creativity in our flow of awareness. Bugental urges us to reclaim our own inner experiencing, our "subjective sovereignty," and with that will come enhanced dignity, choice, and meaningful living.

This perspective from an American pioneer in the existential approach to psychotherapeutic work with individuals enhances the sense of value and meaning in doing careful dreamwork. An existential-phenomenological approach, with its emphasis on a continual return to the phenomena of subjectivity, inviting clarification, description, and explication of the dream imagery itself by the dreamer, gives him or her the experience of responsibility and enhanced freedom as author and creator of the dream imagery and feelings, with their essential meaningfulness as lived experience from within. This approach imposes no meanings or assumptions or interpretations on the dream itself other than those discovered and understood in the processes noted above. Delaney's (1988) descriptive dream analysis technique, with its focus on basic definitions and descriptions ("as if I came from another planet") of objects, people, settings, and feelings in the dream, enhances and extends this phenomenological "focus on the things themselves," consistent with the existential emphasis on the primacy of the subjectivity of the dreamer. As repeatedly noted earlier, we avoid high levels of inference, emphasizing the observed and experienced phenomena. Freud (1914) once wrote, "I learned to restrain speculative tendencies and to follow the unforgotten advice of my master Charcot: to look at the same things again and again, until they themselves begin to speak" (p. 22). If we fall ill from our fantasies rather than from reality, we risk ill treatment of the dream and dreamer when we impose on the dream itself the fantasies of our theories, abstractions, and generalizations.

The Processes of Presence in Working with Dreams

Bugental (1978) has pointed out the importance in clinical psychotherapeutic work of attending to the patient's "presence" and expectancies. Presence he defines as "the quality of being in a situation in which one intends to be as aware and as participative as one is able to be at that time and in those circumstances. Presence is carried into effect through mobilization of one's inner (toward subjective experiencing) and outer (toward the situation and any other persons in it) sensitivities" (p. 36). He believes that when either the patient or the therapist is not truly present, the therapy work will be of less effect in evoking the patient's healing/growth powers. The ways the patient avoids presence are an enactment of patterns that keep him or her from truly living fully with others as well as with the therapist during the session. Bugental believes that much therapy time is wasted when spent on working out a logical and systematic historical account of the patient's dynamics and how they correlate with the theoretical postulates of the therapist's approach to personality. "In such therapy," he states, "the client often attains extensive knowledge (miscalled 'insight') about the self, but little effective inner vision (i.e., a vital sense of one's own intentions and powers in directing one's own life)" (p. 18). The truly present patient is open to discovery within, rather than in "thinking about" or "figuring out" himself or his dreams.[6]

We believe Bugental's emphases have great value for the investigation of dreams in an immediate, lively, and useful manner. The dreamer may tend to relate to his dream as an object, as "out there" to be "figured out." Dream investigation focused on here-and-now experiencing as the dream is told may help to evoke a sense of immediacy and presence. Aspects of presence include accessibility (allowing what happens to really matter, to have an effect on one) and expressiveness (the intention to let oneself be known and to make available to the therapist some of the contents of one's subjective awareness without distortion or disguise). Attention to the processes of presence, to the ways in which the dreamer's flow of awareness is accessible and expressive or not in the time we're together with his dream, enhances the value of the work and may bring vividly into immediate experience the very issues and feelings with which the dream is concerned. An example of this would be a dream revealing in its content distancing maneuvers the dreamer is using in an important relationship, at the same time that those distancing processes are evident in his way of relating to his own dream. The dreamer may also reenact the same distancing process in relating to the therapist. Skillful inquiry at these points can lead to more lasting "visceral" insights of greater use than a more "objective" or figuring-it-out-together examination of the dream.

Attention to emotions and body sensations, questions about how the dreamer is experiencing the process of looking at the dream in this moment, and inquiries about how the dreamer feels about the therapist's questions are all ways of assisting the dreamer to become as fully present as possible with his or her immediate flow of awareness. We should be thinking about the extent to which the dreamer is taking responsibility for using the time to best effect or about his or her basic attitudes toward the dream and toward the flow of his or her own awareness. Is he or she willing to let go of a problem-solving focus in favor of self-exploration and discovery? Is the focus primarily on the therapist when relating the dream, or is it on his or her own here-and-now experience? Is the main purpose clear in telling the dream? Does he or she want the therapist to respond in a particular way or have a particular attitude toward him or her when talking? Is the dreamer needing to defend himself or herself while talking or can the person let go and explore his or her immediate experience? Is he or she relating to the therapist as the doctor, the confessor, a friend, a parent, an audience, or a companion in exploring the inner experience of his or her dream? Sometimes a dreamer will be very present with the therapist as he or she is telling a dream in which a vivid presence is experienced during the dream with clear accessibility to his or her flow of awareness in the dream, and expressiveness in the dream as well as in the telling.

An attractive woman in her mid-twenties is telling her dream. She is animated and immediate, with an intense interest in her own experience as she's talking:

Patient: "I really want to understand this one. It feels very important to me. (She leans back in her chair, relaxing somewhat and attending inward.) The beginning is vague. Somehow in the dream Joe (her fiance) and I have decided not to get married after all. We've opted for something completely different. I've married a guy named Robert with whom I grew up. Joe has married Jane. We're at each other's reception.

It's a double wedding. Joe and I are at each other's side, glued to each other. (She leans forward, smiling with pleasure.) We can't get enough of each other. I never want to let him out of my sight! I think everyone there knew this would happen. There are no presents from others. It's like just the two of us are there."

"Can you remember the setting?"

"It's a typical wedding reception. I can't believe we've made this mistake, marrying other people. (She appears genuinely distressed at this moment.) Nothing else is unusual about it."

"Who is Robert?"

"Ugh! (a look of distaste) Why did I dream of Robert?"

"What's he like?"

"He's a nudge. He says the wrong thing at the wrong time. Thinks he's funny, but isn't. He's not one of my favorites."

"Describe him."

"He has a master's and doctorate from Wharton's, the best business school after Harvard. He's supposedly bright. He's an investment broker. (Shows some interest and a little skepticism.)

"Why might you marry Robert?"

"It's the easy way out. He has no social savvy, but he's very successful. He'll be rich!"

"What's Jane like?"

"Jane is a sweetheart. She's supported her husband, who is a musician. He stays home and cares for the kids while she works and makes a good living. Jane has to compete with her children for his love. Daddy is Mommy. She competes for his love with the kids. There's a role reversal. Jane takes care of her husband musician and supports him."

"Why would you marry Robert?"

"The only reason is security. I'd be safe. For both Joe and me, marrying Robert and Jane would be the easy way out."

"So, what do you think the dream is about?"

"Realizing that opting for the easy way out, for security and money, isn't good. Marrying for financial security would be my major temptation away from Joe. I realize from this dream that it would be a terrible mistake for me to marry anyone other than Joe. I couldn't drink in enough of Joe once I realized what a mistake I'd made."

"What happened last night before you went to bed?"

"Friends were over. I went to bed thinking about what they'd said."

"What was that?"

"They said, 'You can still back out of it, you know. You don't have to marry Joe.' (She laughs confidently.) I really know now how much I want to marry Joe.

One goal of good dreamwork, as of good psychotherapy, is insight, or inner sight of (and within) one's own being. Clearly, this can't be insight from another, however well-steeped in a particular metapsychology about dream interpretation that other is. We hope these final considerations have helped to clarify some of the more concrete ways in which the existential-phenomenological approach to dreams may be useful in the therapeutic situation. We believe that careful attention to a patient's experience of his or her own dreams and to the response to these dreams on waking provides our most firm ground for understanding the patient and for anticipating and clearing the way for the emergence of the dreamer's own authentic possibilities for being-in-the-world. Of course, this project is not something that can be carried out fully in dreaming. Boss (1958) notes that "our life history demands both our waking and our dreaming" (p. 211), but it is only in waking that we can carry the dreamed possibilities forward into our future. As Paul Stern (1972) notes, "The dream for all its luminous power cannot substitute for waking experience. It can illuminate, but it cannot *make* history." We hope our presentation of the existential-phenomenological approach to the clinical use of dreams contributes to this preeminently human project, both in its rigorous respect for the things themselves and in its gentle means for liberating the individual's reality to become more fully what it truly is.

Notes

1. What follows is not a methodological sample of how we proceed when actually working with a dream but rather an organized summary of the kind of unfolding meaningfulness that tends to emerge when the dreamer is given the opportunity to describe and consider his or her own dream precisely as it was "given" to him or her upon waking.

2. *Da-sein* is a term used in the existential philosophy of Martin Heidegger, to refer to individual human existence. Literally, it means "being-there" (*da* = "there"; *sein* = "being") and denotes specifically the fact that an individual's existence cannot be understood exclusive of his or her world; his or her "there." The human being, by virtue of consciousness, exists as a "there,"

as a *realm* of world illumination, as being-in-the-world, *Da-sein*. Boss hyphenates Da-sein here as a way of emphasizing these dual aspects of our human existence.

3. For an illuminating discussion of the relationship between dreams and the therapeutic situation see Masud Khan's (1974) article on dreams and the evolution of the analytic situation.

4. While Freud found considerable "success" with his translations, it is not at all clear whether this effectiveness was due to the reliability of his theoretical code or to some combination of his own personal charisma and his unusual manner of relating to patients. This question of the impact of the relationship on the effectiveness of the interpretation or translation of dream symbols deserves much greater attention than it has received to this point.

5. Naturally, a complete understanding of any dream would parallel the thoroughness and detail of Freud's classical method of dream analysis through free association. Using a phenomenological approach, however, we would systematically *explicate* and *elucidate* the dreamed phenomena, each of the objects, creatures, persons, behaviors, events, attitudes, moods, feelings, and relations that appeared to the dreamer while dreaming. It is also important to explicate and elucidate the dreamers' own presence in the dream including their mood and entire manner of existing in and responding to the world in which they find themselves.

6. While Bugental's contributions mainly concern psychotherapeutic work with less emphasis on dreams than ours, he does believe that dreams (as well as waking fantasies) are "expressions of a larger consciousness . . . [with] clear significance of our truer and larger nature . . . transcending the everyday, preparing the way for creativity, and opening up richer resources for our lives" (p. 113).

References

Binswanger, L. (1963). Dream and Existence. In Being-In-The-World (Jacob Needleman, trans.) pp. 222–248. New York: Basic Books.

Bonime, W., and Bonime, F. (1980). The dream in the depressive personality. In *The Dream in Clinical Practice*, ed. J. Natterson. New York: Aronson, pp. 131–47.

Boss, M. (1958). *The Analysis of Dreams*. New York: Philosophical Library.

———. (1977). *I Dreamt Last Night* . . . New York: Gardner Press.

———. (1963). *Psychoanalysis and Daseinsanalysis.* New York: Basic Books.

Bugental, J. (1978). *Psychotherapy and Process: The Fundamentals of an Existential-Humanistic Approach.* Menlo Park, Calif.: Addison-Wesley.

Craig, E. (1987a). Dreaming, Reality and Allusion: An Existential-Phenomenological Inquiry. In *Advances in qualitative psychology: themes and variations,* ed. F. van Zuuren, F. Wertz, and C. Mook, pp. 115–36. Berwyn, Pa.: Swets North America,

———. (1987b). The realness of dreams. In *Dreams Are Wiser than Men,* ed. R. A. Russo (pp. 34–57). Berkeley, Calif.: North Atlantic Books.

———. (1988a). Freud's Irma Dream: A Daseinsanalytic Reading. In Psychotherapy for Freedom: The Daseinsanalytic Way in Psychology and Psychoanalysis, ed. E. Craig. Special issue of *Humanistic Psychologist* 16(1): 203–16.

———. (1990). An Existential Approach to Dreamwork. In *Dreamtime and Dreamwork,* ed. S. Krippner. Los Angeles: Jeremy Tarcher, pp. 69–77.

———., ed. (1988b). Psychotherapy for Freedom: The Daseinsanalytic Way in Psychology and Psychoanalysis. Special issue of *Humanistic Psychologist* 16(1).

Delaney, G. (1988). *Living Your Dreams,* rev. ed. San Francisco: Harper and Row.

———. (1991). *Breakthrough Dreaming.* New York: Bantam.

Freud, S. (1911) [1957]. The Handling of Dream Interpretation in Psychoanalysis, *Standard Edition,* vol. 12:89–96. London: Hogarth Press.

———. (1900). The Interpretation of Dreams. *Standard Edition,* vols. 4 and 5. London: Hogarth Press, 1953.

———. (1901). On Dreams, Standard Edition, Vol. 5, pp. 629–686. Hogarth Press, 1957.

———. (1914) [1957]. On the History of the Psychoanalytic Movement. Complete Psychological Works. *Standard Edition,* vol. 14. London: Hogarth Press, pages 3–66.

———— . (1923) [1957]. Remarks on the Theory and Practice of Dream Interpretation, *Standard Edition*, vol. 19:107–38. London: Hogarth Press.

———— . (1933). New Introductory Lectures on Psychoanalysis. Standard Edition. Vol. 22. pp. 1–182, Hogarth Press, 1964.

Husserl, E. (1962). *Ideas: General Introduction to Pure Phenomenology*, trans. W. R. Boyce Gibson. New York: Collier.

Jung, C. G. (1934). The Practical Use of Dream Analysis. In The Practice of Psychotherapy. *Collected Works*, 2nd ed., vol. 16:139–61. Princeton, N.J.: Princeton University Press. (1954).

———— . (1944). Psychology and Alchemy. *Collected Works*, 2nd ed., vol. 12. Princeton, N.J.: Princeton University Press. (1953).

———— . (1948). On the Nature of Dreams. In The Structure and Dynamics of the Psyche, *Collected Works*, 2nd ed., vol. 8:281–97, Princeton, N.J.: Princeton University Press. (1960).

———— . (1951). Aion: Research Into the Phenomenology of the Self. In *Collected Works*, 2nd ed., vol. 9, and part 2. Princeton, N.J.: Princeton University Press. (1959).

———— . (1952). Symbols of Transformation. *Collected Works*, 2nd ed., vol. 5. Princeton, N.J.: Princeton University Press. (1956).

Khan, M. (1974). *The Privacy of the Self*. New York: International Universities Press.

Ricoeur, P. (1979). The Metamorphical Process of Cognition, Imagination and Feeling. In *On Metaphor*, ed. S. Sacks. Chicago: University of Chicago Press, pp. 141–57.

Stern, P. (1972). Dreams: The Radiant Children of the Night. In *In Praise of Madness*. New York: Norton, pp. 39–60.

———— . (1979). Introduction to the English Translation. In *Existential Foundations of Medicine and Psychology*, ed. M. Boss. New York: Aronson.

Yalom, I. (1980). *Existential Psychotherapy*. New York: Basic Books.

5

Milton Kramer —————————————————

Dream Translation:
An Approach To Understanding Dreams

Interest in the dream comes from a number of sources. For the neuro-scientist, the dream is one of the two major vehicles for studying the function of the mind, (Foulkes, 1978; Freud, 1900) the other being the study of language (Chomsky, 1968). For the true believer, the dream is the communication pathway between his deity and himself; the Old and New Testaments are filled with revelatory dreams (Kramer, Whitman, Baldridge, and Lansky, 1964). And for the student of human behavior, the dream provides a window through which to glimpse the inner world of the dreamer, a window available to therapists (Hartman, 1973) and dreamers (Ullman and Zimmerman, 1979) alike.

What will be seen if one looks at the premier fantasy production of the individual; if one examines a person's dreams? One gains a view of the subjective aspect of the dreamer's world. One sees the world of the dreamer from the dreamer's highly personal point of view, a view of how do I "feel" the world is rather than how I "think" it is. A night of dreams is more loosely organized than comparable examples of waking thought (Kramer, Moshiri, and Scharf, 1982). Attention to an under-standing of dreams opens up an additional channel of information for the dreamer or the dream interpreter.

The traditional position taken with regard to the dream is that it is of little value in shedding light on the inner life of the dreamer without the dreamer's own associations. Freud warned explicitly that a dream could not be interpreted without the associative assistance of the patient (Freud, 1916–1917). Many psychotherapists are still of the opinion that dreams are not understandable to them without the dreamer's associa-tions (Fliess, 1953). This doctrinaire commitment to the use of the asso-ciative methodology for achieving an understanding of the dream has blocked more effective utilization by the psychotherapist of this impor-tant piece of mental life (Erickson, 1954).

I will attempt to illustrate a method for unraveling some aspects of the meaningfulness of the dream which I have tentatively called "dream translation." I will try to show that the dream, without the explicit associations of the patient, can contribute in significant ways to the dream interpreter's central task, the understanding of his patient's subjective or inner world.

I hope it will be apparent that the dreamer can use this method as well. The technique of dream translation will provide a systematic manner for approaching dreams, which would be available to the dream interpreter, whether he or she is the dreamer or not. I have approached the method from the point of view of the dream interpreter who has no knowledge of the dreamer, as it provides a more stringent exposition of the method.

I have selected the label "dream translation" for the methodology I will describe for three reasons. First, using the term "dream translation" serves to distinguish the method from dream interpretation. The latter is a term that fairly clearly delineates a mode of achieving the meaningfulness of the dream in which a methodology using the patient's associations is used to achieve a replacement of the manifest dream content by the latent dream content (Freud, 1900). Dream translation will differ in that it will not use the patient's associations. Second, I have selected dream translation as an appropriate descriptive designation to call attention to the general similarity between this method and that of symbol interpretation which Freud called a translation (Freud, 1916–1917). And third, dream translation seemed an appropriate designation, as it captures a nuance of the philological difference between interpretation and translation (Webster, 1957) which is present in the difference between the two methods. Interpret, philologically, derives from the idea of an agent between two parties; while translate derives from the idea of "bearing across" or "transferring." In dream interpretation, the psychotherapist or dream interpreter is guided by the patient's associations in negotiating between the two parties, e.g., the manifest and latent content. In dream translation, the dream translator transfers the manifest text into another meaningfulness system without the dreamer-patient's participation.

At this point, a caveat is in order. As will become apparent in the illustrations, the value of dream translation is in the information it provides to the therapist. It is a device to enhance his or her potential knowledge of the dreamer's inner world. One may view it as a hypothesis-generating procedure particularly useful in the diagnostic and early phases of psychotherapy and at points of impasse in the therapeutic process. However, in direct therapeutic work, in the session with the patient, the value of the associational methodology cannot be denied. The associational methodology serves to engage the patient collaboratively in the therapeutic task, lends specificity to the interpretative process, and enhances the patient's conviction of the validity of the understanding of his subjective world that he achieves as a result of the therapeutic process. Yet, I believe the method can be useful as well to dreamers exploring their own dreams.

Before proceeding to the illustrative material, it seems worthwhile for me to attempt to make explicit the assumptions, guidelines, and rules that I believe underpin the method of dream translation. Additionally, I will point out crucial areas of similarity and difference between the dream translation methodology and the premises inherent in the more familiar methods of psychoanalytic dream interpretation. This review will prepare the reader for the case examples.

Assumptions Basic to All Psychological Work with Dreams

There are three assumptions basic to all psychological work with dreams. It seems worthwhile to state these general assumptions, as they provide an insight into the fundamentals of all approaches to dream meaning.

First, all methods of extracting the meaningfulness of the dream assume that there is a dream experience (Jones, 1970). Experimental laboratory research has indeed confirmed that the dream experience occurs (Dement, 1965), is extended in time (Foulkes, 1966), and has a developmental course across the rapid-eye-movement (REM) period (Kramer, Roth, and Czaya, 1975) and during the night (Kramer, McQuarrie, and Bonnet, 1981), and from night to night (Kramer and Roth, 1979).

Second, it is generally assumed in work with dreams that the dream report is an adequate reflection of the dream experience. Again, experimental laboratory research has provided support, if not confirmation, to the idea that there is significant similarity between the dream experience and the dream report (Taub, Kramer, Arand, and Jacobs, 1978). Eye movements and dream action during REM sleep are relatable (Roffwarg, Dement, Muzio, and Fisher, 1962). The intensity of the psychological experience during REM sleep and the dream report of that experience covary (Kramer et al., 1975). Experiments in which stimuli presented during sleep are incorporated into dreams suggest a relationship between the dream experience and the dream report (Kramer, Kinney, and Scharf, 1983a).

Third, the psychological work with dreams assumes that an examination of the dream report leads to an understanding of the meaningfulness of the report. Here again, experimental laboratory work with dreams has demonstrated that dream reports are orderly events (Kramer, Hlasny, Jacobs, and Roth, 1976) relatable to the waking subjective life of the dreamer at both the state (Kramer, Roth, Arand, and Bonnet, 1981) and trait level (Kramer, Roth, and Palmer, 1976). Interestingly, the content of dreams is related to the waking affective state before and after sleep (Kramer and Roth, 1980; Piccione, Jacobs, Kramer, and Roth, 1977).

There is no necessity in psychological work with dreams, at the level of developing their meaningfulness, to make an assumption about the dream playing any functional role in the life of the dreamer. Although all of the classical depth psychologists do, indeed, attribute a function to dreaming (Adler, 1959; Freud, 1916–1917; Jung, 1956), the search for the meaningfulness of the dream does not require a functional assumption about dreaming. The search for the meaningfulness of dreams requires only that the dream be responsive to the psychological condition of the dreamer. This view of the dream as responsive is inherent in our third assumption and supported by studies of cognitive and affective ties between waking and dreaming.

The basic assumptions that underlie all psychological work with dreams are intriguing and well-supported by the evidence. The dream experience exists as a subjective event, is adequately captured in the dream report, and is organized and relatable to waking life such that a search for the meaning of the dream seems reasonable.

Dream Translation Based on Dream Structure

My central supposition in dream translation is that dreams can be understood separate from a knowledge of the dreamer. I am of the opinion that meaningful statements about the dreamer can be extracted from a dream report without his or her associations to the dream and without any information about the context in which the dream occurred.

The reason for examining the dream independent of any knowledge of the dreamer has been commented on earlier. Certainly, knowledge about the dreamer's life and the associational assistance of the dreamer enhances our understanding of the dream and increases the value of the dream to the dreamer. However, if it can be shown that valuable information about the dreamer is available from our examination of a dream even without the additional information provided by the dreamer's history and associations, conviction about the validity of the dream translation methodology should be considerably strengthened.

I believe that dreams can be understood without associations or context because we now have a knowledge of the structure of dreams that can serve to guide us in our dream translation. Our knowledge of dream structure is the result, to a large extent, of the meticulous analysis of dreams utilizing the methods of the various depth psychological approaches (Bonime, 1962; Boss, 1958; French, 1952–1958; Freud, 1900; Fromm, 1951; Garma, 1966; Hall, 1953; Jung, 1964; Shulman, 1969; Stekel, 1967).

In order to undertake a dream translation, one must have available or utilize some appropriate theory of subjective mental processes that has, as part of its explanatory repertoire, paradigms which are potentially identifiable in dreams. The theories of Freud, Adler, and Jung are admirably suited to the task. Meaning does not exist in dreams but is brought to dreams from some external system of meaning.

The scientific studies of dream content, which relate aspects of dream content to other important personality variables, are an additional source of information about the dream that is potentially useful in dream translation. A knowledge of these regularities can facilitate certain aspects of the dream translator's task. For example, it has been shown that strangers are the most frequent characters in the dreams of schizophrenics, while family members dominate in the dreams of the depressed (Kramer and Roth, 1973). It has also been reported that physically impossible events occur most often in dreams of schizophrenics (Kramer, Baldridge, Whitman, Ornstein, and Smith, 1969), and dream content varies as a function of the sex and age of the dreamer (Kramer, Kinney, and Scharf, 1983). If the question the dream translator hopes to answer is a diagnostic one, these bits of statistical information may be of some help.

Laboratory-based studies of the relationship between dreams and waking fantasy and between dreams and personality measures give support to the theory that waking and sleeping mental states bear a continuous, rather than a compensatory, relationship one to the other (Cartwright, 1969). This observation would orient the dream translator to develop his or her textual translation along the lines of the continuity of the dreamer's subjective life, awake and asleep, rather than to infer one as compensatory to the other.

The systematic examination of the dream has called attention to the dream as relating both to the traits (Kramer, Roth, and Palmer, 1976) and states (Kramer and Roth, 1980) of the dreamer. Similar conceptions have been suggested from clinical work with dreams. This body of knowledge from the experimental work with dreams serves not to give specific translational clues to the dream translator but rather to legitimize his undertaking and invites his attention in the translation to both long-range and immediate aspects of the dreamer's subjective life.

The dream experience is responsive to a large number of current psychological forces operative in the life of the dreamer. The dream is linked to the affective aspects of the prior day (Piccione et al., 1977); to the effects of current and ongoing preemptive experiences, e.g., sleeping in the sleep laboratory (Piccione, Thomas, Roth, and Kramer, 1976); capturing interpersonal events (Kramer, Roth, and Cisco, 1977); mood altering medications (Kramer, Whitman, Baldridge, and Ornstein, 1968); and to events presented concurrent with the dreaming period of sleep (Kramer et al., 1983a). To search in one's effort at understanding, i.e., translating, dreams for highly charged, preemptive, and capturing emotional experiences as related to, if not stimulating, the psychological aspects of dreams, is well-supported by the laboratory study of dreams.

Dream Translation and the Manifest Dream Text

In our overall approach to the dream report, we adopt three interrelated hypotheses of a deterministic and causal type which are crucial to our method of dream translation. The three hypotheses are: (1) that the manifest dream report is strictly determined, (2) that the order of elements in the manifest dream report is strictly determined, and (3) that the order or sequence of elements in the manifest dream report are causally related.

We will not try to defend in detail the validity of these hypotheses but argue simply that they are necessary in our method of dream translation. These hypotheses force, or rather demand, that all the material be systematically examined and that the reported relationships in the dream report be taken into account as the data base for the translation process. Without a rigid adherence to these three hypotheses, a dream translation would not be possible.

The first hypothesis, that the dream report is strictly determined, is not, in a general sense at least, at odds with the usual psychoanalytic position about the manifest dream content (Freud, 1900). The elements that appear in the manifest dream content, at least those essential ones not generated as filler by the mechanism of the secondary revision, are presumed to be the product of the basic dream work mechanism and are legitimately considered as determined. In dream translation, we cling rigidly to the hypothesis that all the elements of the manifest dream content are strictly determined. This obviates the necessity for a decision as to what is essential and what is filler, a decision that is not possible when the associations of the dreamer are not available.

The second hypothesis, that the order of the elements in the dream report is strictly determined, is at odds with the psychoanalytic concept of dream formation. The interrelationship of the parts of the manifest dream, its order and sequence, is, in psychoanalytic theory, a result of secondary revision, in the sevice of disguise, and unrelated to the sense of the latent dream content. I am of the opinion that the application of a strict deterministic hypothesis to the ordering of elements within a dream is a productive and revealing approach, which can assist in understanding the meaningfulness of the dream.

The third hypothesis, that the sequences in the dream text are causally related, also is not presumed in the psychoanalytic system. This inevitably would be the case as the order of elements is not presumed to be determined. However, the concept of *post hoc ergo propter hoc* as explanatory of causal relations in the understanding of the interconnection of subjective material is basic to many of the subjective psychologies (Hall and Lindzey, 1957). The test of the correctness of an interpretive intervention is not the assent or dissent of the patient but the meaningfulness of his or her subsequent remarks as they can be understood to be comments on the interpretive intervention. Subjective psychology becomes adynamic without the presumption of "after the fact therefore because of it." We are hypothesizing that this causal connection operates in the manifest text of the dream. We are persuaded it is a useful hypothesis.

Orientations toward the Dream that Guide the Dream Translator

In the dream translation effort, as in dream interpretation, the goal is to understand the meaningfulness of the dream. The attempt is to understand the subjective life or perspective of the dreamer, not his or her objective reality. One is unable in fantasy material to distinguish between the wish and the deed, between the wish for an act and the fear of it happening. The validation point of a translation, as for an interpretation, is not the external world of the dreamer but his or her inner world.

The dream translator can examine the meaningfulness of the dream from three basic points of view: interpersonal, intrapsychic, and narcissistic.

I have adopted an interpersonal point of view as the key to the meaningfulness of the dream. My use of an interpersonal viewpoint will be illustrated in the case examples, where I review the search for basic paradigms in the dream text. My illustrative examples will focus on the attitudes of the dreamer vis-à-vis persons in his or her subjective world. This approach has been, in another context (Dement, 1965), referred to as dream interpretation at an objective level. It is a valuable, and in my opinion often the most valuable, point of view in examining the dream for an understanding of the patient's inner life.

There is an intrapsychic point of view that can be adopted in examining the dream. From this point of view, the dream text is read as if it were a reflection of aspects of the dreamer, or perhaps better, partial aspects of the dreamer. This intrapsychic point of view has been referred to as dream interpretation at a subjective level (Dement, 1965). It is most useful in shedding light on conflicting trends within the individual if one has a conflict view of the human psyche.

There is a third point of view, related to but not identical with dream interpretation at the subjective level, which views the dream text as reflective of attitudes the dreamer has about himself or herself. A dream examined from this point of view would reflect the level, concerns, or changes in self-esteem the dreamer is experiencing. It is this point of view that would reflect the narcissistic aspect of the personality and would be most related to the psychological meaningfulness systems that view the personality of the dreamer as a whole (Hall and Lindzey, 1957).

In attempting the process of dream translation, it is often useful for the dream translator to keep in mind certain possible roles that the dream is purported to play in the mental economy of the dreamer. The Freudian premise that the dream is the protector of sleep is not useful in dream translation (Freud, 1900). The thesis that the dream is responsive to the emotional preoccupations of the dreamer is a useful overall position in guiding the dream translator in organizing the translation, as I have already suggested.

There are two related but distinct approaches to the responsive role of the dream that the dream translator can productively adopt in examining the dream text. One is that the dream simply displays the current preoccupations of the dreamer; the dream is a *reflective* process. The task then is only to recast the metaphorical or figurative language of the dream text in the language of the psychological meaningfulness system that he or she is utilizing to extract the meaningfulness of the dream. The other thesis is that the dream is *reactive* to the current emotional concerns of the dreamer. In this case, the dream translator would attempt, in addition to recasting the figurative language of the dream text, to speculate about to which emotional concerns of the dreamer the dream may be a reaction. This later formulation is the view adopted in the problem-solving theories of dream function (Bregen, Hunter, and Lane, 1971; French, 1952–1958; Shulman, 1969).

The third possible role of the dream which the dream translator may use is one which is not usually adopted by psychoanalytic psychotherapists, but it is more often adopted by psychotherapists influenced by the theories of individual and analytical psychology. In this third role one views the dream as *anticipatory* of the next day's activities. It is an approach to the dream as forward-looking. If the dream translator took this position, then an additional task would be to speculate on the possible sources of anticipation, the specific future goals about which the dreamer is concerned.

I have attempted to compare the responsive role of the dream to the anticipatory role (Kramer et al., 1982) by studying whether the dream, as reported in the laboratory, was more linked to waking thought either the night before sleeping in the laboratory, i.e., responsive, or the morning after, i.e., anticipatory. I found that dreams are connected to both, but they are more linked to prior waking thought than they are to consequent morning preoccupations.

Neither the reflective, reactive, nor anticipatory role of the dream is in itself sufficient, even if any of them could be demonstrated, to attribute a functional role to the dream. In order to have dreaming subserve a functional role in the mental economy of the dreamer, it would be necessary to demonstrate that what we dream about contributes to the adaptive capacity of the individual. In Piagetian terms, one must demonstrate that either assimilation or accommodation or both occurred (Piaget, 1962).

Functional theories of dreaming (Kramer, 1981) that propose an assimilative function for dreaming are geared to account for the totality of the dream experience. In an assimilative theory, the dream functions automatically outside the awareness, i.e., the dream may never become conscious. In these theories, the dream function is reductive in nature, serving to establish the status quo ante.

In the accommodative functional theories of dreaming, some transformation of the dreamer occurs as a result of the dream experience.

The dream must enter consciousness and be understood in order to achieve its special impact.

It is certainly possible that dreams may serve an accommodative as well as an assimilative function. Those dreams that are recalled may reflect special circumstances and are actually or potentially accommodative, i.e., altering, in nature. The bulk of dreaming which we do not recall may at the same time continue to serve assimilative, i.e., homeostatic, tasks.

The function of dreaming can only be explored by manipulating the dream and studying its consequences. Only by treating the dream as the independent variable can a function for dreaming be established.

In formulating as specifically as I can the approach to dream translation, I have tried to offer specific advice that I felt was most useful in each case. Other than discounting as useful the role of the dream as the protector of sleep, I have no advice to offer on whether to operate with the role of the dream as reflective of the current concerns of the dreamer, as reactive to them, or as anticipatory of some future activity of importance to the dreamer. From a functional point of view, one can assume whatever function for dreaming one likes. The choice really may be a matter of the theoretical predilections of the dream translator and the kinds of questions he or she hopes to answer by a careful scrutiny of the dream text.

Rules for Dream Translation

In reading the text of the dream report, the dream translator uses his or her own associational responses to the text to begin the substitutive process. Here, I do not mean the unguided or free-floating approach that the patient would be encouraged to use. The dream translator uses a more controlled and focused cognitive approach that treats the aspects of the dream text in question as if they were figures of speech, e.g., metaphors, and explores the possible meaningfulness inherent in the object of examination. In a sense, one approaches the text much as one would an imagistic poem, and indeed, I have applied the methodology in explicating problems in a Pinter play (Kramer, 1970).

Clearly, one is substituting the associations of the dream translator, even if of a slightly different type, for the associations of the dreamer, and in so doing, one is abrogating one of the basic tenets of dream interpretation, at least of a psychoanalytic sort. In utilizing the associations of the dream translator, one is really much closer to symbol interpretation, which Freud called a process of translation not one of interpretation (Freud, 1916–1917). This substitution of the dream translator's associations is the heart of the method and will be illustrated in the examples given later.

There is a serious danger engendered when an alternative to the classical associative methodology is suggested as a device for extracting some of the meaningfulness of dreams. The danger of a nonassociative method is that ultimately the dream translator will apply some sort of rigidified symbol substitution. We hope it is apparent and will become even more apparent when we discuss actual examples of dream translations that we are not suggesting a symbol substitution approach.

I particularly would warn against utilizing sexual symbols and basic genetic paradigms in the final dream translation unless the context of the dream, its actual form, precludes any other translation. Such an approach leads to translations so far removed from the immediate situation of the dreamer as to be useless in really understanding his subjective experience. Symbolic and genetic translations are too reductive to be useful. They miss the specific nuances that particularize the dream as revelatory of the dreamer at the time he or she had the dream. And as Freud pointed out, sometimes a dream element must be understood in its apparent rather than its symbolic meaning (Freud, 1900).

Rather than symbol substitution, the dream translation methodology attempts to elaborate aspects of the dream text as if the dream language was that of metaphor (Fromm, 1951; Sharpe, 1951). It views the dream as a figurative statement. The dream translator in controlled associative attempts tries to elaborate the maximum number of possible metaphors that the actual text and his or her ingenuity permit.

It is not immediately apparent why the dream should be treated as a figure of speech rather than taken literally or treated as a code. The events of the recalled dream are often so out of keeping with one's immediate reality that taking them literally has never been a very defensible position.

The application of a ciphering strategy to dreams has had a long history that continues to this day (Hiller, 1931). Its highly arbitrary quality was seen by Freud as limiting the usefulness of a decoding approach (Freud, 1900).

The recognition that dreaming somehow invokes a language of its own and that it is organized differently than waking thought has been suggested by a number of authors. I examined the thematic interconnectedness of a night's dreaming as compared with the interconnectedness of samples of waking thought (Kramer et al., 1982). Dreaming is indeed less structured, less connected than waking thought.

The dream is more fluid and not to be taken literally. This lends some vague support to dreams being seen as figurative, and figures of speech often catch the element of fluidity that dreaming has.

It may be appropriate before proceeding to other rules relating to dream translation to comment on the relationship between manifest and latent content as it applies to dream translation. In dream interpretation a latent text is presumed, for which the manifest text is considered a disguised substitute. In dream translation, one makes an analogous but not necessarily identical presumption. The manifest dream is presumed to contain a meaningfulness other than that which is apparent in the dream report. A transformation is undertaken in the dream translation endeavor in which an alternate text, analogous to the latent content, substitutes for the manifest dream content. The methodology does not imply that the substituted text is necessary because the manifest text is unacceptable and must be disguised to reach awareness. However, the dream translation methodology does not preclude that the manifest text is a dynamically disguised representative of the translated text. The methodology is neutral as to the reason or purpose of the metaphorical nature of the manifest dream text—it simply presumes this to be the case. Perhaps some combination of the dreams visual nature, i.e., the need for visual representation, its affective focus, and its subjective nature lay the basis for dream elements to be figures of speech.

The dream translator approaches the total dream text systematically from the beginning to the end. Interestingly, this simple idea of beginning from the beginning in approaching a dream text is not the method of approach generally suggested in "reading" fantasy material for meaningfulness. One approach often used is called "headline reading," (Saul, Snyder, and Sheppard, 1956) and it suggests that the text be read for major themes or trends and that one not get bogged down in detail. The other approach that has been suggested for examining the dream is to search the text for something understandable and work backward and forward from the point of alleged or presumed understanding (French and Fromm, 1964).

In dream translation, it is crucial to begin at the beginning in order to capitalize on the value of our hypothesized causal sequence in ordering one's thinking. To begin at the beginning spurs the generation of as many textual translations as possible and enables one to use later material as confirmatory of prior speculation, thereby assisting the translator in making his or her choice from among the several possibilities.

I have already acknowledged that because of the delineation of dream structure that the associational methods have provided, it is possible to establish at least some of the meaningfulness of dreams without the dreamer's association. It is the recognition of how dreams are structured, an understanding that the dream translator must have, that provides the basis for the more controlled associative approach that would be used in attempting to achieve a dream translation.

The type of structure of dreams to which we are referring is the recognition of certain basic explanatory paradigms that provide clues about the possible concerns of the dreamer. Depending on the explanatory psychological system one would be using, the dream translator attempts to search for representatives of basic paradigms, i.e., structures, in the dream.

The basic paradigm in the psychoanalytic system is the oedipal triangle. Classically, this is expressed in the dream as representations of father, mother, and child. In the dream, the dreamer may appear in any or all of the roles. In a dream translation, any three-person situation is potentially, or at is core, an oedipal one. This presumption, then, permits an analysis of the interaction from the vantage point of the dreamer's oedipal situation. Examining the dream from this triangular position contributes to an understanding of the dreamer's attitude toward other men and women, authority, dependency, sexuality, and other aspects of his or her inner life.

Other paradigms in the dream, for example, are same-sex and opposite-sex pairs. The former situation, at its base, is homosexual, and the latter is heterosexual. No matter what the explicit nature of the situation may be, the basic paradigm is sexual, modified by the social context in which it appears.

Persons of approximately similar age or station are seen as peers, and peer relationships would be seen as siblings from a psychoanalytic genetic point of view. Again, it is the basic paradigm that the dream translator would be attempting to capture. The dream translator would then use the actual dream context to give particular meaningfulness to the basic relationship and its extended psychosocial derivatives.

Movement in the dream (Horney, 1945), toward an object or away from it, has an attraction-repulsion implication. To go toward something not only indicates desire, longing, or wish for it and for what it offers but also the concerns surrounding anticipation. To go away from something or someone has a rejecting implication but also the implications of leaving and separation and their psychological sequelae.

I accept from our knowledge of the structure of fantasy, and particularly of dreams, that the active-passive nature of dream action is potentially revelatory of the feelings and attitudes of the dreamer toward the object of the alleged action or lack of action. Further, it is useful to keep in mind the assertive nature of action and the potentially receptive nature of passivity.

There are other paradigms that have implicit structural components that are helpful in the work of dream translation. For example, the expression of hostility is best conceptualized as having a prior "experience" of expectation and disappointment directed at the object of the hostility, even if the expectation and disappointment are not expressed. This constellation, of which hostility is the final expression, would be a specified example of the more general and basic assumption that behavior is motivated.

Dependency is another example of an important basic aspect of the subjective life of the dreamer in which a constellation approach is useful. It is best to adopt the attitude that if someone in the dream is dependent, he or she is dependent on someone for something. This "on-someone-for-something" formula is applicable to any impulse, desire, or action and is part of the more general conception of an impulse having an aim and an object. The on-someone-for-something phrasing gives a real-life quality to the aim and object concept.

All the paradigms that have been illustrated are suggested from psychoanalytic theory. It may be worthwhile to suggest one or two illustrations from other depth psychological positions. From the vantage point of individual psychology (Adler, 1959), the spatial orientation in the dream along an above or below perspective is a basic paradigm reflecting the striving to overcome. From the position of analytical psychology (Dement, 1965), same-sex unknown figures in the dream may be reflective of the shadow aspect of the personality.

One final comment on paradigms is worth making, recognizing that we have not listed all of the useful basic paradigms. From an interpersonal point of view, the subjective life is concerned with people not things. A dreamer interacting with the inanimate world is most likely relating to a person or some aspect of a person and not really dealing with things.

In reviewing the guidelines and rules for dream translation, I hope I have conveyed the idea that the translator must stay very close to the text. With the exception of the constellation approach, i.e., where the presence of an element suggests or demands the presence of other elements, it is an essential part of dream translation that one translates only what appears in the text. Clearly an inferential process is triggered in the effort to translate a given portion of the dream text. However, in a translation, each step in the inference-drawing process is spelled out.

The inference-drawing process must have an explicit referent in the text and must remain consistent with that referent as one draws higher orders of inference. This demand for a textual base precludes departures into the wild blue yonder of the translator's own private or metapsychological world. What isn't there cannot be translated.

From the position of psychoanalytic theory, there is the recognition that there are omissions in the manifest text as it is created, so to speak, by the dreamwork from the latent text. The process of dream interpretation is capable of recapturing the latent text and supplying the omissions. One of the limitations of the dream translation method is, as has been stated, that it cannot translate what is not present in the manifest text. Accepting this limitation and cleaving to the strict rule of not interpreting what isn't there avoids the errors of wild speculation. It is a price worth paying, even if one loses an occasional brilliant insight (or lucky guess) in the process.

Along related but not identical lines, dream translation cannot really deal with the problem of reversals in dream formation. There are no guidelines or rules to help orient the dream translator to when he or she should "read" the text as is or when the meaning should be reversed. The safest rule to follow is to translate the text as it is given. In utilizing this rule not to reverse aspects of the text, the translator must accept, as with the case of omissions, that he or she may be missing an important aspect of the meaningfulness of the dream. The gain to the translator is that he or she is using a consistent rather than arbitrary approach.

In dealing with the rule regarding reversals, the dream translator is dealing with such issues as the difference between the wish for an action and the fear of the action, the love of an object and hatred toward the object. One should keep in mind that the two aspects of such dichotomies often, if not inevitably, go together. Freud presumed this in his acceptance of the antithetical meaning of primal words, which forms part of the emotional logic for the representational aspects of ambivalent situations (Freud, 1900). However, for the translator, if the manifest text is a wish or a fear, he or she must respond to the explicit first, and secondarily allow for the antithetical pole of the dichotomy.

The task of the dream translator is to provide a coherent substitute text for the manifest dream report that attempts to account for all of the elements in the manifest dream report, including the explicit relationships among the various manifest dream elements. In attempting to provide a coherent substitute, the dream translator often must choose among several possible alternatives for each textual element. His or her guide will be the inferences that most effectively link together the largest amount of the dream material in the simplest possible fashion. The dream translator, in effect, applies Occam's law of parsimony in choosing between alternatives.

We believe explicit note should be made of the potential multiple uses to which a dream translation can be put. The translation, by extension, can be used to contribute to all aspects of the diagnostic process—clinical diagnosis, dynamics, genetics, transference, countertransference, and treatment planning. I have examined in another context (Kramer, Ornstein, Whitman, and Baldridge, 1967) the contribution of fantasy to these aspects of patient evaluation.

The Psychoanalytic View of Dream Formation as Compared with Dream Translation

I indicated that in attempting to spell out the guidelines and rules for doing a dream translation, I would also call attention to points of similarity and difference between the method of dream translation and that of psychoanalytic dream interpretation. This comparative endeavor is worthwhile not because it contributes to the task of the translating process but rather because it sharpens the reader's conceptual clarity in understanding the approach of dream translation by using the more familiar psychoanalytic concepts as a point of reference.

I have not so far examined in detail whether the guidelines and rules underlying a dream translation are similar to or different from the psychoanalytic position with regard to the mechanisms that are postulated as operating in transforming the latent dream content into the manifest dream content. More explicitly, does the method of dream translation view the mechanisms of secondary revision, condensation, displacement, and considerations of representability in the same way one would view them in doing a dream interpretation?

The attitude toward and the manner of dealing with the manifest dream text as sequentially and causally related that I am exposing abrogates the psychoanalytic view of the fourth aspect of the dreamwork, or what may be considered an aspect of the dreamwork, namely, the process of secondary revision. Freud argued that the individual elements of the manifest dream text are strictly determined and formed by three core aspects of the dreamwork—condensation, displacement, and considerations for representability (Freud, 1901). He was undecided whether the organization of the manifest dream text, i.e., the ordering of the various elements, was part of the dream work, i.e., unconscious processes, or whether the bringing together of the parts, with the addition of connective elements, was not more a secondary process guided by reality considerations and therefore more a function of secondary processes best attributed to the system preconscious. His final formulation was to exclude secondary revision from the core dreamwork mechanisms (Freud, 1913a) and to point out that the façade that the secondary revision achieved, under the influence of reality considerations, served to further the disguise purposes of the censorship (Freud, 1913b).

If I accepted the psychoanalytic view, then a dream translation would not be possible. I would have to deal separately with each element of the dream, and there would be no way, without either a knowledge of the dreamer or his or her associations, to order the individual dream elements. I have adopted the position that the order in the manifest text of a dream is as determined and revealing of the dreamer as any of the individual elements. I see no need to drop a commitment to a strict determinism, so useful in so many other contexts, when I deal with the interconnection of the parts of a dream.

My view of the manifest dream elements as sequentially causal is also at odds with the psychoanalytic view of the function of secondary revision, which links the separate elements of the manifest dream together guided by considerations of rationality and disguise, not causality. As I previously indicated the value of "after the fact, therefore because of it" in understanding fantasy material is so useful an hypothesis that I have applied it in the dream translation methodology.

With regard to the aspect of the dreamwork called condensation, the view of the dream translator would be compatible with the position of the dream interpreter. One could consider a single image or textual element as some sort of composite representation. The generation of multiple associations by the dream translator to a single textual element would reflect the possibility that the element is a multifaceted representation—not necessarily having a single bit of meaningfulness. In the sense that an element may be multirepresentational, the dream translator functions with the possibility that the textual element is a condensation.

It seems to me that little effort is made in dream interpretation to distinguish composite images from intermediate common entities (Freud, 1901). Freud did distinguish between the two. For the sake of simplicity we will consider them both as condensations and retain a congruity between the presumptions of translator and interpreter.

When we turn our attention to the aspect of the dreamwork referred to as displacement, another disparity develops between the approaches of dream translation and dream interpretation. The shift in emphasis that can and almost always is presumed to occur between the latent and manifest text, making the central emphasis in the latent content peripheral in the manifest content, is not a usable presumption in dream translation. In dream translation, the manifest dream content is handled or responded to at face value and apparent points of emphasis are accepted as such, although they are, of course, seen as figurative rather than literal statements. In the dream translation methodology, one is forced to accept the text as is, since one is unable to designate whether a shift in emphasis should be made.

The last of the three dreamwork mechanisms described by Freud is the one called consideration or regard for representability. The central notion here is that one of the determinants which accounts for what is chosen to appear in the manifest text as expressive of the latent content is the capability of the element to be visually represented. The dream translation methodology leans most heavily on this presumed aspect of the dreamwork. In effect, the dream translator presumes that the major, if not exclusive, basis for the representability of an idea is that it embodies the literal idea in a figurative expression. This is the basis for seeing the dream text as a figure of speech as so often the dream idea is metaphorically represented. A dream of a lion's heart to represent courage would be an example.

Freud remarked on two other processes that are central to the transformation of the latent dream thoughts to the manifest dream content. These are the mode of dealing with feelings and the complexity of regression in the formation of the manifest dream (Freud, 1900).

Feelings are potentially subject to the same changes as any other portion of the latent dream thoughts. They can be intensified, diminished, displaced, reversed, or omitted. There are no rules that permit the dream translator to choose among these possibilities. Therefore, in dream translations one deals with feelings as they appear in the manifest dream text. Note is made of absent, diminished, or reversed feelings as measured by what the situation in the dream would call for if it were an actual situation. Deviations from the expected then become clues to meaningfulness, and the dream translator gives them some dynamic explanation.

Regression, in all of its aspects, can be accepted by the dream translator as it would be by the dream interpreter. Although the concept of regression is not used explicitly in the process of dream translation, it could be invoked to account for the manner in which ideas are linked together in the dream, the visual nature of the experience of the dream, and the historical sources of the dream content. This view of the potential role of regression in dream formation would be a point of agreement between the method of dream translation and that of dream interpretation.

The review I have provided is the background of the basic assumptions, guidelines, and rules for the method of dream translation. Illustrations have been kept to a minimum. I have attempted, in addition, a comparison of the method of dream translation to the psychoanalytic presumptions regarding dream formation and interpretation. In the second section, I will attempt to illustrate the process of achieving a dream translation.

Examples of Dream Translation

I believe that the choice of examples to illustrate the method of dream translation should come from actual unselected applications of the method rather than from a large series of dreams which were translated and selected for the purpose of providing illustrations of the application of various rules of the dream translation methodology. The use of unselected examples of dream translations will provide the reader with the most realistic appreciation of the method. The two examples presented below are unselected from two teaching conferences taught by the author. Both examples were chosen from the last presentation given in each conference before the author presented the method of dream translation to a seminar.

The first example was presented in a teaching conference for residents on a psychiatric inpatient service at a Veterans Administration Hospital. The patient's therapist selected the dream and wrote up the history and the dynamic formulation of the case in advance. At the time of the case conference, however, the therapist stated only the age and sex of the patient and read the dream, a phrase at a time. The conference leader and participants then attempted a dream translation. When they had finished with their translation and formulation, the patient's therapist then read the history and his dynamic formulation. He commented on where he felt the dream translation had been correct, where it had gone astray, and where it simply did not touch on core aspects of the patient's inner life.

Dream A (26-year-old male)

I dreamed I was back in Vietnam and I had thrown a grenade into one of the Vietnamese huts. I went inside and there was one of the babies blown up all over the inside of the hut. I woke up and was terrified, nauseated and crying.

Translation of Dream A. The patient begins his dream report by placing himself in a foreign environment of danger, i.e., a war zone, and indicates he has been there before. The focus for him may be the fact that this is away from his current setting, and it may therefore have an escape or desirable implication. However, the initial impression of being in a familiar, dangerous, and destructive situation is for me the most striking possibility.

The patient then throws a grenade into one of the Vietnamese huts. The patient, without apparent duress, engages in a hostile, destructive act. Or to be more precise, he engages in an aggressive act, throwing, which is potentially destructive. The grenade has the capability of, and is primarily intended as, a destructive weapon or instrument. If one makes the inference that the patient is in the military, then the act of the aggression and potential destructiveness is a sanctioned act. It is expected behavior, as it would be in keeping with his work as a soldier. It is not then an unbridled outburst of hostility but a controlled and legitimate undertaking.

The controlled or channeled nature of the destructive act may be of importance. It could avoid feelings of loss of control, and it could serve to deal with issues of guilt or fears of retaliation. The plea or rationale might then be, "It was my duty to engage in such potentially unacceptable acts for which I cannot be held personally culpable" or "It is the honorable thing for me to do." It is, in a manner of speaking, the difference between a madman with a butcher knife and a surgeon with a scalpel. The vehicle used for the expression of feeling is likely to tell us something about the person and the feeling because they are determined, not random, choices.

In passing a comment should be made about the attack being at a distance. It is not from direct contact but from something thrown that the damage will come. It is safer than hand-to-hand combat. Must he, for some reason, be distant from his destructiveness?

What then is the object of the aggressive or destructive impulse? One of the Vietnamese huts. I would take note of the fact that it is not his own but that of the other. By this I mean that if I assume that our patient is an American soldier, then the assault is on the non-American object, the foreign, the different, the strange. It is not an American but a foreign object that is attacked. It remains unclear what the foreign refers to at this point.

Further, in speculating about the object that is attacked, it is of interest, I believe, that it is not a person being thrown at, but an inanimate object. I do not pretend for one moment that grenades are usually thrown at empty huts, although that is possible to prevent the later use of the hut. Rather, I would grant the reasonable inference that our patient is overtly concerned about a possible occupant of the hut. Nevertheless, the object of assault is a relatively impersonal, inanimate thing. Is this impersonal assault reflective of some discomfort about or disguise of aggressive impulses directed at some person? Clearly, given our explanatory systems, it is people and not things that matter, so the speculation must be given some credence, but at this time it can be given little further specification.

One further specification could be made in relation to the relatively fragile implication, for most of us, of the idea that a hut is hardly a house. Is some delicacy implied? In addition, it is just one of the huts, not a specific hut, not personal in nature. Does the impersonal nature of the hut indicate that it makes no difference, or does it, perhaps, make too much difference?

It certainly must occur to one that the hut, if the translation effort would allow for symbolic interpretation, can be given some greater specification. The notion of the hut, as a building, being a person is well explicated by Freud in his dream book (Freud, 1900). This speculation would then allow one to recast the dream into a sanctioned assault on a foreign, strange, distant, exotic, and perhaps fragile person.

If the possibility is raised of a man throwing something into a woman that explodes, then a sexual assault is suggested. It would be a destructive view of sexuality that is being represented.

What transpires next? Our attacker from a distance then enters the scene of his destructive or potentially destructive act. Is this simply appropriate behavior? Is it curiosity? The motive is not clear. Nevertheless, he enters the place of his aggressive action.

The scene is one of infanticide. "One of the babies [is] blown up all over the inside of the hut." To everyone, this is a horrible sight; it is not the noble and heroic work of a warrior hero. No affect is expressed at this point, which is not unusual for a dream. Affects, according to Freud (1900), are generally muted in the manifest dream when compared to the latent dream text.

For me, the baby in the hut is confirmation of the symbolic speculation that the hut may be representative of a person and particularly a woman. The assumption that I may be dealing with a woman and perhaps a uterus is simply that the only place, from a biological point of view, that contains a baby is a uterus, and that the only possessors of uteri are women. One should note that it is "one of the babies," perhaps implying others were present.

I will grant that the explication of the hut—baby as pregnant woman—is excessively pedantic. However, the only way that I know to check the inferences in the translation of a dream is to spell out what one grasps immediately. This tortuous and excessive process prevents one from overlooking some points and also serves to insure that the global (or intuitive, if you prefer) grasp is consonant with the manifest content of the dream.

To proceed I must return to the description provided when our patient enters the hut. "One of the babies is blown up all over the inside of the hut." My first association, and clearly I am substituting my own associations for those of the dreamer's, is to the image of something blown up. Here my thoughts were not of destruction but of swollenness and the image of a pregnant woman. I must accept that I am so under the influence of the pregnant woman image that I am gilding the lily and not really moving our efforts at translation along.

The child is splattered over the inside of the hut. If the hut is, as I suggested, a woman, then a splattered child inside is a dead child in a mother, and the next idea is of an abortion or a macerated fetus.

Perhaps I can take our translation a bit further at this point. Our patient has committed a sanctioned, aggressive (destructive) act, at a distance, against a fragile, possibly pregnant woman and caused her (perhaps unborn) child to die or her to abort. Implied again, is the fact that he does not want to be held responsible for the act.

The last line of the dream report indicates that the dream ended in the dreamer awakening, feeling terrified, nauseated, and crying. From a psychoanalytic perspective, these awakening feelings are part of the dream and are not to be seen as reactions to the dream. Either way, the affect did appear and, in my judgment, would be seen as appropriate to the content of the dream. The least disturbed aspect of the dream, Freud says, is the affect (Piaget, 1962). To have been terrified, sick to one's stomach, nauseated, and tearful if one has splattered a baby with a grenade would be considered by all of us the appropriate affective response.

What of the awakening? It is a failure, well recognized by Freud (1900), in the function of the dream. The dream is a protector of sleep and not a disturber, provided it can meet the demands of the censorship and discharge the unconscious without arousing too much affect. If not, the dream fails its sleep-protective function, and an awakening from an anxiety dream occurs.

Constructing the Dreamer

Based on the dream translation, what kind of man is our patient? He is one concerned about his hostile impulses in relationship to mothers and particularly to their children. From a genetic perspective, he is most likely not the youngest sibling. He might well have experienced displacement by younger siblings with relative hostility, at least at the fantasy level, directed at his mother and/or his siblings. I noted the possibility of more than one baby earlier. The anxiety dream and the impersonal, sanctioned, distant mode of the hostility both suggest that he finds the hostility intolerable.

What of his current life? My first guess as to what the dream is dealing with or reactive to, inferring for the moment he is married, is that he is experiencing internal, unacceptable hostility toward his wife, either for being pregnant or for having a child. Why he has this feeling would go beyond the dream. He may have caused her or the child some injury. The anxiety must relate to the feeling or temptation that could cause the destruction to his wife and/or the child.

This would be an appropriate stopping point. One could pursue a number of other dynamic speculations. One could extrapolate from the dream implications for transference, countertransference, clinical diagnosis (e.g., a traumatic neurosis), and treatment planning. I feel that the essence of the translation has been adequately captured and conveyed.

Therapist's History, Formulation, and Comment. This was the first Veterans Administration Hospital admission for this 26-year-old white male. He was brought to the admitting area late at night on 6 September, 1974 in an ambulance by his girlfriend. At that time, he stated that he was afraid that he was going to hurt himself or others. On the evening of admission, he was with his girlfriend at the VFW lodge and was talking about the war. He found himself getting more and more anxious, and he finally went home. The patient stated that he began drinking, became more and more fearful, tried to go to bed and sleep, but had vivid dreams about the war and killing. His girlfriend became afraid and called the rescue squad. They took the patient to the hospital and he was admitted.

Brief History of the Present Illness. The patient was in the army as a rifleman in Vietnam in the latter part of 1970. He enlisted in 1967 because he felt he would be drafted anyway, as his lottery number was low. The last twelve months of his stay in Vietnam were in a heavy combat zone where he was hurt several times, and several of his friends were killed. He got several medals for his service there, and keeps them on his army shirt at home. Now when he looks at his medals, he gets very anxious.

He married his second and present wife four months after coming back from the service. Their marriage went well for the first eighteen months, but they began having arguments associated with his employment and working hours. Although they had two children, the patient moved away from his wife and secured his own apartment. He would frequently return to his family for short periods of time. During this period, he was self-employed and making a good living. However, he sold this business about the time his wife was filing for divorce. He is now doing intermittent painting jobs and contributing two hundred dollars per week in child support.

In late 1972, while bowling with his wife, the people at the bowling alley began talking about the war. He started to get anxious and wanted to leave. His wife did not. He got more and more anxious, and the evening culminated in his hitting her in the back of the head with his fist, causing a large cut. He stated that he went out of his mind with anxiety and fear while he was on the way to the hospital with his wife.

Past History. The patient is of rural background. He is the oldest of nine children. His childhood was characterized by disagreements with his father, who was an alcoholic. His father was out of the home much of the time but would come back for brief periods, often getting his mother pregnant. During those times, the patient would often find himself in a position of protecting his mother and would actually hit his father and run. He ran because he thought that his father would kill him if he ever caught him.

When he was ten, he had to help his mother give birth because the doctor could not come, and they did not get her to the hospital in time. He said that he knew a great deal about the delivery of babies already because of the animals on their farm. He reported that his mother had lost several children in the past through miscarriage, but none of them were the ones that he helped deliver.

Hospital Course. During his admission, the patient talked at length about his army service, of his many friends that he saw killed and mutilated, and of the people that he was told to torture. He stated that at times he would be terrified and confused. In addition, he shamefully noted that many times he actually got pleasure out of the killings and mutilations that he was ordered to do. He often stated that he had a great deal of grief over these feelings of pleasure because this was in contrast to his prewar ideals. He stated that he thought these ideals were now destroyed and he would never really be able to be at peace with himself again.

It is of interest that, just prior to enlistment, he and his first wife were not getting along well. About six months before enlistment, he accidentally caused his wife to lose their baby. He was told the miscarriage was the result of his breaking her membranes during intercourse.

Concluding Remarks. The therapist stated that he was in almost total agreement with my thoughts on the dream, though there was little content about the father. However, that in a sense seemed to be a separate problem to him.

The therapist noted that in session No. 6 the patient had a similar dream to the one presented, which was from session No. 2, only the child in the hut was his daughter, and he was terrified of this dream and revulsed by it.

The descriptive historical material provided by the therapist is provocative and superfically congruent with the dream translation. Unfortunately, no explicit formulation was provided to specify more particularly the correctness of the translation. The therapist was in his first six months of psychiatric training and the lack of a definitive and more sophisticated formulation is understandable. Rather than speculate with the implications of the historical material, I will let the example stand and have the reader draw his or her own conclusions and proceed to the second example.

The second example is from a conference with third-year residents who had asked the author to work with them in developing their skills in dream translation. The format was the same as that used in the inpatient conference. The patient's therapist gave the age and sex of the patient and read the dream to the conference, phrase by phrase. The conference group developed a dream translation and formulation. Then the therapist read her formulation of the case pointing out areas of agreement and disagreement with the formulation.

Dream B (27-year-old female)

I dreamed I was at my roommate's wedding at a music hall–type house with a balcony. There were a lot of servants, men in black outfits, looking through white filmy curtains. Patty was there trying to be helpful. The food was hideous, set up on silver trays. There was a blonde middle-aged German lady, dressed as a maid.

Cadillacs were pulling up. They had to close the front door. I had to go around. I went in and found Jean, who was looking at empty shelves in a linen closet. She took out a yellow nightgown.

Then I met two asexual Munchkins who were named Electricia and Electrician. They were jumping up and down, hugging each other.

Translation of Dream B. The patient is a 27-year-old female. She begins the dream by commenting that she is at her roommate's wedding. I think a fair first association is that the roommate is another young woman, probably of comparable age. It is the roommate who is being married and not our patient. Many things are suggested by this. Let me illustrate a few. First, the pair, patient and roommate, are being separated. No matter what the nature of the relationship, a loss is involved. The patient will no longer have her roommate. Second, certainly associations to the implications of a same-sex pair must come to mind. The homosexual association is indirectly supported by the sexual implications of the roommate being married. Third, the patient is being left behind, and the roommate may be viewed as moving forward or, if moving forward is too big an assumption, moving on. In a sense, then, the loss or abandonment is because the roommate prefers a man to the patient. Shifting our focus slightly, the roommate may have succeeded where the patient has failed; she got a man, and the patient may be left with envious, competitive feelings.

What of the fact that she is at her roommate's wedding? Apparently, despite any feelings of rejection and / or envy, she remains in relationship to the roommate. She can participate in the cause of the disruption. Her feelings, or those we have speculated she has, do not serve to overwhelm her such that she must avoid the situation.

Before proceeding, let us comment on the wedding as an event and the roommate as a person. Neither need really exist. The issue is the patient's subjective reality. Certainly, from the manner she reports the dream, the likelihood that there is a real roommate seems fairly high, but it is not necessary to our translation. The roommate then becomes any same-sex peer person, or even an aspect of herself. Clearly, the same point about subjective reality applies to the wedding.

But what of the setting in which the heterosexually tinged event takes place, "at a music hall–type house with a balcony?" Here I am left with the feeling of a vast, theatrical, cavernous place. The image stirs a feeling of being overwhelmed and left out, or made to feel insignificant. My next thought is that of one attending a performance, since that is usually what takes place at a music hall. Is this our patient's view of what the entry into marriage is like? Does it suggest that she feels small and insignificant, a speculated feeling not in the text, in the face of the big event? Somehow she is not up to it—a kind of "who me?" feeling. Is she for some reason not up to the big heterosexual leap, with all of its implications?

Or, will we find, as we proceed, that it is not that she feels inadequate to the performance, to the task at hand, but rather it is all overdone? Marriage yes, public performances no. I cannot choose, at this point, between these two options, or others I might conjure up; for example, that marriage is just a performance.

I have not addressed myself to the balcony, the protuberance that just out from the upper stories of the building. My first association was a romantic allusion to Romeo and Juliet. A more remote and symbolic one is to breasts—that which juts out from the upper stories of a woman. Another thought is that it is a place to stand, to be above the crowd, but not part of it; elevated but not involved. A vague echo of the rejection, aloneness theme, which I speculated about earlier returns. With further time and thought, with the associative assistance of others, the balcony would certainly contribute more to my translation than I can provide at the moment.

What does our patient comment on next? "There were a lot of servants." Well, she is not totally alone, even if she is not with the other guests or with equals. If this is a continuation of the rejection-abandonment theme, it has a compensatory flavor. She is not abandoned, alone, and helpless; many people are there to be of assistance—people are there to serve her, to take care of our patient's needs, albeit not in a personal way. One could take note of the abundance of servants as reflective of the intensity of the hypothesized need for service, for care.

But who are the servants? "Men," a curious identification. Putting aside a reality explanation based on her actually having gone to her roommate's wedding, and that indeed there were a lot of servants and that these servants were exclusively or primarily men, why does our patient take note of this fact at this place in the dream? Might it reflect the competitive theme we mentioned earlier? Her roommate has a man whom she is about to marry to serve her needs. The patient now has not one man, but a lot of men, servants, who will meet her immediate needs.

There must be some reason, if we are on the right track, as to why the men patient feels are available to her are only servants, and not even her own servants? If she wants a man, it's a party, she could have brought one along, met one as a guest at the wedding, found some other way. She loses her roommate to a man, and the first men she puts herself in relationship to are servants, not equals, not personal. We begin to wonder if there is some problem for our patient vis-à-vis men? Is there something to our homosexual speculation? Must men be depreciated and distanced? Whatever it is, men aren't such a comfortable topic for our dreamer at this juncture in her life.

What else about the men? They are dressed "in black outfits" and "looking through white filmy curtains." For me, this presents a peculiarly sinister and distancing pair of images. Black is a somber, forbidding, and perhaps frightening color. The color of bad, evil, wrongness, etc. Am I overdoing it? What if the patient is black? Am I working with excessive and rather old-fashioned cultural stereotypes? Perhaps, but the night is frightening and the night is black, no matter what one's sense of social justice calls for. If a cultural stereotype has led me astray, then when I attempt to validate my translation with the knowledge the patient's therapist has of the patient, I can later correct the assumptive logic and resolve any differences.

If one grants, for the moment, the forbidding quality of the men, what of their accessibility to the patient? Well, they are looking through white, filmy curtains. Is this a look-but-don't-touch situation? There is an impediment but a transparent and flimsy one. What they are looking at and why they are looking is unclear. Apparently, they are not serving. Men, who may be useful as servants, are forbidding in black and separated from her. They are onlookers rather than participants, although they are potentially available.

A comment on the color of the curtain is in order. Is the curtain white to mitigate the scary nature of the men in black? Is there some latent desire, even if not a dominant push, to find a way to be closer to men? This may be a hopeful speculation if, indeed, our dreamer has a problem with men, who somehow frighten her.

"Patty was there trying to be helpful." The theme of giving, of helpfulness of helplessness, of dependency and its solutions, is brought to our attention again. But who is Patty? A perusal of the remainder of the text does not tell us. Let us make a few guesses. First, she is a girl. Second, she is someone the patient probably knows. And third, she could be a peer.

We would point out that the patient turns from the problematic men, who are the first people she encounters, to the familiar and useful peer female. She certainly speaks better, even if briefly, of the female than of the males. Our patient sees women more positively than men.

She notices that "the food was hideous." Could this be a sour-grapes criticism of her roommate's success? Could it be a commentary on what one gets as part of marriage? If it is, then why bother becoming involved with a man? I cannot pass a food reference without a bow to oral problems. This then permits a comment on dependency, more specifically, a rejection of dependent needs. It is not being waited on, being helpless, being given to, but rather giving that she might prefer defensively. What is offered is hideous. Clearly, she wouldn't or doesn't want it. The previous dependency theme is continued.

Our dreamer notices as part of her disparagement of what is being offered that the food is "set up on silver trays." This implies a certain richness and perhaps opulence that apparently she finds offensive. Is this some liberated rejection of the traditional patterns? A bit of social rebellion? Or, might it simply be that our patient's aesthetic sensibilities are offended? No choice is necessary. They are basically expressions of the same issue. Or is the food and tray a mixed image? The food was hideous, but the silver tray could be construed more positively. Does this reflect her marital ambivalence in one image? We don't know.

Immediately following her critical, rejecting comment on what she might be given, there appears in the dream, "a blonde, middle-aged German lady, dressed as a maid." Why does a woman appear at this point? Following such a forthright criticism of the food, might we not, assuming our speculations about her heterosexual problems are correct, expect some snide or degrading remark directed at men? Our dreamer does not accommodate us. An older woman appears. Who might she be? Our basic triangular paradigm would call for it being mother, an older sister, or perhaps an aspect of herself as older—at heart, all three would be the same.

Assuming this is mother, then the rejection of the dependent gratification, the biting social commentary, might have been done in front of this woman, her mother. This would fit my rebellion hypothesis as a social derivative of the problem. "This is what I think of this show, your kind of show, mother. It's hideous."

What of the lady being German? In our community (Cincinnati), it is simply a high-probability event, but why does she call attention to the woman being German? Certainly it makes the person foreign. This has implications of strangeness, distance, and even for the exotic, although this is less likely. We believe, falling back on the use of cultural stereotypes, that rigidity or some other aspect of the German stereotype might be implied. It is perhaps the rigidity of her mother's expectations that she herself is in rebellion against.

It is interesting to note that the woman is cast in the role of maid, another who serves. This is part of the patient's dependent concerns, perhaps part of the role she fears and rejects. One might stretch for a play on the word "maid," as one who is made—and derive a sexual implication.

The blondness of the middle-aged lady cannot be overlooked. Two beginning speculations might relate to its lightness, its acceptability, its potential for sexual attraction; or conversely, it may be part of a blond cheapness, a thing to be rejected. Or the blondness may be some combination of these possibilities. Our sense of the middle-aged lady as mother, who must be rejected and depreciated, leads us to a negative assumption about the meaningfulness of the blondness rather than a positive one.

I want to mention, in passing, that both the male and female servant figures are described in terms of how they are dressed. One could even infer that the lady wasn't a maid but only dressed as one. A possible inference from the comments on the way they are dressed is that our patient is concerned about appearances, how things and people look. A certain defensive superficiality would be implied, perhaps a need to keep up appearances. A concern about expectations, what others think, or feelings of shame is where this speculation would lead.

Before proceeding to the last two paragraphs of the manifest dream text, let me attempt a condensed summary of my translation. In reaction to the loss of her female friend to a man, the patient attempts to maintain contact with her, although a bit awed and critical of her female friend's decision. She feels needy, perhaps abandoned, and envious. She turns to men to meet her needs, but they are depreciated, forbidding, and not quite available. A peer woman is or could be more helpful. She envisions that what one gets in a heterosexual relationship is hideous and rejects it. This can be seen as part of a more general rejection, perhaps defensive, of maternal values. However, in the course of her struggle she remains concerned that she not be revealed.

Let me now return to the dream text. Our dreamer's attention is attracted to the arrival, I would assume, of the other guests. She does not mention them per se, but experiences the arrival of expensive cars. "Cadillacs were pulling up." An echo of the silver trays, I hope, is apparent. The theme follows what was translated as a rejection of mother and her expectations. It isn't our patient's cup of tea. The social rebellion we speculated on earlier continues in terms of opulence, although a more basic theme, the defensive rejection of the marital expectation, may be what is more subjectively germane. One could pursue a sexual implication in the pulling up, but we will let it pass for the moment.

Then a curious thing happens in the dream. The front door has to be closed. Is the wedding about to begin? If we read ahead, the wedding manifestly never occurs in the dream. What are we to make of their having to close the door? Inside and outside and separated. Free passage is no longer possible. A note of finality is implied. If I presume a sexual allusion, following the pulling up, something is shut—a sexual ambivalence might be extracted related to intercourse.

Let me try another tack with regard to the shutting of the door. Let me say that the rebellion theme related to mother is continued in the image of the Cadillacs and leads the patient, in her protest, to having gone too far. She in effect shuts herself out or ends up being shut out. This may not be a completely tenable position for our patient, who, I am postulating, has had a rejection, feels needy, but must try to keep up appearances. She has or feels she might go too far and be on the outside looking in. If she protests too much, the others will have to close the door.

Her next experience is suggestively confirmatory of our speculations about the closing of the door. It is an impediment, "I had to go around." If one assumes she is on the outside, she is shut out and she still wants in. If she is on the inside, a less likely possibility we believe, she wants to go somewhere, but the closed door blocks her. Earlier in the dream, she seemed to be inside and now, somehow, we would argue as a result of the translated affective meaning of the dream, she has rebelled herself to the outside. If my speculation that she is on the outside, where she doesn't want to be is correct, she goes around, by implication to get back in. The going around (to get in) may be reflective of the interpersonal strategy of using an oblique approach when a direct one is not possible and could offer another line of speculation.

My assumption of protest, of feeling shut out, alone, and wanting to reestablish contact is confirmed by the very next portion of the text and permits a continuous progression of my translation. The patient says explicitly "I went in and found Jean." A contact is reestablished through her effort—again, we infer, with a female, Jean, and possibly a peer female. This contact may be a solution, at some, level to the rebellion against her mother and the loss of her roommate. It is possible that Jean is the roommate, but even if she isn't, this would not change our too-far-out-on-a-limb or let-me-get-back-to-safety (contact) hypothesis.

If I accept that she is reassured by having reestablished peer-female contact, then what do I make of what she experiences Jean as doing, "looking at empty shelves in a linen closet?" The only other "looking" figures were the dangerous male servants. If this permits me to link Jean to men, then I might entertain the possibility that Jean is her roommate who is getting married. Or if not, then a peer-female who is not just for her but is somehow linked to men. Jean is apparently engaged in playing Mother Hubbard, she's got a bare cupboard (closet).

The closet is one in which linens are kept, but there are none. I will not explore the specification of shelves in order to move along. I will comment that linen closet and linen shelves and marriage did occur to me. Why is the cupboard bare? Housekeeping is not an issue. Marriage is empty, a kind of, "Jean you are a fool, there is nothing in marriage but emptiness."

However, what does the potentially heterosexually linked Jean find and take out? She takes out a yellow night gown. Yellow–blonde–middle-aged German lady–mother–traditional values–marriage. Perhaps it is only an idle sequence, but it could be linked to a marriage night and that Jean, and Jean-like figures, are potentially lost to her. If this is the case, despite her warnings to Jean of the potential emptiness of marriage, Jean chooses marriage for sexual reasons. Where does our struggling dreamer turn? The last paragraph of the dream provides us with an answer.

The patient meets two asexual Munchkins. She doesn't have Jean but she has met some new people. What characterizes them? First off, they are asexual. This is an interesting and certainly acceptable turn of events, at least in terms of my thesis. I have been forced in our translation again and again to suggest that sexuality presents a problem for our patient and disrupts her relationship to people. She has solved the problem. She has found some asexual people. Now perhaps she can avoid the disruption that sexuality causes.

What else about these new found friends? They are Munchkins—funny, little, old, make-believe midgets. They are child-adult fusions out of *The Wizard of Oz*. Does this choice of Munchkins serve to resolve the patient's parental tension by making the parental figures more acceptable, more tolerable? After all, it is the child, Dorothy, who saves the Munchkins from the Wicked Witch (Mother). The patient might feel that, "If my parents were more like children, then wouldn't they be more lovable and less fearful?"

It is no small matter that there are two Munchkins who, despite their stated asexuality, have names: Electricia and Electrician, which permit a sexual differentiation. Is this a reference to the Electra complex? Is her father or boyfriend, past or present, an electrician? Is she looking for a charge?

Her asexual solution is paper-thin. Our patient is not at peace with her asexual solution. She has to have her asexuality labeled, but sexually named, friends engage in jumping up and down and hugging each other. Granted, it simply could be childish joy or exuberance. I remain suspicious that, as she wanted back in at the wedding for human contact, she wants to find a safe way, albeit childish at this moment, to enter into heterosexual relationships.

I can now, briefly, give my translation of the dream and psycho-dynamic formulation of the patient's problem. Without repeating the translation and formulation of the first paragraph of the dream, the last two paragraphs point out her concern that in her rejection of maternal values she runs the risk of excluding herself from peer women whom she wants and / or needs. She is troubled that they seek peer men which, despite her warnings, they continue to do. She attempts to find a solution by trying to deny her parental and heterosexual fears by relating to allegedly asexual others. These asexual people, and by implication herself, would want a heterosexual relationship if it were free of adult and sexual fears. She is tempted to seek a childish, regressed intimacy as the current resolution of her difficulties.

I will not attempt a clinical diagnosis or genetic reconstruction, nor will I comment on transference, countertransference, or treatment possibilities. I think that these were indirectly expressed in my translation of the dream.

Therapist's History, Formulation and Comment. The patient is a 27-year-old white single woman. She works as a librarian. She applied for psychiatric treatment complaining of frequent, severe headaches with no organic cause. The headaches had begun in high school but became much worse after her boss became sick. She was first seen in a brief psychiatric treatment service and then she was referred for long-term work. She has been in treatment for twenty months.

The patient is the older of two children born in Cincinnati. She has a brother eighteen months younger than herself. Her father is a retired, blue-collar worker who emigrated from Germany. Her mother was a beautician before her marriage.

An early memory is of being ridiculed by her mother for washing lettuce with soap when she was asked to prepare a salad for the first time. Another significant memory was that she was told not to look at a home movie in which her parents were kissing.

The patient traces the onset of her problems, at the age of thirteen, to her mother's sudden death from lung cancer, with metastases to the brain. She feels that she was catapulted into adulthood then, and adulthood has meant to her a cheerless, perfectionistic world where she could make no mistakes.

The patient is quite an intelligent young woman. She excelled in school and is the first person in her family to get a bachelor's and then a master's degree. This has made her feel different, something she has felt about herself from early childhood. She feels her relatives are "gray," conventional and boring. She feels uncomfortable for earning more money than they do, especially since she is not married. She feels she is rebelling against family values by being intellectual.

She began dating at age sixteen. She felt the need to be chaperoned and was disappointed when her father set no limits on her activities. She has tended to date and have sex with older men from foreign countries. She was briefly engaged once in college. She drank excessively during her college years but does not touch alcohol now.

After college, she was hired as a librarian by a motherly Jewish woman whom she idealizes. While out of Cincinnati, working on her master's, she learned this woman had developed leukemia. It has been very hard for her to work with this woman ever since.

On her return to Cincinnati, after getting her master's, she moved into a house with three other women, two of whom were lesbians. She had an affair for three months with one of them, which ended when her lover's previous partner violently objected. During the affair, she would not eat except when she was with her lover. The leukemic boss was aware of the affair and expressed her disapproval. The patient also felt very angry when the boss made remarks about how barbaric German people are, but the patient did not express these feelings for fear they might cause the boss to die.

In therapy, the central issue has been whether she will get enough and learn enough about herself from the therapist to enable her to deal with the boss's anticipated death better than she dealt with her mother's death. She has been able to express her wish to have the exclusive attention of the therapist. She feels that only when she can deal with losing her mother, the boss, and the therapist at the end of the therapist's residency can she then become an adult.

To go through the translation and formulation of the dream step by step, the therapist felt, would be excessive. She then went on to review some of the major issues. The wedding could refer to the loss of her homosexual lover to the other woman. It could also refer to the fact her actual roommate at the time was heterosexual and would not replace the lover. To complicate things further, the wedding could refer to her going into therapy. Marriage is viewed by her as empty.

The ideas expressed in the constellation of music hall, servants, and cadillacs are reflective of her rebellion against family values. The concern she has about her rebellion is that she ends up feeling alone and ill at ease.

The patient does have a history of turning to men, finding them inadequate for her primitive needs, and then turning to women, whom she views as helpful. Father and brother are viewed, by her, as servants.

A number of other speculations in the translation are also partly or completely correct. The hideous food is denial of her dependency. The middle-aged German lady is probably a composite figure referring to both her mother and the Jewish boss. The young woman who takes out the nightgown is her roommate Jean. The asexual Munchkins refer to her two lesbian friends.

There is no evidence that she has a need for a lot of men as servants. And, no man in her life is an electrician.

Concluding Remarks

The therapist has pointed out areas of agreement and disagreement with the dream translation. Again, it is best, I believe, to let the reader draw his or her own inferences and not attempt a speculative integration of the dream translation and formulation with the formulation from the therapist.

The two examples are neither exhaustive nor ideal. Nevertheless, I believe they provide sufficient illustrative material for the reader to begin to evaluate the method of dream translation which I have attempted to describe.

The systematic, controlled and detailed examination of a dream report does contribute to understanding the inner world of the dreamer. Utilization of the dream translation approach would obviously be useful to therapists in the diagnostic process or early in psychotherapy, as it would suggest immediate leads to the current conflicts or concerns of the patient. This technique would also be useful to psychotherapists at times of impasse in the therapeutic process as it would provide hypotheses to possible sources of the impasse. Lastly, in the work of psychotherapy supervision, the application of dream translation methodology is of great help because it focuses on clues about the patient of which the supervisee may not be aware and offers a systemic method of approach to fantasy material for the supervisee. Therapist's who pay more careful attention to their patient's dreams will be rewarded by having their knowledge of their patient's subjective life enhanced, which should permit them to be more effective in their central task of assisting their patient's in achieving greater self-knowledge.

The methodology is available to the dreamer in examining his or her own dreams. It provides an organized method for approaching the dream. It encourages a speculative but systematic approach which can be quite rewarding. Ullman and Zimmerman (1979) in their dream appreciation seminars point out the value of a speculative and systematic approach to the images and affects in the dream and evoked by the dream in others in helping the dreamer understand his or her dreams. The use of dream translation by the dreamer suggests he or she approach the dream report in an analogous manner—what does it stimulate in him or her? The result will be a revealing increase in the dreamer's worldview.

References

Adler, A. (1959). *The Practice and Theory of Individual Psychology.* Paterson, N.J.: Littlefield.

Bonime, W. (1962). *The Clinical Use of Dreams.* New York: Basic Books.

Boss, M. (1958). *The Analysis of Dreams.* New York: Philosophical Library.

Breger, L., Hunter, I., and Lane, R. (1971). *The Effect of Stress on Dreams.* New York: International Universities Press.

Cartwright, R. (1969). Dreams as Compared to Other Forms of Fantasy. In *Dream Psychology and the New Biology of Dreaming,* ed. Kramer, M. Springfield, Ill.: Charles C Thomas, p.361.

Chomsky, N. (1968). *Language and Mind.* New York: Harcourt, Brace and World.

Dement, W. (1965). An Essay on Dreams. In *New Directions in Psychology,* vol. 2, ed. Carron, F., Dement, W., Edwards, W., Lindman, H., Phillips, L., Olds, J., and Olds. M. New York: Holt, Rinehart and Winston, p.135.

Erikson, E. (1954). The Dream Specimen of Psychoanalysis. In *Psychoanalytic Psychiatry and Psychology,* ed. Knight, R. and Friedman, C. New York: International Universities Press, p.131.

Fliess, R. (1953). *The Revival of Interest in the Dream.* New York: International Universities Press.

Foulkes, D. (1966). *The Psychology of Sleep.* New York: Charles Scribner's Sons.

———. (1978). *A Grammar of Dreams.* New York: Basic Books.

French, T. (1952-1958). *The Integration of Behavior,* 3 vols. Chicago: University of Chicago Press.

French T., and Fromm, E. (1964). *Dream Interpretation: A New Approach.* New York: Basic Books.

Freud, S. (1900). The Interpretation of Dreams. In *Standard Edition,* vols. 4 and 5. London: Hogarth.

———. (1901). On Dreams. In *Standard Edition,* vol. 5. London: Hogarth.

———. (1913a). An Evidential Dream. In *Standard Edition,* vol. 12. London: Hogarth.

———. (1913b). Totem and Taboo. In *Standard Edition,* vol. 13. London: Hogarth.

———. (1916–1917). Introductory Lectures on Psycho-Analysis. In *Standard Edition,* vol. 15. London: Hogarth.

Fromm, E. (1951). *The Forgotten Language.* New York: Grove Press.

Garma, A. (1966). *The Psychoanalysis of Dreams.* Chicago: Quadrangle Books.

Hall, C. (1953). A Cognitive Theory of Dreams. *Journal of General Psychology* 49:273–82.

Hall, C., and Lindzey, G. (1957). *Theories of Personality.* New York: John Wiley and Sons.

Hartmann, E. (1973). *The Functions of Sleep.* New Haven, Conn.: Yale University Press.

Hiller, G.H. (1931). *10,000 Dreams Interpreted.* Northbrook, Ill.: Hubbard Press.

Horney, K. (1945). *Our Inner Conflicts.* New York: Norton.

Jones, R. (1970). *The New Psychology of Dreaming.* New York: Grune and Stratton.

Jung, C. (1956). *Two Essays on Analytical Psychology.* New York.

————. (1964). *Man and His Symbols.* New York: Doubleday.

Kramer, M. (1970). "The Caretaker" by Harold Pinter: An Exploration of an Apparent Paradox in the Theater of the Absurd. *World Journal of Psychosynthesis* 2:31–36.

————. (1981). The Function of Psychological Dreaming: A Preliminary Analysis. In *Sleep 1980: The 5th European Congress on Sleep Research, Amsterdam, 1980,* ed. Koella, W. Basel: Karger, p. 182–85.

Kramer, M., Baldridge, B., Whitman, R., Ornstein, P., and Smith, P. (1969). An Exploration of the Manifest Dream in Schizophrenic and Depressed Patients. *Disorders of the Nervous System.* 30:126–30.

Kramer, M., Hlasny, R., Jacobs G., and Roth, T. (1976). Do Dreams Have Meaning? An Empirical Inquiry. *American Journal of Psychiatry* 133:778–81.

Kramer, M., Kinney, L., and Scharf, M. (1983a). Dream Incorporation and Dream Function. In *Sleep 1982: The 6th European Congress on Sleep Research, Zurich, 1982,* ed. Koella, W. Basel: Karger p.369–71.

Kramer, M., Kinney, L., and Scharf, M. (1983b). Sex Differences in Dreams. *Psychiatric Journal of the University of Ottawa* 8:1–4.

Kramer, M., McQuarrie, E., Bonnet, M. (1981) Problem Solving in Dreaming: An Empirical Test. In *Sleep 1980: The 5th European Congress on Sleep Research, Amsterdam 1980,* ed. Koella, W. Basel: Karger, p.174–78.

Kramer, M., Moshiri, a., and Scharf, M. (1982). The Organization of Mental Content In and Between the Waking and Dream State. *Sleep Research* 11:106.

Kramer, M., Ornstein, P., Whitman, R., and Baldridge, B. (1967). The Contribution of Early Memories and Dreams to the Diagnostic Process. *Comprehensive Psychiatry* 8:344–74.

Kramer, M., and Roth, T. (1973). A Comparison of Dream Content in Laboratory Dream Reports of Schizophrenic and Depressive Patient Groups. *Comprehensive Psychiatry* 14:325–29.

Kramer, M., and Roth, T. (1979). The Stability and Variability of Dreaming. *Sleep* 1:319–25.

Kramer, M. and Roth, T. (1980). The Relationship of Dream Content to Night-Morning Mood Change. In *Sleep 1978: The 4th European Con-*

gress on Sleep Research, Tirgu-Mures 1978, ed. Popoviciu, L., Asgian, B., and Badiu, G. Basel: Karger, p.621–24.

Kramer, M., Roth, T., Arand, D., and Bonnet, M. (1981). Waking and Dreaming Mentation: A Test of Their Interrelationship. *Neuroscience Letters* 22:83–86.

Kramer, M., Roth, T., and Cisco, J. (1977). The Meaningfulness of Dreams. In *Sleep 1976: The 3rd European Congress on Sleep Research, Montpellier 1976* ed. Koella, W., and Levin, P. Basel: Karger, p.314–16.

Kramer, M. Roth, T., and Czaya, J. (1975). Dream Development Within a REM Period. In *Sleep 1974: The 2nd European Congress on Sleep Research, Rome 1974*, ed. Levin, P., and Koella, W. Basel: Karger, p.406–08.

Kramer, M., Roth, T., and Palmer T. (1976). The Psychological Nature of the REM Dream Report and T.A.T. Stories. *Psychiatric Journal of the University of Ottawa* 1:128–35.

Kramer, M., Whitman, R., Baldridge B., and Lansky L. (1964). Patterns of Dreaming: The Interrelationship of the Dreams of a Night. *Journal of Nervous and Mental Disorders* 139:426–39.

Kramer, M., Whitman, R., Baldridge, B., and Ornstein, P. (1968). Drugs and Dreams III: The Effects of Imipramine on the Dreams of the Depressed. *American Journal of Psychiatry* 124:1385–92.

Piaget, J. (1962). *Play, Dreams and Imitation in Childhood*. New York: Norton.

Piccione, P., Jacobs, G., Kramer, M., and Roth, T. (1977). The Relationship Between Daily Activities, Emotions and Dream Content. *Sleep Research* 6:133.

Piccione, P., Thomas, S., Roth, T., and Kramer, M. (1976). Incorporation of the Laboratory Situation in Dreams. *Sleep Research* 5:120.

Roffwarg, H., Dement, W., Muzio, J., and Fisher, C. (1962). Dream Imagery: Relationship to Rapid Eye Movements of Sleep. *Archives of General Psychiatry* 7:235–58.

Saul, L., Snyder, T., and Sheppard, E. (1956). On Reading Manifest Dreams and Other Unconscious Material. *Journal of the American Psychoanalytic Association* 4:122–37.

Sharpe, E. (1951). *Dream Analysis*. London: Hogarth.

Shulman, B. (1969). An Adlerian View. In *Dream Psychology and the New Biology of Dreaming,* ed. Kramer, M. Springfield, Ill.: Charles C Thomas, p.117.

Stekel, W., (1967). *The Interpretation of Dreams.* New York: Washington Square Press.

Taub, J., Kramer, M., Arand, D., and Jacobs, G. (1978). Nightmare Dreams and Nightmare Confabulations. *Comprehensive Psychiatry* 19:285–91.

Ullman, M., and Zimmerman, N. (1979). *Working with Dreams.* New York: Delacorte Press.

Webster's New World Dictionary. (1957). New York: New World Publishing Company, pp.765 and 1547.

6

Gayle Delaney ━━━━━━━━━━━━━━━

The Dream Interview

In the fourth century B.C., Aristotle wrote that "the most skillful interpreter of dreams is he who has the faculty of observing resemblances." When all is said and done, most methods of interpretation aim at discovering how a given dream relates to the life of the dreamer through the medium of symbol and metaphor. I would modify Aristotle's description in one important way by suggesting that the most skillful interpreter of dreams is the one who has the faculty of facilitating the *dreamer's* ability to observe resemblances.

Since 1974, Montague Ullman (1981) and I have been independently devoting our careers to training professionals as well as nonprofessionals in the understanding of dreams. Ullman and Zimmerman (1979) have created an approach to working with dreams in the context of small groups, as described in Chapter 1 of this volume. I have developed the dream interview method of interpretation for work in dyads, in groups, and individual study. (Delaney, 1979, 1988, and 1991). While our methods differ, our years of intensive concentration on teaching dream skills have led us to several common conclusions.

Both Ullman and I believe (and we are by no means alone in this) that a greater general access to the problem-solving, insight-promoting, and creative functions of dreaming would greatly benefit individuals and society. We, along with many of our colleagues, have found that the skill of understanding dreams can indeed be taught to and effectively practiced by nonprofessionals. I concur with Ullman (1981), Boss (1977), and Stern (1972) that an authoritative, indelicate treatment of dreams can hurt a dreamer, but that an approach tempered with humility and the clear recognition that the dreamer is the ultimate expert on his or her own dream minimizes any risk. Describing the dream as an extraordinarily valuable communication intended for the waking dreamer, Ullman (1981) writes that "the rewards of centering serious dream work in the hands of dreamers are generally far greater than the risk" (p. 6).

Perhaps the dreamer is nowhere more vulnerable than in a therapeutic relationship. What can compare to the painful impact of a dream ineptly treated by an authoritative, overconfident, or insecure and dogmatic therapist? At their worst, individual nonprofessional dream partners simply lack the influence necessary to inflict long-term wounds.

Dreams are a part of everyone's birthright. If our society would educate children not only in their native language but in their internal dream language, that of metaphor and of seeing resemblances, we (as impatient adults) would not be faced with the formidable remedial task of learning this exotic language with little or no social support. Had we been taught as children how to sleep on problems by targeting dreams requesting good ideas for, say, a story in English class, we might have a more creative population less inhibited by unreasoning prejudices against dreams.

Prejudice against serious regard for dreams has many roots. On the most superficial level, many people are afraid of looking silly to their peers by being interested in such unreal, unquantifiable, subjective experiences as dreams. Our culture has a long tradition of denigrating dreams. Saint Jerome's sometimes creative translation (circa 386) of the Latin Vulgate, in which he took it upon himself to rank dreams with witchcraft and magic, heralded the end of a rich tradition of respect for dreaming in Western culture. The charlatans who have always flourished outside of the Church and secular intellectual circles have offended the sensibilities of many of those who might have otherwise been more openly curious. For example, during the Enlightenment, the few voices that expressed an interest in dreaming, such as Voltaire, were drowned out by the louder, superstitious voices who believed in dreams as omens or condemned them as the handiwork of the devil. Our present-day physicalism, which would "biologize" dreams into meaningless artifacts produced by random firing of neurons in the brain (Fiss, 1984; Crick, 1983), intimidates some while it reassures others that the puzzle of dreaming is nothing to be concerned about. According to Freud (1900) as long ago as 1886, W. Robert described dreams as "a somatic process of excretion" necessary to unburden the brain of incompleted, unworked-out thoughts and superficial impressions that would otherwise accumulate in the brain causing one to become "mentally deranged."

At a more basic level, I think social resistance to working with dreams is rooted in individual uneasiness in the face of the bizarre, confusing, and seemingly unintelligable quality of dreaming, as well as in the often painful, shocking nature of some dreams. Add to this our human resistance to insight and change reinforced by a culture that provides little support for the journey of self-discovery, and what have we? We have a long way to go toward educating professionals and nonprofessionals alike in the relevance and importance of dreams.

While mental health professionals will usually pay lip service to the idea that dreams are meaningfully related to the dreamer's life, many, many of them have little or no training in dreams and avoid dealing with them in therapy. Both professionals and nonprofessionals have expressed the need for training not in the theory of dreaming but in a specific and practical method of dream interpretation.

The Dream Interview Method of Interpretation: Theory

As Richard Jones (1970) has pointed out, it is important to distinguish between one's beliefs about the psychology of the dreaming process and one's methods of interpretation. The way one practices dream interpretation will be determined by one's beliefs about what the psyche is, how the psyche works, and how dreams function in that psyche.

Regarding the psychology of dreaming, I am a minimalist. Too often, careful observations of dream phenomena are distorted or aborted by the interpreter's adherence to a theoretical superstructure into which, come what may, the dream *will* be placed. This is not always an easy task, and the intellectual contortions required of the interpreter are sometimes mistaken for erudition. The process of using the dream to validate an a priori theory of the psyche steals the dream from the dreamer and steals from the dream its potential for expressing its uniquely constructed meaning.

While Freud (1900) has been criticized for having discarded the dream in favor of its hypothesized latent or hidden meaning, many of his followers (French and Fromm, 1964; Bonime, 1982 and 1971; Natterson, 1980) have emphasized the importance of attending closely to the specifics of the actual manifest dream as the dreamer reports it. In fact, Freud himself wrote, "The technique which I describe . . . imposes the task of interpretation upon the dreamer himself. It is not concerned with what occurs to the interpreter in connection with a particular element of the dream, but with what occurs to the dreamer" (Freud, 1900, p. 130). Jung, (1984), Perls (1969), and Boss (1977) all exhort the interpreter (with varying degrees of insistence) to let the dream speak for itself. Each has pointed out how, in the rush to make the dream fit the theory (to find the repressed wish, the archetypal image, the dreamer in every dream image, and the existential truth), the interpreter may take off on a wild goose chase through the dreamer's psyche while running right past the dream itself. It is, of course, easier to recognize this process in the work of those from schools of thought other than one's own. The degree to which an interpreter is able to follow the advice to let the dream speak for itself depends upon his or her theoretical predisposition, method of interpretation, personal discipline, and style.

My theoretical stance is eclectic and has been shaped by two decades of working not with patients in therapy who sometimes report dreams, but with well-functioning professional and nonprofessional clients who come to my office expressly to explore dreaming. The following assumptions regarding the psychology of dreams have shaped the dream interview method of interpretation.

Basic Assumptions

Dreams are expressions of feelings, thoughts and ideas which are usually out of the dreamer's waking awareness and which, when brought into that awareness, can enhance the dreamer's life. Freud, Jung, Perls, Boss, and many clinicians would agree with this.

The effect of almost all recalled dreams is greatly enhanced by waking efforts to understand the dream in the context of the dreamer's life. With the notable exception of James Hillman (1979), there is general agreement among clinicians on this point. Louis Breger, Ian Hunter, and Ron Lane, after researching dreamers under stressful conditions, go so far as to state that "without work directed at integrating the dreams—at breaking down the dissociations that are present both in the dreaming and the reporting—the subjects do not learn anything about themselves. Just as one must work hard in the real world to transform a creative inspiration into a poem, a painting, or a piece of music or literature, so one must work hard at making individual sense of one's dreams if they are to be more than fleeting, uninformative glimpses of what is within" (Breger et al., 1971, p. 191).

Dreams have a point, a message intended to be grasped by the waking mind and used for the benefit of the dreamer. I concur with Jung (1933 and 1984) and with Jungian analyst John Beebe (chapter 3) that any interpretation is incomplete if one does not get the message, the purpose of the dream, and the purpose to which it can be put. Lowy (1942), Jones (1984), and others would argue that one must not read into the experience of dreams any intent. Jones (1984) summarizes his point in saying that "dreams are of—not for the dreamer." This may be true, although I am inclined to disagree. There is, however, little argument that dreams lend themselves to interpretations that can be very useful to the dreamer. One need not impute purpose to the process of dreaming in order to benefit from interpretation.

The dreamer, upon awakening, has all the information necessary to understand the dream. Because the dreamer may not have the ability to tap that information, an interpreter, whom I prefer to call an interviewer, is usually required to assist the dreamer in unlocking its meaning. Freud (1900), Jung (1984), Mattoon (1978), and many contemporary spiritually oriented dreamworkers not only make interpretations based on systems of thought external to the dream, but they feel justified in explaining the whole or parts of the dream to the dreamer. For example, Freud wrote that "the failure of the dreamer's associations gave us a right to attempt an interpretation by symbolic substitution" (Freud, 1900, p. 407). In this case, he interpreted twelve pears to represent the breasts of the dreamer's mother. Freud went further to say that it is "impossible to arrive at the interpretation of a dream if one excludes dream symbolism" (Freud, 1900, p. 395). He insisted that symbolic substitution was a necessary, if auxiliary, method used to complement his method of association.

Jung and his followers claim that the interpreter must be well-versed in mythology, the history of religion, and alchemy, among other things, in order to properly amplify certain dream images and help the dreamer see their meaning. This can easily lead to the analyst's usurping the private experience of the dream in the name of broadening its scope to the archetypal level. All too often, such calls to mythological, religious, or psychological systems of belief render impossible a recognition of the dream itself and of its highly personal, highly relevant, connection to the individual dreamer. Mini-lectures to the dreamer about how the world (or the male/female psyche, or the spirit) works distract the dreamer from an immediate experience of his or her unique dream.

More importantly, a dependence on external explanations often seduces the dreamer to "take refuge from the personal and the concrete, in something distant and alien which does not oblige the patient in any way to become more responsible for the concrete ways of living his day-to-day life" (Boss 1977). The interpreter, feeling pressure to solve the dream puzzle, is often seduced to take refuge from his or her own anxiety in a prefabricated formulation of the dreamer's experience. I do not believe that adding to the dreamer's associations the "truths" of external explanatory systems adds anything to the immediacy or depth of the dreamer's appreciation of the dream. Quite the contrary. Erik Erikson, in warning his fellow psychoanalysts against too hurriedly dismissing the manifest dream in favor of attending to what they thought might be hidden behind it, said, "So many in . . . [this] field mistake attention to surface for superficiality, a concern with form for lack of depth" (Jones, 1970, p. 102).

If one learns to ask effective questions rather than give interpretations, "both the nature of the dream and its therapeutic message will emerge, contrary to the Jungian viewpoint, without any support from mythology or folklore, without any knowledge of primitive psychology or comparative religion, without any aid at all from psychology. In fact, no doctrine of the psyche is required" (Boss, 1977, p. 168).

The cause and source of dreams is still unknown. I do not think we are in a good position to say where dreams come from; only that once they come into our awareness we may notice how they appear and how they function. The reification of the source of dreams leads inevitably to speculations about its structure, which then return to limit and distort one's powers of observation (Boss, 1977).

Dreams serve many functions. Dreams help us to process new information, correlate it with past experience, make sense of it, and learn from it (Greenberg and Pearlman, 1974 and 1980; Fishbein, 1981; Scrima, 1984). Dreams express instinctual impulses, wishes, and the defenses against them (Freud, 1900). They enable a dreamer to assess conflicts and resources in the context of life-long patterns and past experiences (Delaney, 1979, 1991, 1993; Ullman and Zimmerman, 1979; Greenberg and Perlman in Natterson, 1980; Jung, 1984). They reveal the dreamer's constructive and destructive solutions to problems (Gershman, 1983), and they constitute some of the dreamer's most sophisticated (less defensive, more integrated and synthetic) efforts at problem solving. Dreams can help to crystalize and focus goals, bringing fresh motivation and clearer direction to the dreamer's efforts to change (Bonime, 1958).

Dreams portray the interactions of psychological complexes (Jung, 1984; also see Chapter 3) and lay out in CAT scan fashion the dynamics, origin, function, and results of the dreamer's attitudes and feelings. The honesty with which we look at ourselves while dreaming is of the utmost importance. While sleeping, we seem able to lay down many of our defenses and open ourselves to the quality and depth of our feelings and to new perspectives flowing from them.

Dreams can also introduce the dreamer to undeveloped and previously unrecognized capacities for unfamiliar emotional experiences such as compassion, forgiveness, and tolerance. Some dreams serve as potentially powerful modes of communication to the people to whom we are likely to tell them.

I have worked with many couples whose dreams regularly assist them in communicating difficult and important feelings. Children often seem to produce dreams that communicate vital messages to their parents. For example, a five-year-old girl dreamed that she was watching her two-year-old brother in a small plastic pool while her mother went into the house to get the laundry (as often occurred in waking life). Suddenly the brother began to drown in the water. As the tiny girl struggled to hold her brother's head above water, she cried out, "Mom, he's too heavy. I can't hold him up any more! Mom!" Instead of interpreting the dream as the girl's disguised wish to kill her brother, the mother suddenly realized that she had, indeed, been asking her daughter to take too much responsibility in the care of her son, who was ill.

To close this by no means exhaustive discussion of the functions of dreaming without mention of the important contribution dreams have made to the solution of problems in the creative, scientific, and artistic life of our culture would be to let the extraordinary psychological usefulness of dreams eclipse their concretely innovative, culture-advancing importance. It appears that the famous examples of dream-triggered creativity (Descartes, Kekule, Cannon, Howe, Brahms, Wagner, Stravinsky, Voltaire, Robert Louis Stevenson, Steve Allen, and Richard Bach) are only the tip of the iceberg.

The Goals of the Dream Interview

The goal of this method of interpretation is to assist the dreamer in getting the point, the punch line of the dream, with as few interpretations or explanations from the interviewer as possible. Ideally, the dreamer should be able to arrive at a rich appreciation of the dream without hearing any interpretive statements whatsoever. The interviewer is to let the dreamer be the first to express an understanding of the dream or of any part of it. This requires that the interviewer restrain any impulses to appear wise or insightful by showing that he or she has grasped a connection or meaning in the dream in advance of the dreamer (what Bonime calls therapeutic exhibitionism). This discipline is especially difficult but is of the utmost importance in not distracting the dreamer from his or her thoughts to wondering what might be in the interviewer's mind. This distraction can lead the dreamer to feel insecure, and often aborts useful associative progressions of thought. Hence, interviewers are most effective when they wear curious facial expressions and bend their efforts to devising questions that draw out the dreamer's thoughts.

By resisting the temptation to explain the dream to the dreamer, we avoid making inaccurate interpretations that can harm the integrity and the flow of the dreamwork. By "letting the dreamers get there first," the interviewer is less likely to intrude, and the dreamers are free to express their understanding in their own words. Dreamers who have experienced the exquisite pleasure of figuring out their own dreams are more likely to take responsibility for the resulting insights than are those who receive explanations, no matter how elegant.

Structure of the Interview

To work with a dream, an interview situation is created in which the dreamer is interviewed by a therapist, colleague, friend, or several members of a dream study group. While the dreamer can play the role of his or her own interviewer, this is much more difficult, especially in the beginning. The interviewer asks the dreamer to pretend that the interviewer comes from another planet. In assuming the role of someone from another planet, the interviewer pretends to have little or no understanding or knowledge of objects, places, and people found on planet Earth. This is one of the most important devices of the interview. It allows the interviewer to get at the most pertinent information quickly with a minimum of defensiveness on the part of the dreamer and with minimal intrusion and distortion on the part of the interpreter. This device also helps the dreamer to clarify his or her perception and expression of dream and waking experiences, while it encourages the interviewer to recognize, appreciate, and honor the specific private experience of the dreamer.

Step One: Telling the Dream Story

The dreamer tells the dream in the first-person and present tense and with feeling (Perls, 1969). The interviewer's presence should convey a strong interest in the dream story itself in order to facilitate the dreamer's ability to reenter the dream and recapture as far as is possible the concrete and emotional vividness of the dream. The interviewer might ask brief questions to clarify what is happening in the dream action, but no questions regarding associations or interpretations should interrupt the flow of the dream-telling. Generally speaking, the dreamer should be discouraged from telling more than one dream at a time because this usually results in confusion all around and insufficient time to do justice to any of the dreams. Frequently, the pressured telling of several dreams serves the resistance better than the investigation.

Step Two: Overview of Feelings

The dreamer may be asked to describe briefly the major moods and feelings of the dream and whether these remind him or her of anything in waking life. This is a time of information gathering not of drawing conclusions; therefore, any correspondences are duly noted for fuller consideration later in the context of the dream action. Each feeling is later explored as it surfaces in the dream action or in the discussion of the dream. Feelings are then treated as yet another dream image to be described and bridged (discussed later).

Step Three: Eliciting Adequate Definitions and Descriptions

Settings. The interviewer asks the dreamer to define and/or describe each of the major images in the dream starting with the setting and continuing sequentially through the people, objects, feelings, and actions. With each definition and description, the dreamer assumes that the interviewer from another planet is curious to know first what the place, thing, etc., is like as well as what the dreamer's affective relation to the image is. An adequate (concrete as well as affective) description of the setting framing the dream experience usually helps to localize the dream metaphor in the dreamer's life. For example, a dreamer who dreams of being in Texas and describes the state as one that is run by real, strong, responsible men will be dealing with material different from that relevant to a dreamer who also dreams of being in Texas but who describes the place as one of economic devastation and near hopelessness. This very important aspect of the dream setting is commonly bypassed.

Feelings. The dreamer is asked to describe what he or she is feeling at various moments in the dream as well as what he or she is feeling in the moment of discussing a given part of the dream.

People. The dreamer is asked to describe each character in the dream as if the interviewer has come from another planet and has never heard of the person before. This question is asked even when the interviewer is familiar with the dream character either through general public knowledge or through a knowledge of the dreamer's history. The point is to elicit a fresh description that will be colored by the context of the current dream, the dreamer's current situation, and by the particular words the dreamer uses.

The interviewer then asks what the dream character is like in the context of the dream. It is vital in asking these questions to get the dreamer to include in the descriptions his or her feelings for and judgments of the dream figures. For example, if Nicole dreamed of Margaret Thatcher, her interviewer would say, "Pretend I come from another planet and have never heard of this person. Who is Margaret Thatcher? What is she like?" Nicole might respond saying, "She was England's prime minister. She turns a deaf ear to the plight of the poor; her heart is cold. Now that I think of it, she reminds me of my mother." On the other hand, she might say, "Margaret Thatcher is the most powerful woman in the world. She has succeeded with grace to manage a male-dominated country, to be successful, and maintain her position. She personifies a new and exciting model of womanhood." The interviewer follows the dreamer's direction.

Objects. Approximately the same thing is done with the objects in the dream. The dreamer is asked to define and describe the object generically, e.g., "What is a motorcycle? What are they used for, and what kinds of people ride them?" Then, "What are Harley Davidson cycles like?" Then to the specificity of the dream, "What is the Harley Davidson in your dream like?" Questions like these are very effective in eliciting descriptions and *focused* associations which, when reflected back to the dreamer, rather quickly bring him or her to the point of being able to answer the next question: "Does this cycle remind you of anything in yourself or in your life? These questions are not intended to eliminate free associations but to focus them in the feeling context of the dream. As you might guess, the definitions and descriptions begin by anchoring the dreamers in the concrete reality of the dream experience and carry them soon enough into highly relevant associative material.

Action/Plot. "What is needed more than anything else to understand the gesturing of the dream is an almost childlike, incorruptible simplicity which is not taken in by contrived complexities and is able to see, in the midst of them, the obvious. Such simplemindedness is, among clinicians, a very rare commodity" (Stern, 1972, p. 43).

Remembering this, the interviewer proceeds to ask about the major action in the dream, inquiring as to whether such and such behavior is normal among human beings, and why they engage in such actions. A question like, "Is there any way this is going on in your life?" may or may not be necessary. To many dreamers' surprise, the words they use to answer these questions often trigger a realization of the meaning of the dream. Sometimes it is helpful if the interviewer repeats again the key words used by the dreamer so they can be heard a second and third time, being careful not to be too leading in his or her emphases.

Step Four: Condense and Recapitulate Descriptions

After eliciting an adequate description of one or several images, the interviewer repeats verbatim or in a condensed, distilled form the description the dreamer has just provided. By mirroring the dreamer's response using only the dreamer's words, the dreamer's connection to the image is greatly enhanced, and the dreamer sometimes spontaneously sees the metaphoric resemblance to a life situation. Whether one decides to recapitulate the descriptions after each image or after a scene or the whole dream depends upon the openness of the dreamer, the richness of the descriptions, and the preferences of the interviewer.

Step Five: Bridging to Waking Life

The question that follows the recapitulation of the dreamer's description of the dream setting, feelings, persons, objects, or actions is "Does (this description) remind you of anything or anyone in your life?" In the case of bridging feelings, questions like, "Have you ever felt this way? When? Can you give an example?" are helpful. Bridging questions help the dreamer focus and feel around for the relevance of the dream metaphor to his life. Sometimes, the dreamer is unable to see any correspondences until he or she has explored quite a bit of the dream imagery and action. Patience is a virtue. Let the dreamer get there first.

Too many dreams are only half-appreciated because the interpreter is impatient or at a loss how else to proceed and so jumps to conclusions about the meaning of a dream character before ever exploring the specificity of the image. For example, say a client dreams of her Uncle Joe. Before deciding he represents a father image or an animus figure or old wiseman archetype, we need to know specifically what Joe is like and thereby why she did not dream of her Uncle Mike or Grandfather Patrick. It is hard to find examples of carefully explored dream characters other then family members, even in the literature of the existentialists Boss (1963 and 1977) and Stern (1972). Overlooking the specificity of dream characters has led to much confusion and not a few inaccurate interpretations that result more from the interpreter's bias than from the facts of the dream.

A few years ago, after having used this approach for eight years, I read *Modern Man in Search of a Soul*, a book Jung wrote for a popular audience, which I had ignored in favor of his more "sophisticated" writings. Right there in Jung's own words was the following suggestion:

If we associate freely to a dream our complexes will turn up right enough, but we shall hardly ever discover the meaning of the dream. To do this we must keep as close as possible to the dream images themselves. When a person has dreamed of a deal table, little is accomplished by his associating it with his writing desk which is not made of deal. The dream refers expressly to a deal table. If at this point nothing occurs to the dreamer his hesitation signifies that a particular darkness surrounds the dream-image, and this is suspicious. We would expect him to have dozens of associations to a deal table, and when he cannot find a single one, this must have a meaning. In such cases we should return again and again to the image. I say to my patients: "Suppose I had no idea what the words deal table mean. Describe this object and give me the history in such a way that I cannot fail to understand what sort of thing it is." We succeed in this way in establishing a good part of the context of that particular dream image. When we have done this for all the images in the dream, we are ready for the venture of interpretation. (1933, pp. 13–14)

There is a voice in Jung's writings that cries out for a careful exploration and appreciation for the specificity of dream images. Sadly, this voice is sometimes drowned out by premature and inappropriate explanations and amplifications, which Jung felt to be so important to a "deep" understanding of dreams (Jung, 1984; Mattoon, 1978). To my knowledge, neither Jung nor his followers have developed this line of questioning for dream objects, nor have I seen it applied to dream characters and actions. This is unfortunate because I think one can find out much more that is relevant by employing the dreamer's natural concreteness in the face of a dream to help him or her focus on the relevant associations than one can by moving away from the dreamer into more abstract psychological and mythological constructs. Unlike Freud, who took the lack of associations to a particular image as an invitation to practice his particular brand of symbol substitution, Jung, at least in some instances, used the occasion to better establish the context of the image as the dreamer knew it. However, Jung's venture of interpretation generally included a modified form of symbol substitution, involving his concepts of archetypes and the process of individuation.

Step Six: Summary

Now that all the major images of the dream have been explored (defined, described, recapitulated, and bridged), the interviewer asks the dreamer to retell the dream, describing how he or she understands it so far and to note the parts that remain unclear. This allows both parties to check the dreamer's interpretive hypotheses by seeing if they fit into the dramatic structure of the dream as a whole. If they don't, there is usually a misinterpretation and/or a resistance to be worked out. In this case, one can choose to return to the unclear images and define and describe them again in hope of uncovering or recognizing overlooked information. Alternatively, one might choose to let the dreamer live with the uncertainty until the next session, thereby letting the dreamer's curiosity and perhaps frustration motivate a breakthrough to new insights.

Step Seven: Reflection and Options for Action

Finally, the dreamer and interviewer discuss which images in the dream would lend themselves to fruitful reflection. For example, I often suggest that the dreamer focus during the week on an especially positive dream character by pretending (in private moments or in interactions with others) that he or she really *is* this character. The dreamer thus has the opportunity to get to know the character and to recognize the possibilities for developing these potentials. It is often helpful to encourage the dreamer to keep an eye out or an ear cocked for the appearance of thoughts or actions personified by a negative dream figure. Some dream insights are too new and/or too fragile to merit specific, concrete action on the part of the dreamer. Others, however, are strong and clear and often reinforced by material in therapy or in a series of different dreams. In these cases, the dreamer is asked if she or he would like to do something with the insight and if so, what and when. The collection and hoarding of insights for storage purposes only is to be discouraged. The dreamer's sense of personal power to change his or her own life is to be encouraged and practiced.

The dreamer is almost always asked to reread the dream and any interpretive notes two or three times during the week. It is important not to underestimate how easily a dreamer can forget the insights gained in a session of dream work. By *actively* reflecting on the dream and by taking action when appropriate, the impact of insights gained is enormously enhanced.

The dream interview process should bring the dream to life, not deaden it. The interviewer who can communicate curiosity and a desire to enter as far as possible into the dream and the dreamer's reality will, with practice, do well.

The Dream Interview: Practice

"The greatest wisdom . . . [a dream analyst] can have is to disappear and let the dreamer think he is doing nothing." (Jung, 1984, p. 458)

The following list of questions (a revised version of one published in Delaney, 1988) is designed to help the analyst (amateur or professional) approach that laudable if nearly unattainable goal.

Dream Interviewer's Cue Card

Initial Questions

1. *What are the feelings you are most aware of in the dream? Do they remind you of anything in your current life?* Sometimes, especially when interviewing mental health professionals about their own dreams, it is better to omit this question. Professionals are generally too quick to interpret their dreams before having carefully explored the images. All we are looking for here is a correlation of the feelings in the dream with similar feelings experienced in waking life. This is a warm-up exercise. Even if the dreamer is unable to recognize any parallel at this point, he or she will begin to consider the possibility that there may be a relationship between waking and dreaming feelings.

2. *Describe the opening setting of the dream: place, mood, feelings.* What sort of place is (a desert, a high school gym, a kitchen, your grandmother's house, etc.)? How does it feel to be in this setting? Or how do you feel as you (stand there, ride in the car, etc.)?

3. *Does this (recapitulate the description) remind you of anything?* Does the location or the mood or do these feelings remind you of a situation in your life? Remember to use only the dreamer's words in the recapitulation. Ask Question No. 2 (eliciting a description) and No. 3 (bridging question) about each setting in the dream as they present themselves.

4. *Who is X?* Ask the dreamer to tell you who each person in the dream is. Dreamers will respond best if you remind them that you come from another planet and do not know a thing about Earth life. If you avoid asking "What does X *mean* to you," you can bypass premature interpretive efforts and help the dreamer better explore and experience the image. Keep this response brief. Move quickly to the next question.

5. *What is X like in waking life (or in general)?* This will encourage the dreamer to tell you what she thinks of X. She will usually supply relevant associations automatically. Another way to phrase this question is to ask, "What kind of person is X?" or "What kind of personality does X have?" Encourage the dreamer to give you his or her impressions of the dream persons as they are in waking life and not to worry about being accurate or objective. Ask questions that inquire about the dreamer's feelings, opinions, and judgments about X, such as, "How

do you feel about X? Do you like him, dislike him? What are his most salient characteristics? How do you feel about these?" Some dreamers will describe X in terms of what he does, times they've had together, and "He's the sort of guy who . . . " Descriptions of X's behavior, history, and physical appearance can be very helpful in reconnecting the dreamer with his image of X; however, they can also quickly reach the point of diminishing returns and devour precious time. It is extremely important to help the dreamer distill these descriptions into descriptive *adjectives*, which are much easier to handle and often bring more clarity. Asking a dreamer to provide three adjectives that describe a person who does such things, has such a history, or looks that way can be very helpful getting to the point and in collecting a description that will be more likely to trigger a successful bridge later. If X is a person unknown to the dreamer, ask, "What kind of person would you imagine X might be like, given how X looks and acts in the dream?"

6. *What is X like in your dream? What is X doing in your dream?* By moving from the general to the particular, you can find out what specific aspects of X are emphasized in a particular dream, as well as how these qualities help or hinder the dreamer. In cases where the image is of a major figure in the dreamer's life, such as a mother or a father, the aspects displayed by the dream character can be used to narrow the focus of what could be an almost interminable description.

7. *Does X remind you of anything in your life?* By recapitulating the dreamer's descriptions (using the same adjectives and tone), she will often be able to bridge or to link the description to someone, to a force in her life or to an aspect of herself. By asking the question this way, you leave the dreamer free to relate the image to some part of himself or herself (the subjective level of interpretation) or to someone or something in his or her life (the objective level). Letting the dreamer choose the interpretive level diminishes the interpreter's possible distortion. If the dreamer seems to be avoiding a probable subjective interpretation by rushing to the objective level, you can always ask more pointed questions later. If X does not remind the dreamer of anything at this moment, you can move on to the next image for the time being, or ask other bridging questions such as:

8. *Does X, whom you describe as (recapitulate), remind you of anyone in your life, or is there some part of you which is like X?* You may meet strong resistance with this bridging question, especially if the dreamer has just described someone he or she strongly dislikes. While you may see some of X's characteristics in the dreamer or in someone close to the dreamer,

timing is all-important. An offended dreamer won't talk much. You can always return to this (or any other) question later when the time seems right.

9. *How so?* When a dreamer successfully bridges an image and says something like, "Now that I hear you feed back that description, it reminds me of my first husband!" it is important to ask the dreamer to test the strength of the bridge or to explain his or her connection for several reasons. Some dreamers need to take a moment to clarify and deepen the new perception, while others, upon closer inspection, find that the similarities don't really match. Perhaps they were trying too hard to be good patients or students. In many cases, as in the one just mentioned, unpacking leads to more questions like, "You say X reminds you of your first husband in that he, like X,...Does X remind you of anyone else who is (recapitulate the description once more)?" Not uncommonly, the dreamer for the first time sees similarities with old boyfriends or girlfriends, current spouse, and his or her father or older siblings. This question highlights important emotional and behavioral patterns.

10. *What is a Y?* Ask the dreamer to define each of the major objects in the dream and to tell you what it is used for and how it works. Remind him or her that you come from another planet and have never seen nor heard of a Y. Reassure the dreamer that you are interested not in scientific accuracy but in his or her ideas or understanding of what a Y is and how it works. Again, if you ask what does a Y *mean* to you, you usually get a premature interpretation—get a definition and a description first. Ask questions that elicit whatever value judgments the dreamer has about a Y. Do you like Y's? Do you own, eat, wear, or enjoy Y's? Why or why not? What kinds of people tend to drive, wear, eat, etc., a Y?

11. *What is the Y in your dream like?* This question moves from the general or generic to the specific. When the dreamer describes dream objects, he or she may also add some associations, which you may or may not want to explore further. With experience, you will get a feeling for which trains of association are likely to be productive and which are likely to distract from the dream action and devour time. If the dream Y is oddly different from the waking Y, ask questions which clarify the differences and ask questions like, "How would a Y like the one in your dream look or function differently from a normal Y?" Be sure to find out how the dreamer really feels about Y's in general and about the Y in the dream. If the dreamer is not forthcoming, coax him or her with questions like, "Do you like or dislike Y's?" "Do you think Y's are wonder-

ful, silly, necessary, or creepy?" As soon as possible, cease suggesting words and use those the dreamer supplies.

12. *Does the Y in your dream which you describe as (recapitulate description) remind you of anything in your life?* As when bridging from people in dreams to waking life, it may be necessary or desirable to follow this question with others like, "Does the Y (recapitulate again) remind you of anyone or of any part of yourself?"

13. *How so?* As with any image the dreamer has bridged, asking the dreamer to clarify and confirm by testing the strength of the bridge is vital.

14. *How do you feel at this moment in the dream?* This question can be asked at any point in the dream interview. With experience, the interviewer learns that many dreamers omit mention of important dream feelings and that it is good to ask this question any time there is reason to suspect unexpressed feelings in the dream.

15. *Tell me more about this feeling.*

16. *Tell me about a time (or the last time) you felt this way?*

17. *Does this feeling of (recapitulate the description) remind you of anything in your current life?* By now, the dreamer will be familiar with the feeling and may already have bridged it to a waking situation.

18. *Describe the major action or events in the dream.* This is where the parts come together into a dramatic whole. Here too, it is useful to remind the dreamer and yourself that you come from another planet. If the dreamer has just told you that he was having dinner at his parents' house wearing a coat of armor, you could ask, "Tell me, is that what people usually wear to dinner?" Such simple questions help the dreamer come to an understanding of the dream on his or her own.

19. *Recapitulate all the dreamer's descriptions.* String together the descriptions and bridges made so far in the sequential context of the dream action. You can do this at the end of the dream or as you go along scene-by-scene. Ask the dreamer to correct you if your recapitulation doesn't sound just right. This step is more difficult than the preceeding ones and requires practice.

20. *So in this part of the dream (this happened) which you described as . . . , which reminded you of . . . , then. . . . Does all this remind you of anything?* In practice, question No. 19 (recapitulation) and No. 20 (bridging) may well blend into one. Take your time with this step. Even when the metaphor is obvious to the interviewer, it is important to resist the temptation to provide the interpretation. While making an interpretation can relieve both parties' impatience and make the interviewer look insightful, it can vitiate the impact of the meaning of the dream as well

as reduce the dreamer's readiness to take credit and responsibility for the insight. Help the dreamer to see the metaphor by repeating the dream action while adding the definitions and descriptions (in the form of the dreamer's own adjectives) to the retelling of the dream. This bridging step can be used at the end or throughout the interview in a chronological order.

21. *Now, how do you understand your dream? Tell me the whole dream, adding the bridges and commenting on what you understand and what remains unclear.* Remember to leave interpretations to the dreamer. The interviewer's job is to clarify, to ask questions that will clarify, or to point out inconsistencies. In cases when the dreamer is unable to make important connections, suggesting to the dreamer possible hypotheses regarding possible bridges may be necessary. However, this is a step fraught with danger and should be used only as a last resort. Leaving the dreamer to puzzle out how it all comes together can yield better results, depending upon the dreamer and the situation.

Over the years of working with the dream interview method, my colleagues and I have found the above questions to be the most helpful ones in assisting the dreamer. To some extent the interviewer needs to try to:

1. Reenter the dream experience,
2. Explore and appreciate the vivid existential reality of the images, and
3. Bridge these experiences to ones in waking life in a useful, meaningful manner.

The questions are the reflections of the attitude the dream interviewer assumes and are by no means the only ones needed to conduct a full exploration. Nor need any one interview necessarily contain each suggested question. Because this approach to interpretation depends so little on external explanatory systems and so much on the actual dialogue between the dreamer and the interviewer, the best way to understand and learn it is to observe it in action and to practice it with another dreamer. The cue card of questions has been very helpful to our students.

The simplicity of this approach is misleading. It is more difficult than it looks to adopt the naïve but nonintrusive questioning attitude of the interviewer from another planet. The self-discipline and resourcefulness required of the interviewer who is asked to venture forth into a dream with a minimum of preconceived theoretical notions are considerable.

Things to Avoid in a Dream Interview

In order to present a clearer picture of what we do in an interview it will help to point out what we try *not* to do and why.

Putting Words in the Dreamer's Mouth

Definitions, descriptions, and associations are most pertinent and evocative when supplied by the dreamer. Both professional and nonprofessional beginners in the interview method struggle with strong impulses to help the dreamer or speed the interview by providing factual additions or corrections to dreamer's descriptions of publicly known people, objects, or actions.

For example, a Christian dreamer who describes Passover as the Jewish Day of Atonement might elicit from the interviewer a comment that "Actually, Yom Kippur is the Day of Atonement, Passover is . . . " Now, besides the interpersonal or transference problems involved in an interviewer's correction of a dreamer, such an intervention makes it harder to find out if the dreamer was simply confused or if he was dreaming of issues characterized both by his particular view of Passover and by his perception of Yom Kippur in an ideosyncratic blending of the two. If the interviewer were instead to ask for a description of Passover, the pertinent material would, in most cases, soon surface. If the confusion were the result of a blocking around issues related to Yom Kippur, this would emerge either on its own or with subtle questioning, such as, "You say Passover is the Jewish Day of Atonement. Is there any other name for that day?"

The interviewer tentatively offers a descriptive word only when the dreamer is struck and when the interviewer is unable to think of a better alternative. Actually, at such times several alternative strategies are usually worth trying before resorting to suggesting descriptive words. For example, if the interviewer "guesses" an extremely unlikely association (a strategy we call "guessing the absurd"), the dreamer is often motivated to correct the clearly inaccurate suggestion and is suddenly able to come up with his or her own words. Sheila had a dream in which she was offered the choice of one of three ships in which to take a voyage. One ship had several huge crosses rather than masts on it. After having heard what the crosses were like and how they looked, I asked, "What are crosses?" The dreamer waited a moment then said, "They are symbols." She could not think of another thing to say about them. I asked, as if trying to remember what I had heard about Earth's alien culture, "Gee, are they . . . symbols of . . . fertility?" Immediately, the dreamer fired back, "Of course not! They are symbols of martyrdom!" Thus the dreamer found her own feeling and words and seized the meaning of her dream.

When playing the role of interviewer, it helps to remind yourself that your words will never have the precise emotional fit of the dreamer's words, so it is better not to make a good guess since the dreamer may simply settle for your word and give up the search for *le mot juste*. If the interviewer does happen to guess the exact right word, instead of congratulating himself on his intuition and insight, he might do better to realize that he has just stolen from the dreamer the opportunity of searching a little further as well as the satisfaction of discovery.

Sometimes simply repeating once or twice the descriptions in the context of the dream action (a practice we call "schmoozing with the dreamer") will be sufficient to help the dreamer make a bridge to waking life. At other times, the best strategy with a blocked dreamer is to leave the image or part of the dream after one or two passes at description, recapitulation, and bridging, then move on to the next part. Then each time the interviewer summarizes the action up to the present working point, he or she can ask if any bridges come to mind as he goes along.

One can always return later to difficult images and ask, "Would you tell me one more time, what is a Y?" After a break of concentration on the image and after having explored other parts of the dream, the dreamer is often able to tell you just what he or she needs to know. This also gives the interviewer another chance to listen carefully and devise evocative follow-up questions.

Filling in the Blanks—Even at the Dreamer's Invitation

Even when the dreamer requests it, the interviewer resists supplying any factual information or even any recognition of unexplored images. For example, if Jan dreams about a scene that reminds her of "a scene in that movie about the South and the Civil War. What was it called?" the interviewer who pauses gives the dreamer time to stay with her feelings while hunting for the movie title. When the dreamer finds it and says something like, "*Gone With The Wind!* It was just like that. You know what I mean, you've seen it haven't you?" the interviewer reminds her that he or she comes from another planet and has no idea what it is about. If the dreamer is asked to describe the story, both the dreamer and the interviewer can better see what is in the dreamer's mind.

Falling into the trap of filling in the blanks is very easy. A psychiatrist who was learning this method was working with Michael who dreamed his pancreas was removed. Michael asked the doctor, "What does the pancreas do, anyway?" Just as she was about to give a brief description of the organ, the doctor remembered that she hailed from another planet and said, "On Jupiter we don't have such things. What is your impression of what they do?" When the dreamer said he had no idea, the doctor said, "Well, how is it different from the heart or lungs in fact or in legend?" Michael responded that he hardly knew he had a pancreas but that he thought it was a vital organ. He remembered having read that one study showed that as little as one or two cups of coffee a day were associated with a significant rise in pancreatic cancer rates, and that by the time the cancer is detected, it is too late. When the psychiatrist recapitulated the description and asked for a bridge saying, "Is there anything in your life that is vital to you, but you hardly know you have one, that can become cancerous with just a little coffee, and that by the time you discover the problem, it's too late?" Michael nodded yes. He said that his ability to know what he is feeling and to communicate it to his wife has been, unbeknownst to him, stunted, maybe even killed off by his daily habits of thinking, and that now it is probably too late to do anything about it. It is easy to see how inappropriate it would have been for the dreamer to receive a mini-lecture on the functions of the pancreas.

Telling the Dreamer How He or She Felt in the Dream

We avoid using words not supplied by the dreamer. Remembering this is helpful in recognizing gaps in needed information. For example, Joe dreamed of an uncle who was very nasty and insulting in the dream. The dream analyst made the reasonable statement, "You are angry at your uncle in the dream. Does this remind you of anything?" The dreamer responded with a blank look and then said, "No." If the analyst had first asked, "How do you feel toward your uncle in the dream?" without inserting his own word ("angry"), the dreamer would have been able to supply his own specific words after being called upon to consult and express his feelings. This would have saved time and more directly connected the dreamer to his dream as well as to an analogous situation in his waking life. Frequently, asking the dreamer to state the obvious results in his using words or anecdotes which relate directly to situations and to words he has used to describe situations in his life. Instead of telling the dreamer how he feels, what he thinks or desires or needs, it is usually much more productive to ask him and to assist him in finding out for himself. This takes patience and discipline on the part of the analyst, but the reward is greater accuracy, less time spent, and increased dreamer participation and openness.

Tangential Discussions

With some dreamers it is easy to drown in tidal waves of long, tangential descriptions and descriptive stories. It is important to develop a sense for what is more or less likely to be relevant and to help the dreamer to refocus when he or she strays too far from the feelings and plot of the dream. Such wanderings are not without value. They often reveal or repeat themes that can be of interest in therapy. However, if they are of a nature that moves you away from the issues in the dream, the dreamwork suffers from the distraction and the delay. The dreamer has a limited attention span and can tire of discussing the dream. The interviewer also has his or her limits of interest and more immediately of the time available for the interview. When the dreamer seems to be repeating himself or herself too much or seems to be going off on a tangent, a simple comment like, "Let me interrupt you and bring you back to the dream." usually gets things going again with few feathers ruffled. If you have reason later to think that you prematurely "corralled" the dreamer, you can always return to that part of the dream.

Asking Questions that Are Hard to Answer

Part of the interviewer's job is to ask questions that are easy to answer. He or she needs to remember not to ask multiple questions at one time, to break down complex questions into several simpler questions, and to retreat and step down the threatening aspects of certain questions. Dreamers at work on their dreams tend to be both emotionally tender and conceptually concrete.

Asking "why" questions like, "Why do you think you dreamed of a German Shepherd?" usually lead to blank expressions, trite, premature interpretations, more time lost, and a frustrated dreamer.

In asking questions, we try not to ask ones the dreamer can't answer. If the dreamer knew why he dreamed of a German shepherd, he wouldn't need the interviewer. It usually works better to replace the "why" questions with, "How was it (or how did it feel) when . . . " or "What was it like when . . . " or "Does the dream give you any clue as to what might have led X to do this?"

Too many "why" questions or even too many questions about forgotten aspects of the dream can lead the dreamer to feel inadequate and uncomfortable. Reassure the dreamer that what is recalled is usually sufficient. Add statements like "I just like to ask about the vague parts of the dream to see if you remember more than you realize or if I have missed something you said or suggested." It is worth going to great lengths to help insecure dreamers feel that whatever they say is just fine and that, if they can't answer certain questions, the problem lies with the timing or the questions, not the dreamer. The challenge is to ask more relevant, less threatening, more artful, or simply more interesting questions.

Trying to Bridge before Getting a Good Description

I have witnessed many good therapists say things like, "You don't like this carpenter's attitude in the dream. What does he remind you of?" In trying to bridge the metaphor of the carpenter image before first defining and describing what carpenters are like both generically and specifically, one forfeits an opportunity for discovery of relevant material. Valuable time is usually lost since the dreamer is often unable to make the connection on her own because the gap between her concrete experience of the dream carpenter has not been bridged to her relevant waking experience by her definitions, descriptions, and focused associations.

Shooting from the Hip

It is often very tempting to use a dream or a dream image prematurely to tell a patient something the therapist has been wanting to say without having been able to find a good occasion. Since surprisingly few therapists are well trained in dreamwork, many often succumb to the temptation to grab at any image in a dream that can be turned to predetermined "therapeutic" goals before first thoroughly exploring the images in the context of the dream.

Anyone can "make something" from images taken out of the context of the dream. But to serve the purposes of the dream rather than those of the analyst takes an exploration and appreciation of the dramatic integrity of the dreamer's experience. At first glance, a dream can easily appear to deal with a client's dynamics as the therapist sees them. It is at this time that the dream is most vulnerable to being reduced to a projective test for the therapist. It is at this point that the dream holds the most promise to fulfill the interpretive wishes of the therapist. It is only in exploring the dream in a nonprejudicial way that one can separate the listener's from the dreamer's dream. This is not to say that one cannot learn a great deal about a dreamer by simply reading or hearing the manifest dream account as Milton Kramer has so ably demonstrated in Chapter 5 of this volume. But if one's goal is to assist the dreamer in gaining as much insight as possible from his or her own dream, and if one wants this insight to be as specific and as custom-tailored as possible, there is not substitute for eliciting from the dreamer and then mirroring to him or her the private, sometimes ideosyncratic, associations framed in his or her own words. These practices are good insurance against the risks of misinterpretations and premature interpretations incurred when shooting from the hip.

Asking Leading Questions

Just as a lawyer in cross-examination is not supposed to lead the witness with questions aimed at eliciting certain responses, a dream interviewer must guard against inappropriately pushing the dreamer in a particular direction by asking leading questions. Beginners are especially prone to prematurely jump to an interpretation and proceed to ask questions that are thinly disguised suggestions and interpretations.

Supplying Amplifications

An interviewer resists supplying information on mythological or psychological constructs while the dream dialogue is in progress.

While working with a group of his students, Carl Jung encouraged them to "Be naive about it, please, then you get at the truth" (Jung, 1984, p. 640). However, judging from Jung's writings, the tales about him, and my personal, professional, and social contacts with his followers, while he would often begin the exploration of the uniqueness of a dreamer's image, he often interrupted the process by inserting his perceptions, both personal and mythological.

For example, in discussing a client's dream about a tortoise with a few students, he asks them (without suggesting that he ever asked the dreamer) to describe its salient features. He carefully points out that their descriptions such as, "It's very fertile," and "It has been a mother symbol," do not distinguish the tortoise from other lower fertile animals or the myriad of other animals associated with mother symbolism. But then, unsatisfied with his students' responses, he said, "But the tortoise is a very impersonal symbol. The obvious features are that . . . [it] has an armored house into which it can withdraw and where it cannot be attacked. Then it is amphibious, it is apathetic, it lives a very long time, and it is highly mythological and mysterious" (Jung, 1984, p. 647). These features may be obvious to Jung, but would they be obvious, relevant, or paramount to all dreamers? Would all agree that tortoises are apathetic or mysterious? Jung continued to discuss the turtle's mythological dimension of wisdom and great age. He concluded after all this that the turtle is a symbol of the union of opposites, the transcendent function. Is it accurate, relevant, or helpful to interpret the tortoise as a symbol of the transcendent function?

Jung never tells us what the dreamer thought about tortoises. In her wonderful description of Jung's method, Mattoon (1978) says that "the archetypal parallels are supplied by the interpreter" from his special knowledge of archeology, anthropology, mythology, religious studies, and alchemy. "Jung made no distinction in the usefulness of amplifications already known to the dreamer and those not known to him" (p, 70). Pandora's box is bursting with analysts' associations to other people's dreams. To the degree that archetypal themes are relevant to the dreamer's experience, the dream itself will demonstrate it; and the dreamer in reliving the feeling and meanings of the dream will experience them firsthand, that is, if the analyst does not usurp the dreamer's thrill of discovery by "explaining" the images to him or her. In most cases, discussions of the mythological, anthropological, and archeological dimensions of dreams are best left to mythologists and philosophers. Only after a dreamer has explored his or her experience of a dream and understood its personal relevance, might the knowledge that there are mythological parallels to his or her experience be in order. Even then, there is a great risk that the dreamer will flee from the immediate, real-world experience of and responsibility for the dream insight into a more abstract, less threatening fascination with myths and psychological constructs.

Howard, a hard-working surgeon, dreamed of hooking a big fish while standing at a turbulent seaside. The strike is too big for the tackle. As the line nears its end, he notices that it is frayed and that if it kept going out, it would break. He begins to run along the beach in the direction of his prey to take the tension off the line. He reaches a very tranquil, pleasant beach area and suddenly has control of the line. He pulls in the catch, which to his surprise is a big turtle. Howard awoke and recognized that he was overworked and indeed reaching the end of his line. When asked what turtles are and what they are like, he said, "Why they're just friendly, peaceful little critters. They know how to live; they just carry their house around with them and spend their days basking in the sun. They are such slow-moving things!" He described his dream turtle as very big, slow-moving, and unperturbed at being brought onto the shore. Howard immediately bridged the image, recognizing his own frayed edges and concluded that he should slow down. He was struck by the wisdom of the turtle's attitude toward life. He promptly took a vacation to tend to his frayed edges and to look again at his tendency to overwork. Would it have been helpful, relevant, or profound to look at Howard's turtle as lethargic and armored, or as a symbol of the transcendent function?

Even the existentialist Medard Boss (1977), in a demonstration of his phenomenological approach to a dream about a turtle, violates his own instructions that we not introduce preconceived notions into the work with the dream. In response to his patient's dream of the tearing apart of her beloved turtle Jacob, Boss asked some very leading questions that were thinly disguised interpretations about her existential situation. Instead of first asking her to describe Jacob, he asked questions such as, "Now that you are awake, does the potential for animal-like bearing and for living in the small space of animal, speak to you only from the presence of a cold-blooded armored creature, remote from human modes of existing?" (p. 76). Boss gives us no evidence for assuming that the dreamer thinks of her "beloved pet" as a cold-blooded armored creature, remote from human modes of existence. What if she were to describe her pet turtle as one of my clients described her dream turtle, "Oh, he is so sweet and vulnerable. He is a shy, tender guy underneath that shell"?

My point is that if Freud and Jung had been more willing to let the dreams and the dreamers speak for themselves, their profound insights into the mind would have been even richer. To judge from his extraordinarily insightful and helpful writings, Boss's rare ability to liberate the dreamer from narrow, constricted ways of being might well be enhanced if he would explore a little more and interpret a little less.

Telling the Dreamer What His or Her Dream Means

Most importantly, we try not to make interpretations. It should be clear by now that we prefer to help the dreamer arrive at his or her own interpretation. Even when the dreamer demands your opinion, it is often best to let him or her stew in impatience and curiosity. Sometimes, however, a carefully timed and modest proposal of one or two possible ways of looking at the dream can be very helpful if all other strategies have not brought the dreamer to his or her own interpretation. Suggesting interpretive hypotheses is tricky and generally should be tried only as a last resort.

Demonstration of the Dream Interview Method

Sometimes when reading a text on the interpretation of dreams, I wonder just how the author arrived at a given interpretation. Just what was said to the dreamer? Did the interviewer make interpretations, suggest possible meanings, ask questions, or mostly listen? Were associations liberally explored, or were they controlled or focused in some way? In what way were the questions and interpretations determined by the interpreter's theoretical bias? How often were the dream images used as an opening for the interpreter to comment on something the interpreter had been waiting to communicate? How interested was the interviewer in understanding the dream as a whole before considering its possible therapeutic uses?

One is best able to evaluate and learn a method of dream work after having seen it in action and after having experienced it firsthand. The next-best way to learn the method is to study verbatim (or in this case nearly verbatim) accounts of actual interviews.

The interview that follows is taken from a transcript given to me by the dreamer of a tape-recorded session. Because my goal is to give the reader a sense of the tone of these interviews as well as an accurate account of the proceedings, I have done very little editing. I have followed Dr. Loma Flowers's suggestion of placing my own thoughts and comments on any given exchange between the dreamer and myself in parentheses throughout the edited version. This procedure is helpful in reviewing how and why one asks a given question as well as where one has missed certain opportunities. Our advanced students find this exercise very helpful in developing their interviewing skills. In practice, the tone of the dream interview is neither interpretive nor inquisitional but instead conversational. Therefore, you may prefer to read the interview once without reading the material in the parentheses and then reread it including that material.

Dianna's Hostess Dream

Our dreamer, whom we shall call Dianna, is a consultant in her mid-thirties. At the time she had the following dream, she was divorcing her first husband, Jeff. After five months of marriage, she had discovered that Jeff was a "con man" who had married many women and tricked them into spending large sums of money at his request "until his considerable funds were liberated from a temporary cash flow problem." Dianna was a student in a weekly dream skills training group, and she also had individual sessions from time to time. It was during a private session that we discussed the following dream, which occurred about four months after Dianna realized that her husband of five months was a con man.

D.: We, myself and two others, are in the home of a woman for dinner. Going into the house, I am struck with the oil paintings all about. Someone here is an artist. We go into a den or study. This is a house rich in antique furniture and history. An older man and a woman live here. The man is cordial but passive. The woman, who is a bustling hostess, is the painter. She keeps referring to her husband as being a lot to have to take care of. One of the people with me is Aunt K. We are sitting in the parlor as the woman prepares the meal. She refuses our help. Just before we are to sit to eat, I remember there is something I must get. They encourage me to do so. I leave, go to a house somewhat nearby and return with it. I don't remember what it is. It's a gift that I'm bringing her, though. They are all sitting down, and the lady comments on the loveliness of what I have. The atmosphere seems more relaxed as everyone has been seated at the dinner table. As I leave, I see a current work on the easel. It makes me think the woman must always have a pen or brush in her hand. It is a drawing of shapes and lovely blues and purples, an abstract. She looks and acts quite like an old-fashioned housewife/hostess. I'm surprised.

I.: Tell me about the opening setting.

D.: I am coming into this house. It is like a pretty old English house. It has thick wood and glass windows with little panes, and there are lots of trees around. There are rich tapestries and thick rugs. It has a sort of homey, rich old quality to it.

I.: What sort of people would live in this atmosphere, homey and rich, and old? (Here I repeat or recapitulate the dreamer's descriptive words to assist her in reconnecting with the ambience, mood, and feelings in the dream house.)

D.: I think of people who have had money in their lives for a long time, who are academicians, people who read and write . . . intelligent.

I.: Is that a pleasant environment for you? (It is important to verify that what seems obvious from the tone of voice and facial expression, is in fact so. Frequently, the dreamer will express significant reservations about positive or even almost neutral descriptions.)

D.: Very much so. (Such an affirmative response clarifies affect not only for the interviewer but, more importantly, for the dreamer, who has another opportunity to reconnect with the image.)

I.: Is this a house you'd like to live in or one aspect of a house in which you might like to live? (Multiple choice questions can give the dreamer more freedom.)

D.: It definitely does. I'd like the elegance, the wealth, the intellectual life of this place to be a part of my life. (The description of the setting, its recapitulation, and the bridging has already helped the dreamer recognize the house as an image of something she longs for.)

I.: What is the woman like?

D.: Well, she's very energetic, artistic, productive, but surprisingly like an old-fashioned housewife/hostess too! (This is a good affective description, but I do not recapitulate it nor try to bridge it yet, since there is so much more to hear about the hostess in the dream.)

I.: What happens next? (Even though the interviewer usually has a copy of the dream before her, asking rather than telling the dreamer what happens next allows the dreamer to stay more involved with the dream and offers her a chance to elaborate.)

D.: We come in through the study, where she has all her paintings. It seems we're walking into her room in the beginning, and then we pass through it to the living room and the dining room.

I.: Why do human beings make paintings? (I might have asked Dianna to describe studies, living rooms, and dining rooms and how they appeared in her dream. The next question would have been, "Is there any way that you have come to know someone like the housewife/hostess or the hostess within yourself by first going through the study [might she have described it as a work space?] before entering the dining and living [more intimate or social?] areas of the relationship?" But this might have prematurely identified the qualities of the hostess. Instead, we moved on to the paintings)

D.: People paint to express feelings that they have or to depict a scene that's attractive, to recapture something that's either internal or external.

I.: Does the painting tell you anything about the painter?

D.: Well, usually it does. Usually it tells how they see the world, how they picture it, or how they experience it themselves. (I asked the question on the specific level, but Dianna answered it on the generic level. I am surprised upon reading this transcript to see that I failed to rephrase the question saying something like, "Do these paintings tell you anything about your hostess?")

I.: And is it pleasant when you first go through the study where the paintings are? (Stressing "the detection and identification of feeling, both in the dream and in the waking context" (Bonime, 1982, p. 142) is vital not only for the interviewer but to help the dreamer become more aware of her feelings so that she can make the bridge to waking experience. It would have been better not to put the word "pleasant" in her mouth but to ask "How did it feel to go through the study?")

D.:   Yes, it's quite pleasant. (She settled for my word rather than finding her own.)

I.:   Does that remind you of anything? (The dreamer, looking quite immersed in the feelings of this scene, seems ready to bridge.)

D.:   Well, I think a bit of Aunt K. and Uncle R.'s house in terms of old, sort of rich. I thought a bit of Aunt K.'s place not in terms of the structure but in terms of the feeling of hominess. Part of it could definitely be Nicole (a senior colleague) and her house in terms of the busy productivity and the creativity. It's a blend of different places.

I.:   Is this a blend of things you would like to have? Is it all positive at this point? (Here I was checking for unspoken negative attitudes to the academic, old, rich, environment.)

D.:   Oh yes.

I.:   What is it that's there that you would like to have? How would you put those things into words?

D.:   Well, I don't think that I have as yet found my own creative art. I long for that.

I.:   What do you mean by creative art?

D.:   Artistic expression. I don't feel that I have it and I miss that. Making time for it seems quite hard.

I.:   Let's get back to the dream. (Corralling the dreamer.) Tell me how it feels to be in this house.

D.:   I have a sense of stability. I mean, even though the hostess complains about her husband, there's a sense of their being deeply rooted together, and that feeling is comfortable.

I.:   So there is stability, and there's creativity, and you like it aesthetically. What is it you find aesthetically pleasing about this environment? (Here I'm trying to steep the dreamer in the pleasurable feeling of the scene.)

D.:   Beautiful colors and textures blending, nice lines, nice structures.

I.:   So, there you are, and what happens?

D.:   I'm invited to dinner, and I'm there with Aunt K. and someone else. I don't know who it is. (I decide not to pursue the unknown companion, at least for the present, since he or she does not appear again in the dream action and our time is limited.)

I.:   Why do people invite other people to dinner? (If Dianna had been new at this method, I would have said, "Coming from another planet, I'd be curious to know why humans invite other humans to dinner" in order to elicit a description of this action-image.)

D.: Well, inviting them into your life, come share with me.

I.: Okay, what happens next? (Had this been a novice dreamworker, I would have repeated, "So, this artist/hostess has invited you into her life. How does that feel?" But I could see from Dianna's expression that this was unnecessary, and I decided to keep moving.

D.: The hostess is preparing the meal, and she's complaining. Her husband is quite cordial but very passive. It definitely feels like her house, and she creates the atmosphere there. He enjoys it, has comfort in it, and may financially support it, but it's hers.

I.: Is that a problem in the dream? (To encourage clarification.)

D.: The problem in the dream is his passivity with her. It's a problem to her, and she expresses it.

I.: So, she expresses it as a problem that he's so passive?

D.: Yes. She keeps referring to her husband as a lot to have to take care of.

I.: Does that remind you of anything?

D.: Well, I think of my mother taking care of my father. Almost every woman I know takes care of her husband to the degree of catering to him, trying to treat him nicely. Somehow, the man never seems to come up to the woman.

I.: The men don't come up to the women in what way? (Again, to clarify and elaborate before attempting the next bridge.)

D.: Oh, in dynamism, productivity, self-assuredness.

I.: This seems like a typical configuration?

D.: It certainly is. (Here is a clear statement of the dreamer's perception of the reality of husband-wife relationships.)

I.: Reminds you of your mom? (Since Dianna has already made a bridge to Mom, I invite elaboration.)

D.: Um hmm. Reminds me . . . It's interesting because I think of my sister, I think of her as the active, bustling one in life, whereas my brother-in-law supports the family but isn't very emotionally available in the house.

I.: Is this guy in the dream not emotionally available? (Point of clarification, since this aspect of the sister–brother-in-law relationship doesn't seem to fit that of the dream couple, is Dianna introducing a new descriptive element? This question is asked without any hint in my tone of voice that I note any incongruity.)

D.: No, I don't think he's not emotionally available, but more like he feels like a kid . . . How do I express this? He's passive in a way that keeps saying, "Take care of me."

I.:   Does the way he communicates "Take care of me." remind you of anything else? (The affect-laden "Take care of me." is very likely to evoke a good bridge.)

D.:   It reminds me a bit of Franz, my new boyfriend. It reminds me a bit of Jeff (her con-man husband). It reminds me a bit of my father! It reminds me a bit of Uncle R.! (A little clarification can go a long way! We shall return to this material after we bridge the hostess, so that the dreamer will better appreciate it in the context of the dream and of her life.)

I.:   Before we began recording this interview did you say that the husband in the dream reminded you of your colleague, Nicole's husband Marc, as well? Does that still fit?

D.:   Mark looks to me like someone who is sweet and pleasant, but Nicole's the one who creates the world they live in. (Now we have a good opening to get back to the hostess via the Nicole bridge made earlier and referred to again here.)

I.:   What is Nicole like? (In this case, we need to know more about this figure that keeps surfacing in the dreamer's associations to the house and the hostess.)

D.:   She's very active in her career. She is creative and busy in creating a career she loves. She is also like a housewife to Marc, and they have a warm and stable relationship. They also have a productive home/office combination, like the stable couple in the dream!

I.:   Hmmm. Do you remember thinking in the dream that the hostess shouldn't complain?

D.:   Well, vaguely. What comes to my mind now, as we talk about it, is that what a woman gets out of being with a man like that is a feeling of being powerful, as if she's got it all together. Rather than belittle him, she should acknowledge that that's the payoff. That's what is wonderful about it for her. She should relish it, rather than complain.

I.:   Was she criticizing him by saying that he was a lot to take care of?

D.:   Uh huh. She should get angry with him, so he knows about it. She complains about it rather than getting something either resolved or changed in the relationship.

I.:   Is this a dynamic you've seen in other relationships?

D.:   Uh hmm.

I.:   Is that a dynamic in your relationship now with Franz? (A purposely leading question. I think the dreamer needs a slight challenge to overcome a resistance to exploring in this direction. If the answer is negative, I shall retreat and check it out again later because she has already told us that the Take-care-of-me message of the dream husband reminds her of her current boyfriend Franz.)

D.: Well, there is a degree to which I have always felt with Franz that I'm the mother and he's the son. You know, the mother/son relationship.

I.: And who has the energy?

D.: I definitely have more energy than he does.

I.: You also say that there is a basically good relationship in this house. (My voice suggested a question mark and the end of this sentence.)

D.: Yes.

I.: What was the feeling of it? How do you know that? (We need a fuller description of the relationship.)

D.: It shows in the world that they have created there together. The husband was very solid. I mean, it wasn't as if he was swayed by her complaints too much. The complaints were like a broken record, and they both just lived with it. (With a novice, I would have summarized the dream with descriptions and bridges made up to this point. But Nicole was following the action well.)

I.: Aunt K. is with you. What's she like?

D.: Aunt K. is my father's sister, and she's really down-home. She's not someone who is pretentious or puts on airs. She, above all my other relatives, was extremely supportive of me in the incident with Jeff, my con-man husband.

I.: Supportive of your staying with him and/or of leaving him? (Clarify to see where the support came—again with a tone of curiosity even if the likely answer is known by the interviewer.)

D.: No, of leaving him.

I.: Why did she want you to leave Jeff? (Asking for the obvious will reconnect the dreamer with some important feelings.)

D.: Well, when she found out what was going on, she just wanted me to have the strength to get the hell out and leave him.

I.: And how does it feel to be with her at dinner?

D.: It feels good.

I.: Okay, so maybe you're there with the part of you that's like her, that's down-home, doesn't put on airs and encourages your strength? (Because Dianna is experienced in dream interviewing, I am verbalizing a possible subjective interpretation, since it seemed to be in keeping with the dramatic role (companion) played by Aunt K. in the dream. I was confident that Dianna would stop me if this didn't feel right.)

D.: (Affirmative nod. We have agreed to consider this as a possible hypothesis only.)

I.: Did Jeff (the con-man) pull for that part of you which puts on airs?

D.: Um hmm. (Not much of a confirmation. But the structure of the dream suggests that we should pursue the matter. Aunt K. was Dianna's companion in an environment in which the dreamer is an invited guest surrounded by creativity, beauty, and wealth, and in which she, via her hostess, recognizes the loveliness of what she has to offer. If the answer to this question is yes, Aunt K.'s qualities of *not* needing to put on airs could be Dianna's entrée to this creative, stable, homey world.)

I.: What was it that Jeff promised? "I'll make you a star, and I can do it because I'm wealthy, well connected; I'm hot stuff?"

D.: Right.

I.: How about the pimpmobile? (Jeff had convinced Dianna to buy a huge white Cadillac which she thus nicknamed.)

D.: The pimpmobile, right! And you know (she becomes very animated), he would say, "We're going to have a ranch with Arabian horses and Great Danes and fly down to Peru and do this great expedition. And I'm going to have you out there being the most successful consultant! We'll get these fancy offices downtown, and I'll get you all set up. (Now we're cooking. This material will be useful later in recapping and bridging Aunt K.)

I.: In the dream then, you are accompanied by Aunt K. the down-home support for your being yourself without putting on airs? (A little schmoozing for reinforcement.)

D.: Right.

I.: I wonder, if the Aunt K. in you had been better developed at the time, would you have fallen for Jeff's con?

D.: I wonder.

I.: What happens next in the dream?

D.: I offer help and the hostess says, "No, no, no, I can do it myself."

I.: How do you feel when she says, "No, no, no, I can do it myself?"

D.: I always hate it when hostesses do that.

I.: How come?

D.: Well, they always need help, and I think it's more fun to get in and do it. Sitting around making small talk while you just wait around for someone to prepare the food is boring.

I.: So, you offer to help her, and she won't let you. Does that remind you of anything? (In response to a blank expression suggesting that the bridge was premature, I move back into the dream.) You're willing to help prepare this dinner, but the hostess won't let you help. Why won't she let you? (I return to get a fuller description.)

D.: She's got it organized. But she's also a martyr. She complains but will not let anybody help her.

I.: And who is that true of in your life?

D.: A lot of women I know. I think of my mother as a martyr in a lot of ways, and yet she'd ask me to help. I don't know. (As the dreamer begins to test this bridge, she realizes that perhaps the fit is not so good after all.)

I.: Is it true of Nicole? (Testing the earlier bridge between the hostess and Nicole to see the extent of the similarities.)

D.: No, I don't think that's true of her at all. She definitely asks for help. In fact, she sort of orders, "I need your help. You can do this." (So where does this characteristic of not accepting help fit?)

I.: Do you act like the hostess in similar situations?

D.: Yes, I'll do it myself and just keep going, get wound up and just keep going.

I.: And you don't let Aunt K.–types help you out?

D.: Right.

I.: And then what happens in the dream?

D.: Just before we sit down to eat, I remember there's something that I must get. It's the gift I meant to bring for the hostess. They encourage me to get it. I go to a house nearby and return with it. When I return, everyone is sitting down, and the lady comments on the loveliness of what I have.

I.: That you have brought as a gift?

D.: Right.

I.: Do you remember anything about the gift? (Rather than the more demanding, "What was the gift?")

D.: No. Just that it's in my hands.

I.: Do you remember anything about the house you went to nearby?

D.: No. (The fact that the house is nearby might suggest that the dreamer is not far emotionally from the hostess's house, but one can't follow up every image in a long dream without fatiguing both parties.)

I.: You just forgot to bring the gift? (One never knows if there might have been more to it than that.)

D.: Right. (Given the context of the dream, I accept this thinking that she forgot [has lost sight of] her gift or what she has to offer.)

I.: The hostess comments on how lovely it is.

D.: Um hmm. (Dianna smiles, remembering the compliment.)

I.:   Something that you have to offer? (I keep looking for spontaneous elaboration. Failing that, these comments serve to underline the dream action, so the dreamer will be primed to make a bridge to waking experience.)

D.:   Um hmm.

I.:   Does that remind you of anything in your life?

D.:   I remember very much Nicole's telling me how much I brought in a lovely spirit with me while I was helping her by putting on one of her business-related parties. That was the only time that I have felt that lately.

I.:   So, she's telling you how lovely it is, how are you feeling? (I want her to get closer to the feeling.)

D.:   Very appreciative. It's nice to hear.

I.:   And then what?

D.:   I remember as I'm leaving, seeing a current work on the easel as I'm going out the door to get the gift. I remember that there's a work on the easel, and it's very pretty. It's painted in wonderful light blues and lavenders and purples. It was an abstract. I can remember seeing the oil; it was thick and rich. I remember thinking that this hostess must always be busy painting because this room is filled with paintings, and here's another one on the easel. She looks like such an old-fashioned kind of housewife, you know, cater to the man and take care of him, yet she is *very* prolific.

I.:   What does that remind you of, anything?

D.:   Well, I think about Nicole in terms of writing, getting all that stuff out, and maintaining a devoted-wife stance and a lovely home and all the rest of it. I don't know other people who are that productive. (The dreamer returns again to Nicole in connection with the characteristics of the artist/hostess/housewife.)

I.:   How about the mood of the colors? What does that communicate? How do you feel when you see them?

D.:   They are real calming colors—lavenders and blues and purples. They're colors that I like. When I had my color chart done by a professional, I was told that they are very good colors for me. I find them very attractive. They have a very calming, gentle flavor to them.

I.:   Does it remind you of a feeling, or of a feeling you'd like to have more of?

D.:   It's definitely a feeling I'd like more of. I think Nicole has got some of those colors. She wears some of them.

I.:   In the last scene you're sitting down with your gift?

D.: I bring in the gift, and I give it to her. (While it may seem tedious to come back to each dream event, restate, and explore it, in practice it rarely feels that way because a good interviewer knows that surprises can surface at any point and that the dreamer, who is traveling long distances emotionally and conceptually, needs to proceed step by step.)

I.: And what's the very last thing that happens in the dream?

D.: That's it. (You never know when the dreamer will recall an unmentioned last event or feeling, or when she will omit the last action.)

I.: Is that where she says she likes the gift?

D.: Right.

I.: What happens last? You give her the gift, or she says, "What a lovely gift?"

D.: She comments on the loveliness of what I have, and as she's doing that, I'm noticing as I'm coming in . . . yeah, that's it! The thing that I notice as I come in the room is that everything is more relaxed, and everyone is sitting down eating.

I.: (I missed the opportunity to say, "So the feeling is more relaxed now that you have remembered you have a gift to offer and have brought it?") I was thinking of the part that does not seem to fit Nicole, your asking to help and the hostess saying no. Is there any way that this happens in your relationship with Nicole, where you'd like to help or wanted to help with something to which she says no? Did you ever ask her if you could join her in her work, or did you want to do that?

D.: I remember thinking about how to work with her and make her work part of mine, but I didn't ask her anything specific.

I.: It's as though you're being kept out of the action a bit within this nice environment. Have you felt that? (Restatement of same question.)

D.: I felt that when I put on the party at Nicole's house. Nicole said at one point that she had put on the party, and I felt like I'd put it on. I didn't feel that I had been acknowledged. So that may be it, but it doesn't really speak to the fact that Nicole asked for my help with one of her big projects.

I.: (Had Dianna wanted to ask to be included in Nicole's career and guessed she would get no for an answer?) I don't know what to make of that moment in the dream, but I don't believe it's coincidental. It's as though you wanted to be in on it? (Expressing confusion and restating the issue sometimes trigger a useful response.)

D.: Yes, definitely. As I watch Nicole doing all her career stuff I think, "That's something I need to be more involved in." I need a larger arena. I'm not getting out into the world. I don't have my package together to get out into the world, and I need to get out there. It's as if I have things to say, but I don't have it organized. Nicole is organized, productive, and recognized. I'm not a part of all that.

I.: How do you understand the dream at this point?

D.: Well, I definitely feel that in my relationship with Nicole, I've gotten a lot of acknowledgement for my loveliness or my spirit or what I have to give. And I've also been quite aware of (in terms of what Nicole is putting out in the world) what I could be doing and I'm not. I'm being much more the hostess than I am the artist and creator.

I.: Why might you have created such a dream? (i.e., What can you learn from this dream?)

D.: To point out that one can do both.

I.: Both being . . . ? (An invitation to the dreamer to clarify and reinforce her insight.)

D.: Both being the hostess, having the home, having the husband *and* being prolific, putting one's self out in an artistic way in the world.

I.: Could it be pleasurable, as it is in the dream?

D.: Yes. (I had hoped for a little more than this.)

I.: And it can be a calming place. Maybe that's something you can remember that's important?

D.: It is because every time I think of putting myself out in the world, I feel anxiety. It makes me anxious. I won't be good enough, I won't be well received. I won't have the right things to say, or there'll be criticism.

I.: What if you did it with the feelings of the blues and purples and lavenders?

D.: That would make it quite peaceful, quite healing, quite gentle. I have never framed it like that before! I have always framed it as caution, almost militaristic. So, if I could be more like the hostess and more like Aunt K., could I pull it off *and* be happy with a sweet but somewhat passive man? My boyfriend, Franz, is like that. I just seem to find that type of man most attractive.

After the Interview

The most important work one does on a dream is accomplished in the week and months following a successful interpretation. As Jung

(1984) wrote, "Full recognition of the meaning of a dream comes in waves" (p. 651). It is in living the dream, in trying out the new feelings and insights gained from it, that one manages to incorporate the benefits of the dream into the way one experiences and lives life. I encourage dreamers to keep the feelings and insights of their work on the dream in the foreground of their awareness for the next few weeks. I suggest that the dreamer reread the dreams we have worked on, along with their notes on our interview, and note any new ideas or feelings that surface. Listening to tapes of interpretation sessions takes time and patience but can be extremely helpful in assisting dreamers not only to recall forgotten connections and relive the pleasure of hitting upon insight but also to witness how they avoid, resist, and distract in the course of the interview. More importantly, adjustments (from fine-tuning to major corrections) in the directions taken and conclusions arrived at can be made as the dreamer (or interviewer) reviews the session.

Perhaps the easiest way to carry into daily life the work one has done on a dream is to select one or two major dream characters and keep them in mind for a week. In the case of a negatively charged character, I suggest, "You might keep a lookout for the feelings of the exuberant, foolish woman in your dream. Notice at what moments you feel like her. You needn't do anything differently now, just watch her and get to know how she operates. Pretend you are a psychologist and consider why she might have turned out the way she has. Eventually, you will have a better sense of how you can deal with that part of yourself."

In the case of a positive image, I would say, "Why don't you play with the image of the hostess this week? You could pretend that you are this person several times a day. At neutral moments, say, when you are walking down the street or talking to a friend, pretend that you are she for a moment and see how it feels. If that is rewarding, try being your hostess-self at work. Ask yourself questions like, 'What would the hostess say or do or feel at a moment like this?' " With practice, pretending can evoke a solid awareness of and comfort with previously disowned and unappreciated aspects of one's self and of one's repertoire of possible experience.

The Pivotal Importance of the Dramatic Structure

As Jung was fond of pointing out, dreams often begin with an exposition of the dream theme, proceed to the development or entanglement, and close with the catastrophe or solution (Jung, 1984, p. 241). When the catastrophe (as in some nightmares) or the solution alone is reported, one wonders if the rest of the dream has been forgotten. Such dreams can be enormously useful but do not offer the same opportunities for discovering the dynamics of the waking situation as do dreams that include a development of the plot. For example, if Dianna had reported only that she had forgotten to bring a gift to her hostess, we would have missed the insights offered by the setting, Aunt K., the paintings, the relationship possibilities portrayed by the host couple, the personal development possibilities shown in the hostess, and Dianna's recognition via the hostess that what Dianna has to offer is lovely. When training students in dream interviewing, we encourage them always to work within the context of the entire dream (or as much of it as is recalled) and to respect its dramatic structure. A number of therapists who are new to this discipline have commented that they never knew how much one could learn from a single dream.

Structure as Frame of Reference

The dramatic structure of the dream, what happened and in what order, provides us with a frame of reference against which associations and interpretations can be evaluated for their relevance and usefulness.

A respect for the integrity of the dream so elegantly emphasized by Stern (1972) and Boss (1963 and 1977) can save the interpreter from both slight and serious misinterpretations. A psychiatrist once told me his dream with the interpretation he made of it. His account went something like this: "I dreamed of sitting in a chair in front of my bookcase. A snake came down from the shelves to the floor and moved up between my legs. It was about to bite me as I awoke. I understood the dream to be a very special one of the Uroboras, the mythical symbol of wisdom and integration. It comes to me from my study of the psyche." The dreamer saw this as a sign of his increasing mastery and insight. I asked him, "Yes, but the snake was about to bite you in the dream. Wouldn't that suggest a problem somewhere?" He had taken the snake out of the dramatic context of the dream and had applied an external symbol system to it. (In response to this account, Walter Bonime commented that "This is a beautiful caveat regarding plundering dreams for ideological support.")

Image Interpretation versus Dream Interpretation

One of the dangers of using images out of context of the whole dream to make a therapeutic point to the dreamer is that of forfeiting the actual message of the dream in the assumed service of a therapeutic goal. The interpretation of a dream and the therapeutic use of the dream or of its images are not the same thing. While any dream image can be used to highlight or trigger the discussion of a therapeutic issue, this is not the same as interpreting the dream qua dream. My preference is to first understand what the dream has to say before using its vocabulary out of context. Too often, the interpreter plunders the dream for his or her own preconceived therapeutic purposes by using images out of context.

Once one has let the dream speak for itself, one is in a position to employ the dream images and insights in a more nearly accurate and appropriate manner. This minimizes interpreter/therapist distortion and thus speeds the dreamer on his or her *own* way.

Settings and Scene Changes

"The description of the locality is very important; the place where the dream is staged, whether hotel, station, street, wood, under water, etc. makes a tremendous difference in the interpretation" (Jung, 1933, p. 38). By investigating the setting of a scene, the dreamer is often able to indicate the issues the dream will deal with. In Dianna's hostess dream, the house descriptions she gave acted as signposts to key goals she used the rest of the dream to explore.

Abrupt scene changes are often confusing, and a number of researchers point to them as signs of the random, irrational nature of dreams. If, however, one takes the time to explore a dream step by step, following the sequence of the dream, the scene changes reveal themselves to be elegant tools to express psychological transitions, developments, and results. "The irrational sequence is to be understood as a *causal* sequence" (Jung, 1984, p. 21) While in waking logic *post hoc, ergo propter hoc* ("because B follows A, B is caused by A") is indeed a fallacy, in the associative logic of dreaming it is a general rule.

Subjective versus Objective Interpretations

Regarding the question of whether to interpret a given image on the subjective level (as an aspect of the dreamer) or on the objective level (as the thing or person it manifests as or as a representation of a person or force in the dreamer's life), there is much confusion. Jung (1984) suggests as a rule of thumb that, in the case of persons, one employ an objective interpretation if the person is "in close relationship to the dreamer" (p. 457) and a subjective one if the person is not. He further suggests that one should try out subjective interpretations with even close relatives because they might well represent internalized psychological characteristics of the dreamer (Jung, 1984, pp. 29–31). Fritz

Perls (1969) and many of his followers have insisted that all dream images (plates of spinach, open garage doors, etc.) are subjective and represent an aspect of the dreamer.

We encourage the interpreter to consider and explore both levels for any image if and when the dreamer seems open to the exploration. The definitions and descriptions of the image, when placed in the dramatic context of the dream, will usually make it clear whether one or the other or both levels are appropriate and fruitful. The questions in the dream interview provide a method for making these important distinctions with regard to dream objects, forces, and actions as well as to dream persons.

Judging the Quality of an Interpretation

"The initial concepts of a dream's meaning, elaborated by therapist or patient are . . . not interpretations, but interpretive hypotheses, which are then modified, replaced, or validated as the analytic process moves ahead" (Bonime, 1982, p. 142). Those who have experience working with individual dreamers over time know that the initial understanding of the dream is just the beginning of the process of refinement, integration, and discovery of new dimensions of insight. I am not at all convinced that there is such a thing as a complete interpretation. A more realistic goal would be to arrive at a good and useful interpretation that does not do violence to the dream itself.

There are those who suggest that dreams do their work while the dreamer sleeps and that waking interpretation is unnecessary, especially in the case of certain lucid dreams in which the dreamer either conquers or removes troublesome dream figures. My experience of reviewing the dreams and dream journals of dreamers over several consecutive years has convinced me that relatively few recalled dreams accomplish their mission of providing insight without the dreamer's active participation in a waking interpretive process.

Time and again I see dreamers who feel that by controlling and modifying the dream action they have solved the problem or integrated the insight of the dream. Generally speaking, these same issues surface again and again, like a broken record, in subsequent dreams until such time as the dreamer comes to a conscious recognition of the dream message. This recognition might come through vehicles other than the dream such as therapy or the school of hard knocks. This broken-record phenomenon suggests that positions such as Lowy's (1942) that the fruitful interpretation of a dream is but a secondary gain to the primary functions of psychological integration, which are achieved while the dreamer sleeps, should be modified.

One might instead state that, while one of the primary functions of dreams may be the achievement of psychological integration and information processing, the fruitful interpretation of dreams provides practical insights relevant to and useful in improving an individual's degree of self-knowledge and the quality of his or her daily life experience.

I think one can consider a dream well interpreted when it: (1) opens the dreamer's eyes to a new or more profound aspect of the dreamer's self, motives, behaviors, attitudes, hopes, fears, or relationships; (2) solves a concrete problem or provides a novel idea; or (3) provides the dreamer with a new experience of and appreciation for qualities of being and experience, such as acceptance, joy, compassion, responsibility, or peace.

Dreamers often have small "ah ha" experiences (French and Fromm, 1964) that indicate they have reached a pertinent interpretation. However, these can be misleading efforts to please the interviewer or to avoid a deeper, more threatening realization of the meaning of the dream. Asking the dreamer to "unpack," or elaborate on, an "ah ha" will usually provide both the interviewer and the dreamer with the information necessary to discard, modify, and/or enhance any given "ah ha." John Beebe said it best: "A good interpretation often feels more like a whole-body *thump* than an 'ah ha' " (personal communication, 1985).

> The content (dreamer's response) that follows a successful interpretation is of a special *quality*. . . . Essentially it comes from a feeling of intelligibility, meaningfulness, and coherence. . . . So what feels like new content . . . is, more accurately, a realignment, a bringing together of warded-off or defended thoughts, feelings, fantasies, impulses, views of oneself and important others. (Breger, 1980, pp. 10–11)

The rush of confirmative associations and vignettes that often follow a good interpretation have a quality of sureness about them that one can generally depend upon. In fact, after a dreamer has really grasped the meaning of a dream, he or she usually wonders how he or she didn't see it before. "It is so obvious! How could I not have seen it?" is a frequent exclamation that usually, but not always, indicates a bull's-eye interpretation. Given time to actively reflect upon the dream and to explore other dreams which follow and which treat the same subject, one can modify or gain confidence in an interpretation.

References

Aristotle. [1941]. On Prophesying by Dreams. In *The Basic Work of Aristotle*, ed. Mckeon, Richard. New York: Random House.

Bonime, W. (1958). The Use of Dream Evidence of Evolving Health as a Therapeutic Tool. *Psychiatry: Journal for The Study of Interpersonal Processes* 21(3): 000–00.

———. [with Florence Bonime] (1982). *The Clinical Use of Dreams*. New York: Da Capo Press.

———. (1966). The Role of Dreams in Psychoanalysis. In *Development and Research*, ed. Jules Masserman. New York: Grune and Stratton.

———. (1969). A Culturalist View, The Dream as Human Experience. In *Dream Psychology and the New Biology of Dreaming*, ed. M. Kramer, Springfield, Ill.: Charles C Thomas, pp. 79–92.

———. (1971). Dreams: Affect and Interpretive Limitations. In *Science and Psychoanalysis*, ed. J. Masserman, vol. 19. New York: Grune and Stratton.

Boss, Medard. (1977). *"I Dreamt Last Night"*. New York: Gardner Press. (Original edition, 1963. New York: Basic Books, out of print.)

———. (1963). *Psychoanalysis and Daseinsanalysis*. New York: Basic Books.

Breger, Louis, Hunter, Ian, and Lane, Ron. (1971). *The Effect of Stress on Dreams*. New York: International Universities Press.

Berger, Louis. (1980). The Manifest Dream and Its Latent Meaning. In *The Dream in Clinical Practice*, ed. J. Natterson. New York: Jason Aronson, pp. 3–28.

Crick, Frances, and Mitchison, Graeme. (1983). The Function of Sleep. *Nature* 304 (14 July): 111–14.

Dane, J., and Van de Castle, R. (1985). A Comparison of Waking Instruction and Post-Hypnotic Suggestion for Lucid Dream Induction. *The Association for the Study of Dreams Newsletter* 1(4): 4–9.

Delaney, G. (1979, 1988). *Living Your Dreams*, rev. ed. New York: Harper and Row.

———. (1991). *Breakthrough Dreaming*. New York: Bantam Books.

————. (1993). *Sexual Dreams.* New York: Ballantine Books.

Erickson, E. (1954). The Dream Specimen in Psychoanalysis. In *Psychoanalytic Psychiatry and Psychology,* ed. R. Knight and C. Friedman. New York: International Universities Press.

Fishbein, W., ed. (1981). *Sleep, Dreams and Memory.* New York: SP Medical and Scientific Books.

Fiss, H. (1984). Personal communication, 1984.

French, T., and Fromm, E. (1964). *Dream Interpretation: A New Approach.* New York: Basic Books.

Freud, S. (1900). The Interpretation of Dreams. *Standard Edition.* London: Hogarth Press. 4:1–338 and 5:339–627.

Gackenbach, J., and La Berge, S. (1988). *Lucid Dreaming: New Research on Consciousness During Sleep.* New York: Plenum.

Gershman, H. (1983). Current Application of Horney Theory to Dream Interpretation. *American Journal of Psychoanalysis.* 43(3): 219–29.

Greenberg, R., and Pearlman, C. (1974). Cutting the REM Nerve: An Approach to the Adaptive Role of REM Sleep. *Perspectives in Biology and Medicine* 17:513–21.

————. (1978). If Freud Only Knew: A Reconsideration of Psychoanalytic Dream Theory. *International Review of Psychoanalysis.* 5:71–75.

————. (1980). The Private Language of the Dream. In *The Dream in Clinical Practice,* ed. J. M. Natterson. New York: Jason Aronson, pp. 85–96.

Hillman, J. (1979). *The Dream and the Underworld.* New York: Harper and Row.

Jones, R. (1970). *The New Psychology of Dreaming.* New York: Grune and Stratton.

————. (1984). *Dreams Are of—Not for the Dreamer.* Paper presented at the first annual conference of the Association for the Study of Dreams, San Francisco.

Jung, C. G. (1984). *Dream Analysis.* Princeton, N.J.: Princeton University Press.

————. (1933). *Modern Man in Search of a Soul.* New York: Harcourt, Brace and World.

Krippner, S. (1981). Access to Hidden Reserves of the Unconscious Through Dreams in Creative Problem-solving. *Journal of Creative Behavior* 15(1): 11–22.

Litman, R. (1980). The Dream in the Suicidal Situation. In *The Dream in Clinical Practice*, ed. J. M. Natterson. New York: Jason Aronson, pp. 284–99.

Lowy, S. (1942). *Foundations of Dream Interpretation*. London: Kegan Paul, Trench Trubener and Co.

Mattoon, M. A. (1978). *Applied Dream Analysis: A Jungian Approach*. Washington D.C.: Winston & Sons.

Natterson, J. (1980). The Dream in Group Psychotherapy. In *The Dream in Clinical Practice*, ed. J. M. Natterson, New York: Jason Aronson, pp. 435–43.

Perls, F. (1969). *Gestalt Therapy Verbatim*. Moab, Utah: Real People Press.

Robertiello, R. (1968). *Use of Interpretation in Treatment*. New York: Grune and Stratton.

Scrima, L. (1984). Dream Sleep and Memory: New Findings with Diverse Implications. *Integrative Psychiatry* 2(6): 211–19.

Stern, P. J. (1972). *In Praise of Madness*. New York: Norton.

Ullman, M., and Zimmerman, N. (1979). *Working with Dreams*. New York: Delalorte Press.

——— . (1981). On Deprofessionalizing the Dream. *Academy Forum* 25(4): 2–4.

7

Loma Flowers ━━━━━━━━━━━━━━━━━━━━━━━

The Dream Interview Method in a Private Outpatient Psychotherapy Practice

In 1976, when I read Gayle Delaney's newly formulated dream interview method of dream interpretation (Delaney, 1979), I promptly began to learn the technique because it seemed so adaptable to clinical psychiatry (Flowers, 1988). Prior to that time, I had spent very little time on dreamwork in psychotherapy for two major reasons. First, dream interpretation was addressed only peripherally in Stanford's eclectic psychiatric residency training program that I completed in 1972. As a result, I never developed a truly satisfying technique of dream interpretation to add to my professional skills despite the dreams and interpretation theories that had flitted through the various readings and seminars on Freudian, Jungian, gestalt, interpersonal, and other psychopathological theories.

Second, even various expert demonstrations of dream interpretation methods did not convince me either of their fidelity to the patients' dreams and issues or of their relevance to the patients' pragmatic concerns that led to their seeking psychotherapy. As a result, dream analysis rarely seemed to me to contribute any more useful material than what could be elicited from a thorough exploration of the issues, and therefore I never became very motivated to learn and utilize any of these methods of dream interpretation consistently.

To this date, I have not seen a single method that surpasses the dream interview method with respect to fidelity and relevance to both the patient and all the elements of the whole dream. Many methods contain similar ingredients, but the entirety of Delaney's technique is its unique, essential feature, which lends itself extremely effectively to psychotherapy and psychodynamic formulations. Over the years, I have kept my ears open for further ideas which I have gratefully con-

241

sidered in refining the fabric of the applied dream interview method. These ideas frequently arose from discussions of dreamwork with many experts, including Bonime (1989), Hartmann (1984), Hunt (1989), Kramer (1987), Maybruck (1989), Moffitt (1991) and Ullman (1979), who have presented their work at the annual meetings of the Association for the Study of Dreams. Various other applications, and further examples of oneirecriticism (dream interpretation) are explored in this book.

The dream interview method of oneirocriticism was itself developed from traditional techniques but contains two clinically crucial, innovative steps. The first is the complete descriptive definitions elicited entirely from the patient and not from theory, unless the patient himself believes the theory. The second step is the final synthesis, or bridging step, which remains true to the entire plot of the dream with all its twists and turns and accompanying feelings.

The dream interview method is more structured than most because it requires the therapist and patient to unravel the creativity of the dream, rather than create their own interpretations. It demands a collaborative style with patients that is very compatible with goal-directed, insight-oriented psychodynamic psychotherapy. The completed interpretation often presents patient and therapist with a succinct and useful psychodynamic formulation of an issue on the level it is being worked by the patient at the time the dream was dreamed.

The dream interview method has a remarkable conceptual elegance and simplicity that make it attractive to a wide variety of therapists and patients. It does not require the therapist to invoke concepts such as reversal, condensation, displacement (Cavenar, 1978), or archetypal myths, even though they may be operative. Rather, the derivation of each interpretation from the dreamer's beliefs is immediately apparent to any observer witnessing a few demonstrations, and the power of the application of the interpretation is often very convincing to the therapist and the patient, not only at the time but in the succeeding weeks and months. However, like any skill, dream interviewing requires considerable practice for mastery. Interestingly enough, alert beginners can soon recognize a problem long before they may be able to correct it, which is not my experience with other methods. This is a useful self-regulating factor in learning this technique.

In the dream interview method, the psychotherapist is the dream interviewer who elicits facts, ideas, beliefs, associations, and feelings from the dreamer about each symbol (noun, occasionally verb) used in the dream and synthesizes these into a succinct descriptive defini-

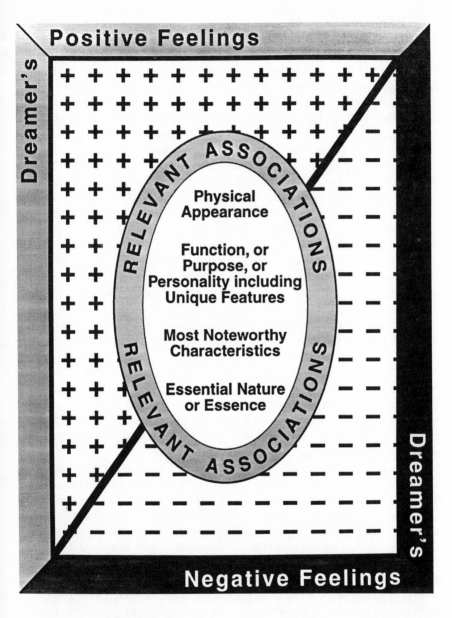

Figure 7.1 This diagram illustrates a descriptive definition of any dream image. It includes the seven components of the verbal portrait elicited by the dream interview method. Notice particularly the four core components which are frequently less emphasized or omitted in other methods.

tion. To me, this descriptive definition is like a verbal portrait (see figure 7-1).

Next, the therapist integrates these definitions into the sequence of actions prescribed by the dream and asks the dreamer to bridge this as a metaphor to his or her everyday life. The therapist may have to rephrase questions a number of times, remaining faithful to the descriptive definitions, the feelings, and the plot of the dream throughout, just as one rephrases questions in the normal course of therapy, especially when dealing with resistance. When the dreamer recognizes the metaphoric bridge, he or she will confirm where the dynamic of the dream is operative in some way in an aspect of his or her life that is concurrent with the dream, and *not* necessarily current with the dream interview or discussion. A day note is often helpful here. This is a brief note written in a dream journal at bedtime; it is a summary of the major feelings, issues and events of the day. It helps orient the dreamer to the events concurrent with a particular dream. In my experience, dreams deal with issues current in the dreamer's life and mind, somewhat similarly to newspapers and magazines in a community. This recognition of the dynamic is frequently quite visible as an insight.

In this chapter, I detail my application of the dream interview method to a variety of therapeutic situations. The patients whose dreams are reported have all agreed to be anonymously included, and I am very grateful to them for permitting such a choice of examples from which to demonstrate the method and the various approaches involved. I am also indebted to the many astute questions posed by the therapists in my professional seminars which challenged me to clarify my thinking and to extend my conceptualizations about the application of this method to psychotherapy.

The dreams and analyses are reproduced as close to verbatim as I could from process notes usually written during the therapeutic hour. This may reveal some poor sytrax which is not unusual in normal conversation, but I have tried to keep the meaning clear. Incidentally, I write the dream double-spaced and frequently use colored pens to distinguish one descriptive definition from another and to record different interpretive remarks. Whenever I thought it might be helpful to the reader in describing the examples in this chapter, I have included some of my thinking in parentheses to indicate why I selected one possible direction of questioning over others. To get the flow of the dream interview method, just reread it, ignoring the parentheses. The chapter concludes with the indications and contraindications for this technique in the clinical practice of psychotherapy.

Application to Modes of Therapy

Individual Psychotherapy

Examples No. 1–5, 12, 13, in this chapter come from individual psychotherapy encounters. It is perhaps the easiest setting in which to do dream interpretation because there are not other people to consider with regard to either the amount of time that a particular descriptive definition consumes or their feelings and reactions. I find my patients vary considerably in their interest and motivation in recalling dreams and using them as part of their therapy. Some can bring in three dreams a session without a single note, and others have not recalled more than two or three dreams in years of therapy. Occasionally, I negotiate with patients about the use of dreams, sometimes to avoid the use of old dreams as resistance to current issues, and sometimes to encourage them to help themselves through a difficult phase or to promote a faster resolution of a symptom. Speed can be particularly important to people facing deadlines, limited financial resources, or racing their "biological clock." It is also of significance to third-party payers.

When using the dream interview technique for the first time with someone, I usually introduce it briefly by name and may mention that Delaney's books (1981 and 1991) are available if he or she is interested to pursue it further. Many of my patients are constantly seeking new psychological readings. I explain that this method involves a series of questions designed to help them describe the people and things in the dream in such a way that someone could distinguish them clearly from something or somebody similar, hence, the term "descriptive definition." Then, I explain, I will recapitulate their dream to them in segments, using their descriptions somewhat like translations, so that they can see if any segment of the dream fits any aspect of their current waking life. If they are willing to give it a try, we move into the questions. I always ask patients to work with the dream interview method whenever they bring a dream to therapy for the first time with me, and to date, no one has refused.

Patients who have been in therapy before may already be familiar with a method of dream interpretation, but that is not a contraindication for using the dream interview method. If a patient has incorporated certain beliefs about symbols from previous dreamwork, then these beliefs become part of the descriptive definitions—but only part. In addition, I elicit the full description of the symbol in order to ensure the completeness of the definition. For example, if the dreamer believes that snakes are sexual symbols, then this would be perhaps the "relevant association" or even the "essential nature," depending on the strength and nature of his or her belief. One would still need the other six components for a complete descriptive definition of the particular snake in the dream. In contrast to Jungian and Freudian techniques, the therapist's beliefs and knowledge about symbols are totally irrelevant with this method: the dream and its images belong entirely to the dreamer. Instead, the therapist's role as a dream interviewer is that of an experienced traveler (a Martian even!) in the unknown land of the patient's dream. The traveler knows of probabilities and possibilities, but has to consult a local (the dreamer) for the 'facts,' and of course, has to ask with sensitivity and tact but also the determination to discover.

In practice, I find I scan dreams for pivotal images or distinctive feelings or turns in the plot as soon as the patient has told me the whole dream. Focussing on these can lead to a rapid bridge that condenses the interpretative process into less time; this is frequently an important consideration for therapists in a 45–50 minute session. The risk is that one may miss an important detail or even bridge inaccurately from too narrow a premise. However, any minor image can provide a descriptive definition that will serve as a quick check for precision because when the bridge is correct, every single detail, color, or sequence, when descriptively defined, will also fit the identified circumstance. One or two discrepancies could be accounted for by an incomplete descriptive definition or the dreamer's lack of awareness. Too many unplaced details indicate we're probably on the wrong track and need to reexplore the bridge. This is a very similar process to differential diagnoses and rule outs in medical practice.

The most common difficulty that arises is with people who want their dream interpreted but resist the technique's direction and want to control and limit what they explore. They resent the constraint of formulating a complete definitive description and often prefer flights of associations. I usually explain that my skills are limited in other techniques (with the reasons if they ask for them) and have them consider their priorities and choices—even changing therapist's if they really want expertise in another method of dream interpretation. No one has terminated over the issue to date, though a few keep to their preferred method, foregoing much help from me. Many have come to recognize their resistance to the specific clarity of insight that this method can offer in contrast to other techniques; some elect to do fewer or no dreams; others resign themselves to the rote quality of the technique for the results, "Oh yeah, the Martian business!"

Consultation Liaison

Many of the interventions used by psychiatric consultation liaison services are based on someone's character and pathology, which determine his or her responses to certain situations. Dream interviewing can sometimes facilitate the process because it not only effectively focuses attention on the specific psychodynamics of a problem and delineates the appropriate level at which the patient is probably ready to address it, but it also introduces the concepts with which to tackle it. Unlike long-term psychotherapy, where one would use this insight to open further exploration, in consultation, one uses dream interviews to design a strategy to support existing strengths and useful defenses that facilitate patient management and recovery. The first dream example demonstrates this clearly.

Inpatient work, moreover, deals with hospitalized people who have ample time to sleep and dream, and once they are not acutely ill, they often have little else of interest to compete with their dream recall. They readily discuss dreams with staff and medical students who ask, so this technique can be of use to nurses and students on these services as well as the consultation liaison professionals. In addition, in both leading support groups and teaching seminars on coping and the psychiatric aspects of medical practice at the University of California at San Francisco, I found dream interviewing of additional benefit in helping medical students and residents deal with their own countertransference to medical and surgical patients (Smith, 1984).

Example No. 1. I was asked to do a second-opinion psychiatric consultation on a hospitalized patient suffering from severe nausea and vomiting following abdominal surgery for colon cancer resection with an initial good recovery and a subsequent relapse. Her medical and surgical work up was entirely negative, yet the severity of the medical situation was such that without symptomatic resolution within a few days, she would have to undergo a laparotomy. The surgeon wanted to avoid that in her debilitated state if at all possible. I saw her once for a history, then discussed her case with the previous consultant. The obvious issues about her very stressful job situation had been well covered, and the symptoms were unabated. So in desperation, since I was still only learning dream interview skills, I asked if she had described any dreams, and indeed she had described one to the consultant. Accordingly, on my second visit, we discussed her despair and then:

L. K. F.: I heard from P. (consultant) that you've had a dream since you've been in the hospital about being in a pit with a faceless woman at the top with a whip? Is that right?

H. O.:   Yes, I'm in a pit, and this woman is at the top, whipping me.

L. K. F.: When did you have this dream?

> (I was orienting myself to her life in order to reconstruct a day note for the dream. Patients commonly do not consistently keep the written record that Delaney suggests, even when familiar with the recommendation.)

H. O.:   Two weeks ago.

> (Two weeks ago would be just before the beginning of the symptoms and about the time the nurses noted increasing depression in her postoperative course. Therefore, I thought the dream was likely to be related to the symptoms, a major event in her life at the time. Thus it was worth interpreting to see if further insight could be gained beyond the work she had already done with P. I had to begin by getting the definitions of symbols. She was so sick I didn't explain anything but plunged right in. She was also so resistant to being referred to a psychiatrist that I wanted to keep it as brief as possible.)

L. K. F.: Let's look at this dream a bit more. What is a whip? Pretend I am a Martian and have never seen one before. Can you tell me what it is?

H. O.:   Well, this was a horse whip, the kind you use to train animals.

L. K. F.:And who is the faceless woman? Describe her in the same kind of way.

H. O.:   She looked like S. (her boss).

L. K. F.: Who is S.? Tell me about her again.

H. O.   She is evil and deceptive. She carries a sweet smile and then secretly attacks people. She's a very insecure woman, very inferior, no education, dull. She seems stupid and malicious.

> (The description of S. was consistent with the work events we had already discussed and fit precisely her feelings about her boss, so I doubted this was an intrapersonal [subjective] representation of this very intelligent, highly educated, patient who had been very direct in her initial attack on me. Therefore, I assumed that it was an interpersonal [objective] representation of S. as H. O. experienced her in her everyday life and I moved on to the action in the dream. Some issues, of course, may be both intrapersonal and interpersonal, but the patient will bridge to them as they are able to see them, at the time they are working on the dream. This may include a recognition of both levels, and reworking an old dream can therefore be very helpful.)

L. K. F.: What were you doing in the dream?

H. O.: I wasn't fighting back. I was trapped in the pit. I couldn't get out. I couldn't fight back because the whip was coming down on me.

> (She had vividly dramatized the helplessness she was experiencing consciously about her work situation, so I thought I was right about the dream relating to her work. I decided we would work with the dream image for a few more minutes to see if there were any possible courses of action that might now be suggested by the new conceptualization presented in the dream—namely, her relative passivity in the face of this whip. I chose to do this before bridging to the interpretation because she was both so sick and feeling defeated and initially so resistant. I wanted her to find or devise her own way out of the work situation that she had so clearly pictured in this dream metaphor. I find that staying with the dream image sometimes seems to allow more psychological freedom to explore alternative behaviors.)

L. K. F.: Was there anything that you could have done in the pit?

H. O.: Maybe cover up—but there was nothing there. I was frightened and getting licks and dodged and ducked and danced, not maimed—like I was her little tiger.

L. K. F.: (Aha! The first power image, though "little.")
A tiger? Not a pussycat?

H. O.: No, a tiger.

> (So she has stated it again, but she still does not see the power yet).

L. K. F.: What do tigers in the circus do when they don't like what the trainer is demanding, and he or she cracks the whip at them?

> (I still chose to stay with the dream symbols because it was moving well and she was most cooperative between vomiting and retching and excessive salivation.)

H. O.: They catch the whip, and pull it. They bite at it.

> (By her face I could tell that she was now making the emotional connection to the power and the bridge to her working life.)

L. K. F.: Do you think you could get a little more in touch with the tiger in you in this work situation and maybe jerk the whip a little bit yourself?

> (At this point we had finished the dream, and I needed to check out the image interpretation and the suggested course of action.)

H. O.: Smile.

> (This was the first time.)

This led to an active discussion of such courses of action represented by "pulling and biting the whip" that she might employ when she left the hospital and went back to work. By the next day, she had reestablished her assertiveness and mobilized her defenses against the kind of abuse to which she had been subjected at work. Her symptoms were considerably better, the nurses were pleased, and the surgeon was relieved, although the vomiting was not completely resolved.

The dream interview, however, had been so complete and effective in the area of the work problem, that I was then convinced that the symptoms were indeed fundamentally psychologically rather than physiologically based. There had to be a second issue we had missed and that had been obscured by the very significant work conflict. Entirely based on this conviction, I went back over the history on the third visit and uncovered a major secret issue of fifteen years' duration that had been disturbed by the prospect of death from cancer or anesthesia.

When I began to explore this issue with her, the retching increased significantly, blending with sobs and completely interrupting our conversation. With the help of a second incubated dream that night, we did substantial work on this exquisitely painful area of loss on the fourth day. When I walked in on the fifth visit, she was sitting in a chair, drinking liquids. The physical symptoms were completely resolved. She went home three days later after a final session in which she was able to satisfy her curiosity about how we had come to uncover an issue she had so skillfully masked for so many years, and which would probably have remained buried without the pit dream.

Brief Psychotherapy

The dream interview method of dream interpretation lends itself naturally to brief therapy that is designed to resolve problems using limited insight. It is invaluable for resolving small or immediate issues and reestablishing emotional equilibrium. In addition, both brief treatment and the dream interview method can model for patients an approach to problem solving that they can subsequently apply to a variety of situations, independent of therapy.

Example No. 2. A fifty-year-old, overweight woman called me to see if I was available to work with her in brief therapy for "blocking" on a job-related examination that she had been strongly encouraged to take by her supervisor. She had not yet written for the application for the exam, which was to take place in a few weeks. She explained that she had had considerable therapy in the past and only wanted a brief course for this specific problem of procrastination.

L. K. F.: (Phone call.) That's something I can work on with you. What's your schedule?

M. R.: Saturday is best for me.
   (A usual workday for me.)
L. K. F.: O. K. (We arranged a time.) You know, there's a dream technique that can be very useful in dealing with issues you're blocked about. It's called incubation. Are you familiar with it?
M. R.: No.
L. K. F.: What you do is, ask yourself a question before going to sleep. In your case you might ask, "Why am I blocking on this exam?" Then you write down any dream you get when you wake up, even if it seems totally unrelated. Incubation can be really useful if it works and you remember the dream—and you've got nothing to lose if it doesn't. What do you think?
M. R.: Sounds interesting. Now, what do I do?
L. K. F.: Formulate a question that you really want to know the answer to, such as "Why am I blocking?" or "How can I get started on this exam?" Something like that. Be sure it's one you're comfortable with, otherwise you won't remember the dream. Then write the question down verbatim before you go to sleep because the dream answer depends on the specific question you asked. OK?
M. R.: Yes.
L. K. F.: Then keep a pencil and paper by your bedside and write down any dream or dreams you remember when you wake up. *Any* dream, even if it's about giraffes! And bring it in to your appointment, and I'll show you how I work with dreams. The technique I use is Gayle Delaney's, if you've heard of her book, *Living Your Dreams*?
   (She was someone familiar with therapy and might already have some knowledge in this area.)
M. R.: No, I haven't, but I'll try it.
L. K. F.: Fine. See you Saturday and bring the question and the dream if you get one.
   (In manipulating dreams with incubation or lucidity (Gackenbach, 1989; LaBerge, 1985), I recommend, like Delaney, against any approach that is essentially blind repression or escape. Lucidity is an awareness during a dream that you are dreaming. You can use it to take control of the dream action. I encourage patients to collaborate with their unconscious and to seek understanding, direction, clarity, or motivation, not destruction or avoidance of images. This leaves the unconscious free to design an answer or strategy that takes into account deep issues totally outside conscious awareness.)

[At the first session.]

M. R.:   Well, I got a dream.

L. K. F.: What did you ask?

M. R.:   Why am I blocking?

L. K. F.: OK. Do you want to tell me the dream?

M. R.:   I was with N. walking. She is much older now, but in the dream she was seven or eight. We were trying to go someplace in P. and I had a map, but I could not read the map. I am real directional. I looked at the map more closely, and it was like a city but without names and lots of culs-de-sac around the edges, and that scared me. I then awoke and realized the map was of B., the town I am originally from. That put me back into the realization of an old dilemma that I had. And I had been priding myself on having moved past this!

   (Clearly, the patient had already begun to work on this dream and the issue of immobilization. I wanted to proceed with the definitions, however, in order to get the more detailed information and the clues for action that she might not yet have access to.)

L. K. F.: Who is N.? Can you tell me a little more about her? What was the most striking thing about her at age seven or eight?

M. R.:   N. was a large child, a tall, rather pretty woman, the remnant of a life that I once had and whom I now live with. She is my companion of a kind.

   (This reflects relationship and physical characteristics but not personality, so I tried again. I did not get distracted with exploring what 'companion of a kind' meant. It may not be relevant to the interpretation of her blocking dream.)

L. K. F.: What kind of character is she?

M. R.:   Charming socially, friendly, full of fun, with a determination and anger underlying that is startling when you first encounter it. Right now, she is angry because I want more separation from her.

   (If this had been someone familiar with the method, I might have stopped here and tried a intrapsychic-subjective bridge interpretation because we now have enough information to form a hypothesis of the psychodynamic. However, because she was unfamiliar with this technique and with me, I chose to continue with the definitions until she was comfortable with them and then move on in to the interpretation or bridging stage. This seemed less confusing.)

L. K. F.: What in your life now is seven or eight years old?

(Distortions are often a clue to a particular circumstance and are important to explore, as Example No. 4 with K. N.'s mother and No. 10 with K. E.'s boyfriend on the waiting room floor show. Noteworthy too is that age is handled differently in dream interviewing than it is in many other methods. It is not assumed that the image is of the patient at age seven or eight, but that the seven- or eight-year-old was born seven or eight years ago and, as such, is a part of the dreamer or someone else. The descriptive definition of the characters at the age in the dream is then particularly important.)

M. R.: I began this job seven or eight years ago.

L. K. F.: So the employee in you, at this particular job, is seven or eight years old?

M. R.: Yes, I suppose so.

(Her caution was secondary to the new perspective not a disagreement in fact. I suspected now that since the age had been distorted, N.'s traits belong exclusively (in this psychodynamic) to that part of herself that is the seven- or eight-year-old employee on this job. Dream distortion thus adds to the information about the situation in an extremely concise and specific way. But we're not finished with the dream.)

L. K. F.: What is P.? Tell me what kind of a town that is, as if I had never heard of it or been there. How would you describe it? How is it different from Y. or D.?

(Other similar, familiar towns.)

M. R.: P. is when I worked in the county, and my baby-sitter was there. It is a small suburban town. I liked it—I really . . . I had an enthusiasm about my work and where I was going that has never been as clear and as strong and satisfying since. It was the beginning of my transition and escape from being married and from isolation. I lived in S. at the time when there was a very artificial quality to that life and a husband who made a lot of money.

(She had given me all I needed to now summarize her description and associations into the complete, unique, but succinct descriptive definition.)

L. K. F.: So P. is a small, suburban town where your baby-sitter lived and that represents a time in your life characterized by enthusiastic, satisfying work and a transition from artificiality and isolation.

M. R.: Yes.

(This setting description firmly sets the stage for the dream and its meaning, similarly to a day note but more certainly because it is part of the dream itself. It is not limited by facts but includes misconceptions, feelings, functions, beliefs, and personal significance. I now expected the dream to deal with career identity and perhaps a personal identity as it relates to work, or artificiality or isolation, or help with childcare. I also felt sure this was the dream related to her incubated question.

Since people dream four or five dreams a night, occasionally the dream they recall after an incubation may be unrelated to the question asked. Yet I find that the dream is, almost always relevant. When teaching workshops, Delaney and I sometimes interpret an incubated dream before the dreamer reveals the question in order to dramatize the precision of this technique. It is noteworthy here too that 45-minute naps (non-REM) can also produce useful dreams, even though dreams are more frequently reported from REM sleep. This, incidentally, is clinical evidence to support the sleep research that points out that REM sleep is not equivalent to dream sleep, despite the frequent misnomer (Othmer et al., 1969).)

L. K. F.: Let's move on.

M. R.: OK.

L. K. F.: What about B.? What kind of a place is that?

M. R.: My childhood, my mother; it was also the place to go when you were upwardly mobile and black. It was where I lived when I was first married, where my first two children were born, and where I moved from a parental situation into my own home.

(She had described the particular phase in her life that the town B. depicted, and strictly speaking, that's all I needed for the dream interpretation. But this is someone on whom I had absolutely no history yet, and I wanted to orient myself to her life so that I could remember the details later.)

L. K. F.: When did you live there?

M. R.: After high school.

L. K. F.: And you left?

M. R.: About ten years later.

(Back to the dream. Her description had lacked feelings of any sort, I realized, and had more associations than definition yet. I needed something to tie the associations together into a definition. Questions about images are commonly answered with associations by patients who have previous experience with either Freudian or Jungian methods of dream interpretation. Their experience often provides motivation to look at dreams, but it often impedes the collection of the concrete information necessary for descriptive definitions.)

L. K. F.: Do you like B.?

M. R.: I'm mixed about B. It was a place that nearly broke me emotionally. It's draining, blankness, emptiness, gutted.

(That's feelings! Now I think I have enough to bridge.)

L. K. F.: If we were to translate this dream and use the descriptive definition that you have provided in the place of symbols, would it make sense for your examination block? Let's try it. Is there a part of you that is on the surface socially charming and friendly and full of fun and yet underneath is extremely determined and angry (N.)? Are you in a place in your life where you have a real sense of direction about your life, and yet, although you have available the tools you need—the map—to get where you are going, you can't understand it because it is blank, as in blocked?

M. R.: (Nod's.)

(She had obviously followed me through a huge amount all at once, so I went on to the part she had already figured out. It was now in context and I expected she could use it to undo the block when we had finished with the dream.)

L. K. F.: In addition, the blankness is similar to the kind of blankness you felt in your twenties when you lived in B. Does this seem to fit your life now with respect to the exam or work?

M. R.: (Big sigh.) Then I was depressed and naïve and enmeshed in my family at the time I lived in B. I wonder if that fits my current job family.

(Once one is in the correct life context with the dream, all the details should firm up the details of the dynamic, like the last pieces in a partially completed jigsaw puzzle.)

L. K. F.: And do N.'s qualities—especially the underlying anger—relate to the job?

M. R.: You know, I'd not been aware that this was frightening to me, but I suppose it is. I like what I do, from day to day, but I have difficulties with the system.

(I assume she is extrapolating from block and anger to fear, but I need to be sure.)

L. K. F.: How?

M. R.: Well, the job is dead-end.

L. K. F.: As in culs-de-sac?

M. R.:   (Chuckle.) I suppose so.

We spent the rest of the hour discussing the job situation generally and used the image of N. in the dream to explore the anger she felt, knowing it was associated with her inability to read the blank map because, in the dream, she was walking with N. and carrying the blank map. Since this was her first session and we had unearthed an enormous quantity of material rapidly, I checked out her response.

L. K. F.: How do you feel about all this in your first session?
M. R.:   We've jumped in the middle. But if I didn't, it would take me forever to get into it, and I sense some relief. It doesn't kill me; it allows me to live.

We then explored any reluctance she might have to giving up her old pattern represented in the dream by B. She looked at whether or not there might be some way she could both get where she wanted to go (pass the examination) and avoid the dead-end aspect of this particular job. In fact, by the second session the following week, she had discovered what she was angry about at work and had begun dealing with the issue with her supervisor. She had also written for the examination application, something she had been unable to do for months before. We had a total of four sessions, and she was kind enough to call me later in the year to let me know she had passed the preliminary examination and had lost considerable weight! She wrote eighteen months later to give me permission to use this dream and to say that she felt the gains were lasting, despite the rapid dream-dependent insight to which she had been unaccustomed. She had also passed the final examination.

Long-Term Treatment

Early Stages of Therapy. In this phase, the task is to formulate the problem, and dreams interpreted by a dream interviewer are especially helpful because they do just that.

Example No. 3. A 31-year-old woman office technician began therapy three months before this dream, wishing to deal with a chronic sense of dissatisfaction and depression in her life, particularly with a relationship that had ended recently and then restarted. She was on jury duty when she had this dream. She mentioned having slept badly because of the jury duty disrupting her life and then remembered this particular fragment. Because of the instructions for the jury, she was looking at all judgments in her life, wondering what their bases were and becoming aware of her prejudices. This day-note information set the stage very specifically for the dream. Such orientation is especially helpful when there is only a dream fragment.

M. G.: We were in a jury setting and demonstrating talents, and G. started singing like a bird. It was a nice dream. People were laughing and talking.

L. K. F.: Who is G?

M. G.: G. is engaged to a friend's friend. I saw her at a barbecue, and she had written some poems about freedom. She's political and devoted to the struggle. She's overpersonal. I don't know G. that well. She must take a tremendous amount of responsibility in her life.

> (This is a scanty definition, which often happens when someone has only limited information about a person. It was sufficiently like the patient, however, that I thought she would easily recognize G. as a part of herself from this description and left it. Again you will notice I avoid the temptation to explore the details eg. 'the struggle,' 'overpersonal.' My agenda now is the dream dynamic. The rest can wait.)

L. K. F.: What is a bird?

M. G.: A bird is pretty; it's free; it has a good time flying around and gets to sing. It was beautiful trilling in the dream.

L. K. F.: Do you ever feel like the feeling you had in the dream?

> (An early bridge try from feelings alone sometimes works and saves time when it does.)

M. G.: I occasionally . . . I felt that way before I left work to go work on the jury.

> (Her bridge was vague and not explicit enough to be sure of the specific dynamic referred to in her life. So I elected to keep it in mind and get more data.)

L. K. F.: What is a jury?

M. G.: A group of people going to judge somebody and determine his or her future. I felt this guy was guilty, and I felt sympathy for him.

> (Not a complete definition but specific enough that I was willing to try another bridge.)

L. K. F.: Do you feel you are currently sitting in judgment on somebody for example? Perhaps yourself?

M. G.: Yes.

L. K. F.: Are you aware of a part of you that might be like G.? Devoted and passionate and that you do not know very well. It seems that she is able to enjoy the freedoms of a bird with its beauty and fun.

M. G.:   When we were talking last week about my future and competition and stuff, I did feel like a bird.

(This was news to me, and very helpful because it was the first indication to both of us of her recognition of a way out of her chronic depression through a part of herself, represented by G.)

L. K. F.:   You seemed more in touch with your fear of failure and your concerns about the burdensomeness of the responsibility last week.

M. G.:   Yes, it's interesting to think about it not as success or failure, but about the fun in trying. It's a free thing to be free of the judgment, and then I can move as I want to move.

This outlined a broader aspect of her difficulty in life, not restricted to her relationship, which had been her topic to date. Not surprisingly, it has proved to be the more basic issue, and throughout the subsequent months of therapy, we have continued to pursue these issues of responsibility and guilt and sympathy, fear of failure versus passionate involvement, freedom and fun in the context of her internal jury.

Middle Stages of Therapy. Dreams in the middle stage of therapy can address any of the issues being discussed or those being avoided. Example No. 5 is a case of the latter. These middle-therapy dreams can be difficult to understand, especially without a day note because of the number of possible bridges and levels. When there are parts of a dream that never do fall into place, a general impression of other parts can still be helpful. Prior to using this technique, a general impression was the best I ever achieved, and it always seemed incomplete and left me feeling vaguely thwarted. I suspect that it is this frustration that leads some therapists to accept what seems to me to be projecting meanings onto a dream from a theoretical framework. In my view, this just leads further and further away from the patient and his or her own capabilities of mastery of issues, the essential foundation for a successful course of psychotherapy. However, when one has a method of oneirocritism that opens many dreams so beautifully to interpretation, the occasional incomplete interpretation is not unexpected and can be tabled with its meaning still obscure. I have also been startled to find that months and years later, when other issues have surfaced and I look back at a patient's old dreams in my notes, the totally opaque parts of a dream are sometimes suddenly quite transparent.

The following example demonstrates how the dream interview method can produce specific, usable information in the course of long-term intensive psychotherapy.

Example No. 4. A 27-year-old professional man from a violent home had been in therapy for two years, initially for depression, which had considerably resolved. More recently, he has been working on his interpersonal relationships, a frequent source of his depressive episodes. A couple of weeks before this therapy appointment, he noticed he had begun to obsess. He was exploring the possible sources of this increased anxiety and suspected that it came from his current close relationship with D. He began this session with a dream, as he often does. He has remarkable recall without notes, despite intermittently strong denial in other areas of therapy, and finds dreams the fastest way to discover what he feels. He is usually impatient about resolving issues.

K. N.:   I want to start with this dream. I was back home in my house that I lived in during high school. My mother and stepfather were fighting. It was so real. He was drunk or high and lying down. She was cutting him, and he got up and asked her why she was cutting on him. I was listening in the next room, and I ran in and said, "Y'all don't realize what this is doing to me. STOP!"

L. K. F.:   Oh my!

K. N.:   Yeah!

(Dramatic material like this, even when not totally new, is very attractive to therapist to immediately explore, so one needs to make a decision at this point, as a dream interviewer: are you going to interpret the dream or not? K. N. and I had already done lots of dreams using the dream interview technique. He had set the agenda, and I saw no reason to object. The dream usually leads to specific information that enhances the general information one gets from open exploration.)

L. K. F.:   Who is your stepfather?

K. N.:   Immature—he was a heroin addict, weak. A pretty-boy kind of person. Kind of wild. He was trying the best that he could to be a productive person.

L. K. F.:   And your mother? How old is she now?

(His mother is involved only peripherally in his current life, and she has changed a lot over the years, so I needed to know which definition to seek, since I suspected a subjective interpretation.)

K. N.:   Fifties.

L. K. F.:   And in the dream?

K. N.:   Forties.

L. K. F.: What was she like then?

K. N.:   She was real frustrated then, feeling rejected, and she would try so hard to make him what she wanted.

L. K. F. What was that? A husband and father?

> (I sometimes suggest things when I have an idea or hypothesis, and want to rule it in or out. I also do it to facilitate the process, but I try not to do it with a suggestible person or someone reluctant to assert their own opinions and ideas over mine. K. N. is very frank.)

K. N.:   A husband, never a parent! And he would do it for three or four weeks and then he would backslide. She saw his problem as a personal assault on her. She was possessive too.

L. K. F.: When did you have the dream?

> (When I work with dreams in therapy, I commonly establish the day context later in the interpretive process. By then the definitions may have jogged the dreamer's memory and evoked some recall of the day's events preceding the dream. We both suspected that these characters were subjective representations of parts of himself, since neither figures a great deal in his current walking life. Whenever such difficult material surfaces from a dream, I like to have as much of the day-to-day reality setting and context available as possible. This allows us to move easily from the insight derived from the dream into its application to the patient's current life. In this case, all I knew so far was that his increased anxiety was leading to the distressing obsessive symptoms, and I needed more specific information.)

K. N.:   I had gone out with D. Saturday night to the beach. It was real nice and I didn't stay. He was hurt and disappointed, and I was guilty, but not wanting to give in to this relationship. I want to keep it where I need it. It's not a matter of want.

> (This gives enough information to try a bridge. I try to use words from the patient's definitions and dream wherever possible and perhaps include hypotheses I have. He has mentioned in therapy an internal conflict, with much less affect than in the dream, but it fits the quality.)

L. K. F.: I wonder if you have been beating up on yourself? For not performing up to expectations, perhaps? For being addicted to this relationship with D.?

K. N.:   I have been feeling weak over the past few weeks, and I have been pounding at myself for my difficulties in making this life transition that I'm in now and for my need for this relationship.

(Note how he amends my hypothesis to fit his own experiences of the issue more precisely.)

L. K. F.: But at present, it seems this relationship is valuable to you.

(Hence the conflict. We went on to discuss the dynamics, which he now understood, of his recent obsessional thoughts.)

It can be invaluable for someone to be able to conceptualize various constellations of feelings as one particular person. Whenever K. N. began to be self-critical over the next few days and weeks, he could conceptualize that part of himself as his mother at forty, a frustrated person who personalized events and felt rejected and then in turn "cut" and "pounded" the weak, immature stepfather in him who was doing the best he could.

The relationship with D. meets his need despite its inherent inadequacies, i.e., it takes care of the stepfather in himself. It is destructive to his present-day self—the observer in the other room—when his "mother" attacks his "stepfather." It would be more productive for the "mother" in him to look inward and grow and develop independently, as his real mother has done in the last ten years, and for the "stepfather" to confront his limitations and begin maturing. This is the long-term process, of course.

This dream clarified another piece of his understanding of his internal dynamics and their origins and present expression. Following the dream, he began to feel better, more content, and calmer, with fewer anxiety symptoms, and decreased use of alcohol, cigarettes, and drugs. He explored his concerns about using the relationship with D. until he didn't need him anymore and his wish to be fair. He explored some of his current relationships with women and why they were not adequate, and he examined how he felt during high school, where he always felt rejected and alienated.

L. K. F.: How could your stepfather have done better in life?

K. N.:   He needed to invest himself in relationships with people and love, and he couldn't do it because of his past.

This is, of course, the long-term theme that we are working on—his own difficulty with interpersonal relationships as a course of his depression. He is aware that he has far more resources than his stepfather but similar limitations.

End Stages of Therapy. I use the end of the termination phase of therapy to review the progress made, to identify any unfinished business that is apparent, to evaluate the current status of the patient, and to extrapolate a little as to what might be anticipated in the future. Dreams interpreted at this time can be very helpful in summarizing these four areas and providing a simple format by which such issues can be recalled.

The following example illustrates issues in which progress had been made as well as area's of unfinished business, which would be important in the patient's future. It is also an example of significant resistance to working with a dream.

Resistance can occur at all stages of the dream interpretation process and must be distinguished from inexperience, performance anxiety, lack of conceptual skills, and incomplete or erroneous interpretations. They can present similarly because resistance can appear as an inability to recall any dreams, a refusal to write down dreams that are remembered on awakening so that they are forgotten, losing or forgetting the book or paper on which the dream has been recorded, omitting a crucial part of a dream, the inability to define something, or a total lack of recognition of issues worked on for months. This patient was familiar with the method and was not particularly anxious about her performance with me. She was denying familiar connections and resisting the dream interpretation process itself.

I address such resistance like any other, recognizing that it serves a valid function of defense. When the overt content looks ominous, I sometimes discuss the worst possible interpretation suspected about this dream. The patient is then free to take a look at the actual interpretation, which can be less frightening than their suspicions and often includes resources, options, and implications for action, as in Example No. 1. The reverse also occurs when patients plunge into a dream with no awareness of how upsetting the new understanding might be. It is the therapist's job—as the experienced traveler—to monitor how much anxiety the patient is feeling and titrate the amount of insight tolerable at any one time. In this example, because it was the final termination visit, I only tackled the resistance lightly.

Example No. 5. This woman was a single, unmarried graduate student completing her degree who had begun therapy with unresolved issues around her mother's death. She said as she came in for her last visit, "It's our last session—I'm finishing everything." She described the final process of her degree, the termination of her relationship with her boyfriend Joe, and the reappearance of a number of "old ghosts," namely, people that she had not seen for years. She discussed her friends who were seriously ill and noted her own good health and current athletic activity. She then mentioned that she had lots of dreams last night.

P. N.: I started to wear my black suit today, but my white silk blouse is dirty. (Smile.) I'm in touch with termination, but I'm not sad about it.

L. K. F.: What was the dream? Tell me one of them.

> (Since she had said there was a dream, I elected to choose this route through the resistance to her sadness about termination, since I hoped it might be a shortcut.)

P. N.: Mom and I were in a train station. It was raining inside and the place was packed. She held the umbrella real high, and I couldn't see anything but bodies and feet moving in a small shuffle because of the press of people. My mother was in front. She found a small space, and Ralph was with a white woman. (I got drunk with him after I broke up with Joe. It was fun.) I pointed him out to my mother, who said, "Eh?" She was not impressed with him. He came over and greeted me with a brief kiss and left.

L. K. F.: Who is Ralph?

P. N.: Ralph said, "Don't have kids without a man," and that's bothered me.

L. K. F.: Can you describe him as you would to a Martian?

> (I find that it is important when doing a dream not to be distracted by enticing associations, such as this remark of Ralph's. If they are relevant, they can be added to the definitions. Pursuing every association leads to information far too diffuse to be useful. She knows this, so she must still be resisting. I therefore chose to refocus her in the basic, concrete way.)

P. N.: He's an interracial man struggling with racial identity. He's very successful in his career and personally fucked up. That's like Joe.

> (Joe had been an interracial relationship about which she had had a number of concerns.)

L. K. F.: Who is your mother?

> (Deceased people are used in dreams similarly to people still alive but who are no longer in a person's current everyday life. They may be subjective intrapersonal parts of the patient or someone else in his or her life or, less commonly, objective parts that represent the residual relationship when a patient has not accepted his

or her death and behaves as if still alive. Therefore, I needed her definition of her mother now at the end of the therapy.)

P. N.:   Just my mother—nice, someone I looked up to. whose judgment I respect. She was trying to find a place less crowded and did, though I didn't realize she could see where she was going.

(This is exactly how she views many of her older women relatives, so it is far too generic a description to be definitive. She was being so resistant that I shifted to a less cathected topic after a few abortive tries to get more descriptions about her mother. She did add dream detail, though, which often happens. In the course of therapy she had often discussed using me in lieu of her mother, so I doubted that transference was all the dream had to say. I thought it was addressing a different level of mother issues more relevant now. Either way, it will be revealed by the bridge after I get the definitions. A key question to distinguish these levels would have been "Are you and your mother traveling together?" If they are, then this is probably not primarily a transference, dream since we are in reality separating. In my experience with the dream interpretation method, the dream deals with reality as it appears to the patient at the time of the dream.)

L. K. F.:   Tell me about the crowd.

P. N.:   They were all waiting to go somewhere. It didn't bother me, I wasn't pushed out—I was just blinded, and it impeded my progress.

L. K. F.:   Has your life been crowded recently?

(In the past, this patient has repeatedly dealt with difficult feelings by denying them and getting very busy, so I framed a shortcut speculative question that I expected would not be hard for her to acknowledge.)

P. N.:   Yes, I've been going out a lot—movies, dinner, it's so nice! Friday . . .

(She went on to describe a number of events and some anxiety she was having about where to go next in her life.)

L. K. F.:   So the train has not come yet?

(I wanted to try again to focus on the dream. I hoped the digression had decreased her anxiety, so I linked her current concerns about her next goal to the wait for the next train.)

P. N.:   No.

L. K. F.:   Do you feel that you have a Ralph in you? Someone who feels you shouldn't have children without a man and who is successful in his career and personally fucked up, struggling with racial identity?

P. N.: I don't like to admit it, but I guess I do. I have been aware of it, but I'm not paying any attention to it.

(So she is labeling this piece of unfinished business. Now I elect to see how far she would take it in this last session.)

L. K. F.: Was that the part of you that was involved with Joe?

P. N.: No, I was with Joe for the books and the foreign films, and I want to do more of those kinds of things.

(She has told me she sees books and foreign films as inconsistent with her own racial identity, so she is now denying her racial identity conflicts in her relationship with Joe. I still think I'm right, but I have to concede to her level of awareness—the dreamer is always right!—so I try another part of the dream. It should corroborate the actual theme and indicate the dynamic depicted by the dream.)

L. K. F.: In your dream, it looks as if you were taking care of yourself with the umbrella and that your mother was teamed with you quite successfully. How does this fit?

P. N.: My mother was much more integrated racially than I am. I think maybe I reacted and went overboard against her position before.

(Now we have the crucial description of mother. This was also a first admission of such an idea about her own racial identity. This bridge is consistent with the dream plot; her blind, slow progress in mother's wake, previously unaware that mother can see. Ralph is her first sighting—and a white woman whom we did not have time to explore. Because she denied my previous suggestion, I was careful to make this next question very open-ended.)

L. K. F.: So what do you think this dream tells you about your therapy and where are you now?

P. N.: Well, I think I'm better! I have enjoyed therapy, it was the usual kind of painful, (you'd expect from therapy) but it's a luxury. If you were closer (geographically), I'd have to come up with more symptoms to keep coming.

She is clearly not prepared to look further at this unfinished business in her last session, so we left it. We went on to review her first visit and the changes she had experienced since then. My private speculation was that she had now effectively teamed with her "mother" and was encountering the more racially integrated part of herself, instead of just rebelling, while she waits for her next move in life, exposed to but protected from rain inside (sadness?). This brief dream encounter with her racially conflicted, professionally successful part (Ralph) also revealed restrictions on childbearing; I suspected that issue might recur in the future. (It did.) She ended the hour by checking with me that I would still be available if she chose to return, a direct but not specific acknowledgment of more unfinished business.

Couple Therapy

I use the dream interview technique perhaps the least of all during couple therapy because couples work focuses on their interactions with one another, and dreams are uniquely personal. In addition, when a spouse dreams of a partner, a frank and complete description is sometimes impossible to obtain when there is limited openness in the relationship. Similarly, couples in therapy are often so significantly estranged that it is impossible to interpret dreams together at home or in the office because of the conflicts.

However, dreams about the marriage relationship are invaluable, and of course, dreams about partners often come up. When the partner is used interpersonally, like Perlmutter and Babineau (1983) I find it very helpful. The spouse is less likely to feel manipulated by the dreamer's pain described in a dream. However, whenever one can obtain a bridge to an intrapersonal interpretation of a spouse, it is also quite therapeutic because it reveals a constellation of traits common to both. Working on a dream in couples therapy permits both partners to begin to learn the process, so in relationships that can tolerate it, they can work at home with one another on their dreams. In my experience, well-functioning or open couples are more likely to share their dreams and their interpretations with one another, and they can use them for preventive and maintenance care of their relationship.

Example No. 6. The following dream is from a couple who had just been married after living together for a number of years and who returned to therapy because of a recurrence of their chronic relationship difficulties.

T. S.:   I was with my wife in a room after Alice's death. I was remembering Alice and feeling sad for my wife and the loss of Alice.
(This dream seemed to be about the relationship since they are both present and possibly in their own home—I'll need to check. Alice was a former relative, now deceased. I chose to explore this dream with this therapeutically experienced couple because both husband

and wife are quite frank, despite their severe relationship difficulties, which stem from lack of individuation.)

L. K. F.: What kind of room?

T. S.: A living room or den.

L. K. F.: Where you spend your time, socialize together?

(I was checking out my guess about his definition of a setting. I had heard about their room usage in the course of therapy, so I had a basis for my guess, but it is crucial not to project one's own ideas or to assume their ideas have not evolved or changed in the course of therapy.)

T. S.: Yes.

L. K. F.: Who is Alice? Pretend I've never heard of her.

T. S.: She was close to my wife. A nice lady in her own right. I knew her in high school. Spunky, interesting. Very unorthodox. Her death was a loss my wife felt most.

L. K. F.: Have you been recently grieving the loss of a spunky, unorthodox part of yourself?

(I could have added, "or your wife.")

T. S.: I was very upset the other morning. I was burning waffles in the kitchen and my wife had her hair in rollers and was looking fat! (Laughter.)

I suspected this husband was grieving the loss of their unorthodox living arrangement. It might therefore be important to him, and the dream suggests even more so to his wife (in his opinion) that they retain some interesting, unorthodox ways to keep the interest and spunk in their relationship. This had also been one of the difficulties before the marriage. Because dreams are not limited by reality, I could suggest that they look for ways to resurrect Alice in their relationship.

Group Therapy

My experiences in this context have come from three types of therapy groups. Dreams have been presented at will or on request in the course of both goal-oriented, long-term, psychodynamic psychotherapy groups and support groups. The third type of group had Gayle Delaney as a permanent oneirocritic consultant. Thus every member knew that dream interpretation was one of the major techniques to be used in this outpatient, insight-oriented, psychodynamic therapy group. As a result, members expected to bring in dreams, to learn the technique, and in due course to be able to work on one another's dreams both in and out of group if they chose. The telephone can be very useful for a half-hour of dream work.

As one would expect, there were more dreams presented in the third group. In the therapeutic support groups, the members seem initially to be more passive in their dream interpretation but soon participated in the same way as they would in any work by another member using interviewer questions. There were no other obvious differences.

We found group participation extremely productive during and after the bridging phase. Such interaction occurs (1) when the subjective part of a patient is discussed, particularly if it is symbolized by another group member; and (2) when confirming a symbol as not characteristic of the dreamer, and therefore objective or revealing subjective material previously concealed. These discussions were especially fruitful among the support groups formed of medical students, who are more closely acquainted with one another in their lives outside the group than are the strangers gathered to form most outpatient groups.

The major difficulty in using the dream interview method in groups is the monopolization of group time by a long dream. Even short dreams can be used to monopolize group time. It is important for the members to assert themselves appropriately and for the leaders to facilitate the group process in a way that is therapeutic for everyone. Although any work can be helpful, it will probably not yield the richness of a completed dream. This may mean that only one symbol of the dream can be explored, or just the plot or feelings, but the descriptive definition must be exclusively that of the dreamer to preserve the benefits of the dream interview method.

Dream interviewing sharply contrasts with Ullman's technique (1986). He encourages group members to associate to and project onto a dream, although the dreamer reserves ultimate possession. I encourage group members to approach someone else's dreams with questions so that the group becomes the dream interviewer. I encourage them to deal with their associations and projections personally, similar to Kolb (1985). This often includes their feelings of relief that someone else is on the hot seat, of resentment that someone is getting all the attention, or of amazement at another's descriptive definition of a cat and their recognition that people's viewpoints are indeed unique.

Example No. 7. This example was presented to the psychodynamic therapy group by a man having difficulty in his relationship with his wife following the birth of their first child.

M. Y.:   I had a dream that the union had won an election against management! I go for the prize, and on the way I get a sexy lady and feel her up while she has her legs wrapped around me and is also beside me at the same time, if you understand what I mean.

Group: (Lots of laughter.)

(This patient has had difficulty with assertiveness and anger in his marriage and had recently presented a dream to the group of bowing down to his mother. The dynamic in this one is less autocratic, so it sounds as if he is making progress.)

L. K. F.: What happened the day you had the dream?

Group
Member: Sounds good!

(This member—*not* the dreamer—also has trouble with assertiveness and yet is able to see a bridge for the dreamer towards increased assertiveness. This is a common phenomenon in group and is very therapeutic.)

Group: General laughter.

M. Y.: I had a fight with my wife last night and afterward felt more sexual than I had been feeling toward her. I'm also not flirting with other women since I've been married, and I'm pleased about that.

L. K. F.: It sounds as though the woman could then also be your wife? Both sexual partner and companion beside you? Or perhaps a part of yourself?

(After I had asked the first question so specifically, I realized that I had better broaden the options for this nonassertive man.)

M. Y.: Yeah, that seems right. (Nod.) My wife.

(A specific choice.)

As with any material raised in group, there are always issues that relate to more than one member, and assertiveness is a common problem, so this union-management dream image was very helpful. It also seemed to represent the group dynamic around this issue, and the less assertive members all recognized that M. Y. had designated his wife as management when in reality that was not mandatory. Similarly, the group members treat the leaders as management in situations where it is not required. This was briefly explored, and we left the interpretation at the level comfortable for the patient and the group at the time, knowing it will come up again.

Example No. 8. A medical student in a therapeutic support group devised the question, "What should I do with this relationship with my boyfriend?" for a dream incubation. Everyone was familiar with the repeated ups and downs of this relationship.

B. R.:   In the dream I am cleaning out the refrigerator, and the leftovers are there. I am surprised that some are still left. I had thought that they were all used up. I am pleased because they will tide me over until I can cook again.

Group: (Lots of laughter.)

B. R.:   But wait, wait. You know, I redid the incubation the next night because I didn't believe it, and the first part of the second dream I have to tell you because it is so funny. I am returning to a place to get another pair of glasses because I didn't like the first pair!

Group: (General laughter.)

L. K. F.: Well, let's take a look at the first one anyway. Maybe you can get some information out of it. What's a refrigerator?

B. R.:   Where you keep food to eat to take care of yourself.

L. K. F.: Care-taking source, then. Are you feeling too busy to cook or make something fresh?

B. R.:   I really am. I have so many decisions to make right now and so many things to consider.

She had not consciously been using this leftover relationship to tide her over. As a result, she was more distressed at each cycle than her friends would have expected, and the dream indicated she was making a deliberate choice for leftovers until she had time to create something better, and need not be distressed but rather pleased that it was available and adequate. This reconceptualization was very hard for her to accept because she's a perfectionist, but it made the relationship more tolerable over the next few months until she had time to invest in creating something new.

I couldn't resist the temptation to take a look at the second dream, and it appeared to be a much more detailed view of why this relationship was not her final choice and of what was missing in it for her. The second dream represented the relationship as a convenience stop along the way to a place which she defined as very satisfying. As the other group members participated in the interpretation, they were also able to see her close the gap between their perceptions of the relationship and her perception of it, which rewarded them for their consistent support for her during these repeated crises. They were also free to use the image of the leftovers, without appearing judgmental since it came from her whenever the next down cycle came.

Application to Symptoms and Situations

Depression

Some of the previous examples also come from people suffering from depression, such as the bird-trilling (Example No. 3), the dream of Alice (Example No. 6), and the union-management dream (Example No. 7). One case of special interest to me was that of a depressed man whose dream colors changed as his depression lifted. The gray and dark colors so characteristic of his earlier dreams gave way to more varied and vividly attractive colors in his later dreams, as his depression resolved.

Example No. 9. This dream came about a year after a 46-year-old man began therapy for chronic depression. He was feeling some progress, and at the end of the last session, had been wondering "how many layers of the onion are left to peel," i.e., how much more working through did he have to do before he would be finished with psychotherapy.

B. R.: Frank Sinatra is in a wheelchair and I am pushing him around. He knew my name too—I was surprised. I talked with him.
(This seems a little sparse. I wonder if there is more.)

L. K. F.: Where were you going?

B. R.: Maybe into or toward a hospital. Boy, I don't remember. I should have written it down. There, I'm being perfectionistic again.
(I deal with fragments just as if they were complete dreams, keeping in mind that the bridge may be harder to make because the dream is incomplete.)

L. K. F.: That's O.K. We can work with what we've got. Why is he in the wheelchair?

B. R.: It seemed a natural circumstance. He wasn't uncomfortable.

L. K. F.: Who is Frank Sinatra?

B. R.: I enjoy his toughness—when necessary. He's a mature man. His singing is a very pleasant skill. I used to love singing. There is lots of joy in it.

L. K. F.: So you recognize a Sinatra in you?

B. R.: I suppose in that way.

L. K. F.: But you have him in a wheelchair. He's disabled. Maybe we need to get him out of the wheelchair?

In fact, it was not until two years later that the patient began singing again and loving it. Three years later when he terminated therapy, he was considering developing a singing group tailored to his own needs.

Anxiety

Just the other day, a patient called in a crisis. He had an attack of dizziness with headache and malaise for which he had been seen in the emergency room the previous night. When nothing physical was found, and Tylenol was prescribed, he had the following dream that night, and so called me up very concerned about his health. The dream focused the primary cause of the anxiety attack clearly on the relationship he was in and showed the minor roles of two other possibilities: the shambles of his financial affairs (of which he was quite tolerant) and the total absence of his examination preparation. The possible courses of action were easily inferred from the dream, and a brief discussion of them was all that was necessary for the patient to again feel in control. Further discussion was left for the next appointment, and what might have been a prolonged conversation was over in twenty minutes. Example No. 4 (the parents' fight) also addressed anxiety.

Example No. 10. I had just seen the patient recently in a support group session and was familiar with the fact that she was getting along well with her boyfriend and might move in with him. She called me in a crisis.

K. E.:   I was so petrified. I'm so confused! I don't know whether I'm overreacting to making a commitment or whether it's real. I'm premenstrual, too. Anyway, I have had this dream, and I just can't stand it anymore, so I hope you don't mind, but that's why I called you.

L. K. F.: It's fine. Tell me the dream.

(I felt the dream would automatically delineate feelings for us. In my experience, premenstrual tension increases the intensity of feelings, but does not generate new conflicts, so I expected the fresh dream to depict the problem.)

K. E.:   I was in this room, a waiting room. There were three couches. I was in one corner. Next to me on the couch was this Vietnam vet without legs and on the floor next to him was my boyfriend. A second Vietnam vet was in the corner of the couch adjacent to mine. We're all small and talking about things, and the conversation leads to F. (A town). The other people in the room are losers. I quipped that "living in F. is like living in a

Third-World country where there are ninety different Third-World groups with less than two hundred people in each."

L. K. F.: What's a waiting room?

(I saw no easy way to shortcut this one as I scanned it, since the impact of the quip was not clear to me or the action particularly distinctive, so I used the methodical approach to each image that works well with any dream—beginning with the setting in order to place the issue in her life.)

K. E.: Where you anticipate or get ready for something to happen.

L. K. F.: Does this fit part of your life now?

(I knew it did, but I wanted her to frame the bridge and get in touch with that waiting room aspect of her life.)

K. E.: Oh everything, residency, moving, my life, a man.

(I had not realized that she felt it was her entire life. It always pays to ask and not assume!)

L. K. F.: O.K. So it's about what's happening to you right now in general. What is this guy without legs? What is significant about such a guy?

K. E.: Sad. Not much to offer, not much to look forward to. Unimportant and out of it. Couldn't walk away if he wanted to.

L. K. F.: So he's trapped?

K. E.: That's the way I feel a bit now. A hint of it. And it's definitely what I fear if I were to move in with my boyfriend.

(She has made the jump to subjective interpretation without a word from me, and it fits. Remember this amputee is between K. E. and the boyfriend, separating them. Her boyfriend's position is a departure from the usual waiting room behavior, which is always an informative point in a dream.)

L. K. F.: Now, what's your boyfriend doing on the floor?

K. E.: He's feeling separate, a little bit hurt, like he was yesterday. Oh, I was so mean to him!

L. K. F.: O.K. So that fits him clearly. Now what's the crack about F.? I'm a Martian, and I don't know what you mean.

K. E.: Well, my boyfriend used to live and work in F. It was a dig, the kind of thing I say when I'm anxious.

L. K. F.: Like you did yesterday when you were mean to him?

(An action tie-in to real life, perhaps.)

K. E.: Yeah, that's right.

L. K. F.: Who's the other guy?

K. E.: I don't know. He's just a shadow.

L. K. F.: So what's a Third-World group?

(I am switching to the plot here because we have now defined the people and the entire action of the dream is in the quip. The rest is a still-life scene. It is crucial that people be frank about their prejudices when defining political, ethnic, or racial groups in order to get a meaningful and accurate definition.)

K. E.:   They are foreign people, transplanted. They live in their own little societies and cultures not shared by others. I dislike some—I feel I don't belong with some, but I'm fine with the Blacks and Irish, for example.

L. K. F.: And F. itself?

K. E.:   Another place I'm afraid of going. Not just because of an old boyfriend but because it's boring, flat, ugly, narrow-minded, and socially unaware. My boyfriend wants to go because it will be good for his career. I don't want to go.

L. K. F.: And two hundred people. Is that too few, too many, enough?

K. E.:   Enough.

L. K. F.: So let's see if we can put this part together. Let me make a jump from what I know about your past that you've talked about in group. Was your mother's married life like F.?

K. E.:   Oh yes, exactly. That's what is foreign to me. I'm not that way. Everyone in my family was isolated, narrow, enclave, and my boyfriend is a lot narrower than I am.

L. K. F.: Are you afraid that you will get absorbed or lose yourself if you get closer to him?

K. E.:   I am asserting myself as different from him. That's why I am so critical of him. I told him his hair was to short. Oh my!
          (She recognized here the connection of short hair and what she considered to be narrow-minded and socially unaware.)

L. K. F.: You sound like you're determined not to be subsumed by that narrow-mindedness and become powerless like the vet.
          (Just a restatement of what she said and implied, which was intended to help her continue.)

K. E.:   I've had this problem with men before. I drive them away. I'm not comfortable being happy. Thank you. That really helped. I feel better now. I'll think about it.

L. K. F.: Maybe you should get your vet a motorized wheelchair for the time being!

K. E.:   A "Huh" of new awareness.
          (This may seem rather insensitive to people with disabilities. However the legless vet is *her* choice of image and the interviewer has to work with that, and not be influenced by political and social cor-

rectness, or he/she will lose the dreamer and any hope of their psychological growth. So 'a motorized wheelchair' is a metaphor for outside help, or for a management tool for a disability until 'the vet' obtains some kind of new legs because *anything* is possible with a dream image! I wanted to indicate clearly that this part of herself needed some help and perhaps some major work sometime in the future, but our contract is therapeutic support, not intensive psychotherapy, so I felt comfortable leaving it with a joke. She was obviously more in touch with what the anxiety was about, but I was not as clear as she was. There were certainly a lot of issues here that would take a lot of work. I did understand that she was distancing her boyfriend by being very critical of him and that she was doing this because she feared being trapped in a relationship like her mother's. This conflict was producing the anxiety, and her insight into this diminished her confusion and made her feel less panicked.)

Psychosomatic Symptoms

Visible physical symptoms provide some of the most obvious indications of the effectiveness of oneirocriticism because the symptoms resolve when they are accurately understood and the issue is successfully addressed, such as occurred with the vomiting surgery patient in Example No. 1. Even though alexithymic patients with psychosomatic symptoms such as asthma are often able to recall only white dreams (i.e. awareness of dreaming with no dream content), (Monday, 1987) when they do actually recall dreams, dream interviewing can provide a beginning feeling vocabulary for them. I have also explained to such patients how to enhance their recall with a day note at bedtime and a paper and pencil beside the bed to make a daily awakening note. This almost always produces results within two weeks. The area of dreams and somatic symptoms also provides interesting possibilities for research on comparison of techniques of dream interpretation and for even more basic documentation of the relevance of dreams themselves to everyday life, especially to illness (Sabini, 1981). The following example is quite typical of my experiences.

Example No. 11. This 33-year-old woman had developed angioedema in the previous few months. She was appropriately treated medically, with some improvement, but in her attempts to control the disabling symptoms, she incubated the following dream: Why am I allergic?

F. W.:   I am in a big banquet room trying to set the tables. I am a waiter or something. There is a big stage, and the show is going to start any minute. These two Laurel-and-Hardy types keep throwing the silver on the floor in slapstick comedy. I am furious. Others are enjoying the humor. I hate slapstick! As I try to squeeze out of the room at the last minute, the chorus on stage appears with the finale of the song from *Oklahoma*, "I'm Just a Girl Who Can't Say No!" (Laugh)

L. K. F.: Who are Laurel and Hardy?

F. W.:   Two silly comedians. Lots of people like them. I never find that stuff amusing.

L. K. F.: Are there two such people in your life who make you work harder, not maliciously, but in a slapstick kind of fun? What you hate?

F. W.:   Not that I know of.

L. K. F.: Think about it.

F. W.:   Well I don't know. Any ideas?

(Patients genuinely interested in insight may ask for suggestions when they hit a blind spot, and it can be useful to suggest ideas. Resistance is the trap, of course, in this area too. This patient was open enough to give it a try.)

L. K. F.: What about your sons?

F. W.:   I don't know. Maybe, I guess my two boys would fit that. They're two and four and always messing things up, as toddlers do. I do get furious. I have no patience with this stage of development.

(Pretty good acknowledgment for a first pass.)

L. K. F.: And the song?

F. W.:   I've always liked that song and the charm of the words. She doesn't want to say no. It's just that the long-term consequences of the yes that are damaging to her, so she knows she ought to say no or has to say no or pay severely later.

L. K. F.: Does that fit you? Not wanting to say no, and yet knowing when you don't . . .

F. W.:   Oh yes. I always want to do more than I can, and I have real trouble deciding, and I hate to give up things.

L. K. F.: Well, it seems that this may be connected with the development of the allergies in the context of your two new sons and their demands, and your waiter job. It might be worth trying a few more no's and some long-term examination of the consequences before you say yes to things. What do you think?

In fact, it was a very helpful approach. Recognizing the stress of the children, she was able to make other interventions in that area which were helpful, including not being so formal while the children were at that slapstick stage of development. Her symptoms dramatically decreased in the next two months. Interestingly enough, future recurrences were almost always traceable to a conflict between two desirable choices that were mutually exclusive. Resolving the conflicts led to remissions. I have subsequently confirmed this dynamic with two other people with spontaneous angioedema.

Borderline Traits

Dreams, especially nightmares, can be very helpful for patients with borderline traits who are subject to psychotic episodes. They indicate the impending onset of a psychotic episode by their changing character (Hartmann, 1987). For one such woman patient of mine, they served as a very accurate early warning signal that some defenses need to be mobilized to avert the danger and keep her functioning.

In my experience, nightmares, when interpreted by dream interviewing, seem to be invoked when the usual dream communication has been ignored or a trauma has been experienced. One recurrent post-traumatic nightmare actually showed an evolution of detail, which dream interviewing showed to be parallel to the patient's working through of the trauma. This method might therefore be used to expedite the mastery of the experience and to minimize the residue in post-traumatic stress syndrome.

M. G., a woman with borderline traits, came to me for brief treatment to help her through a relocation crisis after "lots of therapy" in the past. "I have been able to come through with an identity of my own. I have enormous problems with relationships and locating how I feel about things. I'm not a basket case, but I lose it with people. I want something practical, down-to-earth, and someone to help me focus." This seemed to me to be an ideal opportunity for her to work with dreams, using the dream interview method.

Example No. 12. This was one to two dreams she presented on the second visit.

M. G.:   You'll love this one! I'm at the beach, back up on the dunes. All my favorite stuff is by the water—my blanket, my books, etc.— and there is a twenty-foot wave coming. I ran to save my stuff, but I couldn't, and I said, "I can freak out or I can go with it."

And I did go with it. I had time for two big breaths and enjoyed it and rode it out.

> (This one has a happy ending, but it sounded pretty severe nonetheless, and I wanted to estimate the damage.)

L. K. F.: What happened to your stuff?

M. G.: The blanket was still there, and my friends were putting the stuff back in place after the wave passed. Now I know the wave is feeling and emotion, and I do just try and go with the feelings now.

> (She is presuming a belief about the wave, and I need to check it out without devaluing it, so I elect to start at the beginning with the setting and later move into describing the wave by following the routine of the method, rather than challenging her beliefs.)

L. K. F.: What's a beach?

M. G.: It's the nicest, safest place in the world. It's a source.

L. K. F.: What's a wave? Remember I am a Martian.

> (She is new to the method.)

M. G.: Well, Ms. Martian, a twenty foot wave is awesome, destructive, or wonderful and beautiful, depending on where it is, a big-time megapower—it's beauty, splendor, and danger.

L. K. F.: How is it different from any other megapower, like a volcano, for example?

> (It was very descriptive, but not specific enough.)

M. G.: It moves. It's water and wind; its element not its quantity distinguishes it from other things.

> (That was exquisitely precise and complete, so on to another point.)

L. K. F.: So what were you doing at the beginning of the dream?

M. G.: I was wandering around, curious and happy, exploring.

L. K. F.: That fits where you are now in your life, doesn't it?

> (She had said as much last visit.)

M. G.: Yes.

L. K. F.: And the wave—can we do more with it than general emotion? Does this definition tell you more—a moving, awesome, destructive, or beautiful megapower? Do you have a feeling now that emotion comes in massive waves that catch you off-guard and threaten to freak you out?

M. G.: The sadness. I'm surprised by its power. On the bus coming here, I was thinking, "San Francisco is so beautiful—I hope I can stay," and I started to cry.

L. K. F.: Why?

M. G.: I feel unsafe, unentitled.

> (So this fits the dream action, and we can move on to the rest of the dream bridge. This issue is now apparent, and we can return to it whenever indicated.)

L. K. F.: What is interesting to me is not only do you ride out the wave and enjoy it even—and you do seem to me to have an unusual capacity to enjoy the experiencing of any emotion—but that your stuff is intact at the end, surprisingly, and that your friends are there to help you. Could you recognize any?

> (I was wondering if these friends might also be parts of herself that she could learn to rely on.)

M. G.: No, they weren't recognizable. They were just friends. I knew they were friends.

L. K. F.: So even with your relationship difficulties, you seem to have the capacity to conjure up supportive friends when you need them.

> (I wanted her to be conscious of this valuable resource in the face of her sadness issue.)

She was intrigued by her deliberate choice in the dream not to decompensate as she has in the past. Consciously, she said she was feeling freer and safer to explore and experiment now that she was in therapy. This was what the beach represented for her.

Addictions

My least successful interventions from dream interpretation have been those related to ending addictions, which is consistent with the literature on substance abuse treatment. Although the dynamics of someone's drug or alcohol abuse may be clear from the dream interpretation and the implications for action are obvious, the addicts, smokers, and overeaters usually only decreased their habits, sometimes just transiently. Delaney (1991) suggests that dreams incubated to motivate one to stop might be more effective than ones designed to explain overeating, or drinking excessively. For example: "I need a dream to help me get back on my diet" led one 46-year-old woman to have a dream fragment of a 44-year-old colleague who had let his weight get out of control and who had died of a heart attack two years previously. She was then highly motivated through the hardest first four or five days of her diet.

I expect more precise applications of dream interviewing must await additional work with larger samples of patients. I have not yet had the opportunity to work with enough patients in this way to even formulate a hypothesis on the efficacy.

In the meantime, I have seen that dreams can provide warnings for patients in recovery who must remain vigilant about possible relapse. The following is an example of this.

Example No. 13.

L. K. F.: Hi, how are you?

R. R.:   I haven't been depressed, but I'm not happy either because my husband is depressed.

> (We go on to discuss her response to her family situation briefly, and about twenty minutes later in the session she mentions she had a dream about cocaine.)

R. R.:   My mother is in the bathroom brushing her teeth, and she said while snorting cocaine, "For one minute in my life I want to be happy!" I was sympathetic, but I said, "Mom, that's not the way to do it."

L. K. F.: Are you using it again?

> (One never knows with addiction problems whether the answer will be true, but in the absence of evidence to the contrary, I accept it as a working hypothesis.)

R. R.:   No.

L. K. F.: Who is your mother? I know we did her before (i.e., formulated a descriptive definition of her mother), but let's do her again, quickly.

> (Family members especially evolve within their descriptive definitions as the relationships ebb and flow with time, so an update is usually advisable.)

R. R.:   Someone who has been depressed for ever and ever and has given up trying to improve, even though she knows I'm better and my uncle's better, and we've done it with therapy and the antidepressants.

L. K. F.: So your mother is someone who's chronically depressed and has given up hope of improvement despite evidence of your success with psychotherapy and medications?

R. R.:   Yes.

> (Her mother's definition, which had changed considerably, was so close to a description of R. R. herself that I did not wish to pursue it at this point until I had more of the dream to work with.)

L. K. F.: What is brushing your teeth?

R. R.:   She was in a nightie, so she was getting ready to go through the day, doing her grooming. That's when I used to use cocaine.

L. K. F.: And cocaine? What's that?

> (This question was to cover the chance that cocaine might be symbolic of something else, though it was doubtful to me.)

R. R.: A white powder that makes you euphoric and real jittery.

> (I saw she still had some negative affect associated with the cocaine, which was a good sign for her staying away from the addiction.)

L. K. F.: Well, if we put that together, I have to wonder if the depressed part of you that has given up trying to improve, the part that is not happy, is at least considering using coke again? It could even be a part of someone else?

R. R.: Well, yes, it did come up again the last time I was really stressed on the job. I'd forgotten. It was a painful urge, and I had forgotten to supply myself with my substitutes, my cookies and stuff. As you know, I've been thinking more about my depression and my reasons to be depressed.

L. K. F.: So we need to talk about this because your dream states it very clearly, much more clearly than you sounded when you came in today.

We where thus able to quickly cut through substantial denial and deal with her recurrent depression and pain that she was feeling before she acted on her drug dependency. By taking advantage of this precious opportunity, she handled this episode of stress without drugs. She did not use cocaine again in the subsequent year. When she did use it again, it was two years later in a deliberately planned, circumscribed, and openly discussed way to facilitate study and despite my strong counter recommendations. She stopped again promptly, exactly as she had planned. There were no dreams presented about it that time.

Decision-Making

This is the most universal use of dreams in and out of therapy. It is commonplace to remark that one is going to sleep on a decision or an idea, and a number of spectacular insights have come in dreams. Incubation is just a more directed use of this faculty. Examples No. 2 and No. 11 were also incubated.

Example No. 14. I heard this dream during a public dream interpretation seminar I was teaching. People tend to be more resistant in such situations because of the public exposure, but this woman was quite open.

F. O.:   I incubated a dream, as you suggest in the workbook, and I asked how shall I rank X hospital in the fall? I'm a medical student. I dreamed that I was in an institution, probably a hospital. I was walking along with a very familiar, close, shadowy presence, maybe my boyfriend, but I'm not sure. I was having a good time because he was with me, but whenever people asked me questions, I answered them, but the answers were wrong, not what they wanted to hear.

L. K. F.: Who is your boyfriend?

F. O.:   Someone who is very comfortable in X. He likes it.

L. K. F.: What is the most striking thing about him?

F. O.:   He's very familiar, and I'm close to him. We've been together awhile.

>   (Her description was very emotional rather than factual, but it seemed as if it might be adequate. She had in fact said the same thing in three different ways.)

L. K. F.: Could the institution have been X?

>   (A shortcut to a specific bridge—risky but we'll see. If she bridges "wrong," none of the other details will fit.)

F. O.:   Oh yes, easily.

>   (No need for a shoehorn to make it fit here, so keeping to my working hypothesis, let's test the details.)

L. K. F.: Do you feel at X that you don't follow their expectations? That you give the "wrong" answers, not what they want?

F. O.:   Yes I do. I have never felt I belong there. I always feel out of place.

L. K. F.: In the dream, the only reason you are comfortable there is because of your relationship with your boyfriend. You could take him as himself or as a part of you that is familiar with X, so the familiarity itself is an attraction to that place. What do you think?

F. O.:   You mean I am comfortable at X because it is familiar and I have been there awhile, not because I fit?

L. K. F.: I don't know. That might be what the dream suggests. What do you think?

>   (A common trap is to have someone ask you to tell them what their dream means, especially when it's already all laid out. It sometimes seems so obvious that one is tempted to do it, and at times I may, but I am always reluctant to fit someone with a dream interpretation they do not espouse themselves. This is especially true in the absence of a relationship. Such interpretations tend to be less

useful because the dreamer cannot work with them in such a passive position. Additionally, the interpretations have much less chance of being badly fitted than when dreamers themselves discover the application to their waking lives.)

F. O.:   Well, it could be true. That's interesting. I could be comfortable because my boyfriend is there or because I am familiar with it. Thank you.

We left if here, but she was not convinced. Later I heard that she had become more and more sure that X was not the place for her, and she therefore chose to go elsewhere. This evolution in one's insight following dream interpretation is very common and seems easier to make than with general insights. This is perhaps because the dramatic presentation of the concepts stays more easily in the conscious mind. About a year later, F. O. was working at a different hospital, convinced she made the right choice to leave X.

Indications and Contraindications for the Use of Dream Interviewing in Psychotherapy

Contraindications

The most obvious contraindication for the use of the dream interview method of dream interpretation is the presence of any thought disorder severe enough to prevent concentration, abstraction, or coherent speech. These render the technique useless. Similarly, I have experienced an obsessive patient so extremely anxious, suicidally depressed, and blocking on his speech that he was unable to express anything sufficiently coherent to generate a descriptive definition. As his symptoms improved, he became more able to make use of his dreams.

Secondly, a persuasive contraindication to dream interviewing is when dreams are used as resistance to the actual work of therapy. One patient with an addiction occasionally brought in a dream and then used the process of defining the symbols as an opportunity to struggle with me about the worthlessness of dreams, my severe limitations as an interior decorator and a psychiatrist, and the doubtfulness of psychotherapy in general. He rarely gave more than one complete definition, and the dreams were basically untouched when we abandoned them. He and similar patients need to address their resistance to therapy directly before dream interviewing could possibly be of any use to them.

A different form of resistance is when a patient presents a very long dream that he or she wishes to work on exclusively for two or three sessions, and the dream obscures the very real events occurring in his or her daily life and which should probably be dealt with more promptly. In general, I prefer to use no more than half of a fifty-minute session for dream interpretation with one dream, though there are periodic exceptions. These exceptions rarely happen in more than one or two sequential sessions and are most frequent with people who are fairly compulsive about completion rather than resistant to discussing the other issues in their life. In those cases, I will reserve ten minutes, often at the beginning, to discuss significant life events.

My patients are also soon aware of my particular interest in dreams, and therefore, they bring in dreams to please or confound me and withhold dreams to resist therapy, to express anger at me, or to induce me to solicit them. They also bring dreams in to distract me. I try to deal with these problems as one deals with similar situations of resistance in psychodynamic psychotherapy.

A final reason to avoid using the dream interview method for interpreting dreams in psychotherapy is when the therapist or dreamer does not find it helpful. Therapists who prefer to be passive and nondirective can have great difficulty with this technique and may choose not to use it. My experience prior to the use of the dream interview method was that very few dreams added new information, although they were often very interesting, and I felt this to be a contradiction to my doing dreamwork with these methods. Perhaps I was reminded of my clinical professor who declared, "Therapy is not an archaeological expedition!" Currently, I think I learn something new from most of the dreams I discuss with patients, and frequently I understand the basics of the psychodynamic addressed in the dream and many of the details. My patients vary from understanding almost all of their dreams that we work on to the patient I mentioned earlier who resisted them all and only learned a morsel from the odd one or two. If the dream interview method is rarely helpful to you and a particular patient, I feel this too is a contraindication.

Indications

I think the primary indication for using the dream interview method in therapy is patient interest. There are other places, such as the Delaney and Flowers Dream Center, where I can indulge my own interest in dreams and the techniques I've described in this chapter, and this helps me stay honest in this regard. Fortunately, many people are vitally interested in their own dreams, and it is a common assumption in our culture that dreams are of interest to psychotherapists, so patients and clients frequently bring dreams into therapy. The dream interview technique has been effective for me with men and women, heterosexuals and homosexuals, African-Americans, Asians, Hispanics, white Americans, Europeans, and Indians as well as with a wide range of occupations and educational levels (e.g., secretary, student, welder, attorney, business executive, accountant, physician, veterinary assistant, waitress, and bus driver) and various ages (elementary school to postgraduate) and with a range of psychiatric diagnoses.

The dream interview is also indicated for overcoming resistance and blocks in the progress of therapy. One dream may be all that is needed to penetrate some resistance and get the therapy or one's life moving along again, as with Example No. 2 (examination block) and Example No 13. (the cocaine dream).

Because the dream interview method can rapidly touch issues that might otherwise remain buried for some time, a third indication for dream interpretation is a need for speed in the psychotherapeutic process. This can be because the patient has a deadline of some kind, such as M. R. in Example No. 2 had with her examination application and H. O. in Example No. 1 with her need to safely avoid a second surgery. In addition, psychotherapy is an expensive, time-consuming endeavor, and there is no need to prolong it, particularly when one can expedite it without sacrificing the quality of the outcome for the patient. Patients sometimes choose to initiate their dreamwork at home by beginning their definitions, and I find this generally facilitates the process. Some actually bring these descriptions in with their dream, written or typed with a copy that I include in my process notes. Since I have a copy machine in the office, I occasionally copy a dream from someone's dream journal to circumvent writing it from dictation, if a patient is agreeable to this.

In the course of long-term psychotherapy, patients who come in for a specific issue and its resolution bring in dreams that often relate to areas of their lives other than the central issue of therapy. Their interpretations can be used almost as brief therapy asides while the main thrust of the therapy pursues the chosen theme. Thus, the peripheral issues are not neglected despite such an in-depth focus, nor do the subsidiary matters detract seriously from the longer-term problems. I find this use of dreams facilitates an effective balance, so that one need not choose between suspending one's life during the course of long-term treatment and risking impulsive or unexamined decisions.

The dream interview method has yet another indication, namely, that it is possible to use it without a therapist. It does not require a formal therapeutic training, although similar skills are essential. I find people work most effectively with someone else, such as fellow group members or another dream interview student rather than alone where resistance can more easily defeat them.

In this context, I wish to make explicit extremely important cautions, which I don't consider actual contraindications. The specificity of this technique creates a very powerful tool that needs to be handled with care and respect. The implications for action found in most dreams are just that—implications, not orders, directions, or even recommendations. The dreamer must consider each life action in a thorough, conscious fashion before making any decisions or changes in behavior based on a dream's interpretation. Understanding the simplicity of the concept can easily be mistaken for mastery. This can lead to misplaced confidence in erroneous interpretations. If an interpretation is correct, there will be many events and feelings that will support the understanding. Further confirmations often surface over the week succeeding accurate work on a dream, and sound decisions for action seems to grow as much out of these subsequent revelations and recognitions as out of the original dream interpretation. Inaccurate interpretations begin to feel more and more awkward, irrelevant or magical, though they may be fondly treasured. Supporting evidence in reality is noticeably scarce. These misinterpretations are to be carefully distinguished from uncomfortable insights.

There is one last indication for use of the dream interview method that I wish to emphasize. If one is careful in one's use of the method, then dreams provide a vehicle to move rapidly with mastery in therapy and they can be used this way by the therapist. It is rare in psychotherapy to have a technique equivalent to a chest x-ray, a laboratory test value, or a CAT scan to confirm one's clinical judgment. Dreams interpreted by this dream interview method can provide such confirmation and occasionally even the sense of certainty I felt in my treatment of the surgical patient in Example No. 1, which led to her dramatic return to recovery. What a gift!

References

Bonato, R. A., Moffitt, A. R., Hoffmann, R. F., Cuddy, M. A., and Wimmer, F. L. (1991) Bizarreness in Dreams and Nightmares. Dreaming: J. of the Assn. for the Study of Dreams. 1:53–61.

Bonime, W. (1989). *Collaborative Psychoanalysis*. Cranbury, N.J. (also London, England and Ontario, Canada): Associated University Presses.

Cavenar, J. (1978). When the Psychotherapist Is Black. *American J Psychiatry* 9:1084–85.

Delaney, G. (1979). *Living Your Dreams*. New York: Harper and Row. (hardback)

———. (1981). *Living Your Dreams*. New York: Harper and Row. (paperback).

———. (1988). *Living Your Dreams*, 2nd ed. New York: Harper and Row.

———. (1991). *Breakthrough Dreaming*. New York: Bantam Books.

Flowers, L. (1988). The Morning After: A Pragmatist's Approach to Dreams. *Psychiatric Journal of the University of Ottawa* 13:66–71.

Gackenbach, J. (1989). *Control Your Dreams*. New York: Harper and Row.

Hartmann, E. (1984). *The Nightmare: The Psychology and Biology of Terrifying Dreams*. New York: Basic Books.

———. (1987). Who Has Nightmares. *Archives of General Psychiatry* 44:49–56.

Hunt, H. (1989). *The Multiplicity of dreams: Memory, imagination, and consciousness*. New Haven: Yale University Press.

Kolb, G. (1985). The Dream in Psychoanalytic Group Therapy. *International J of Group Psychother.* 33:41–52.

Kramer, M. (1987). A Selective Mood Regulatory Function For Sleep. Presented Fifth International Congress of Sleep Research. Copenhagen, Denmark, 1987.

LaBerge, S. (1985). *Lucid Dreaming*. Boston: Houghton Mifflin.

Maybruck P. (1989). *Preganancy in Dreams*. Los Angeles: Jeremy Tacher.

Monday, J. (1987). Dream Process in Asthmatic Subjects With Noctournal Attacks. *American J of Psychiatry* 5:638–40.

Othmer, E., et al. (1969). Encephalic Cycles during Sleep and Wakefulness in Humans: A 24-Hour Pattern. *Science* 164 (April):447–49.

Perlmutter, R. A., and Babineau, R. (1983). The Use of Dreams in Couples Therapy. *Psychiatry* 46:66–72.

Sabini, M. (1981). Dreams as an Aid in Determining Diagnosis, Prognosis, and Attitude Towards Treatment. *Psychotherapy & Psychosomatics* 36:24–36.

Smith, R. (1984). Teaching Interview Skills to Medical Students: The Issue of 'Countertransference.' *Journal of Medical Education* 59 (July): 582–87.

Ullman, M. (1979). *Working With Dreams.* Boston: Houghton Mifflin.

———. (1986). *Access to Dreams. Handbook of States of Consciousness.* New York: Van Norstrand Reinhold, pp. 524–52.

8

Ramon Greenberg *and* Chester Pearlman ▬▬▬

An Integrated Approach to Dream Theory and Clinical Practice

In this chapter we try to demonstrate that sleep and dream research in recent years provides a basis for the modification of classical psychoanalytic dream theory. We will then show how this new, research-based theory can facilitate the clinical use of dreams. We assume that there is no totally atheoretical clinical approach and that the more explicit the theory, the more helpful it can be. In order to achieve this goal, we will begin with a review of sleep research which, in our opinion, presents a clear foundation for a theory of dream function. We will then show how this theory has been tested with dreams collected under controlled conditions. Finally, we will present material from therapeutic interviews that illustrate the application of our theoretical framework.

Research

The findings of recent sleep research suggest that information processing is a function of REM sleep and dreaming. In order to understand this, we must consider the meaning of "function" in relation to higher nervous system activity, the relations between REM sleep and dreaming, and finally, what studies of REM sleep and dreaming tell us about the nature of the information processed. We feel this will provide a coherent picture derived from a number of different perspectives instead of the usual one-dimensional approaches.

Let us begin with some thoughts about the nervous system and function. Two authors will be of great help here. One is Aleksander Luria, the Russian neurologist, and the other C. R. Gallistel. Luria, in his book *Higher Cortical Functions in Man* (1980), discussed the concept of function and of functional systems. He considered the problems with attempts to understand function on the basis of anatomical localization in the nervous system. Instead, he suggested that function is organized in relation to *tasks*, such as locomotion, perception, or even intellectual activities. Because these acts can be performed in different ways, he postulated that they must be based on a dynamic constellation of connections situated at different levels of the nervous system. Gallistel in *The Organisation of Action: A New Synthesis* (1981) expanded on these ideas by using a concept of interconnecting hierarchies of units of behavior, from simple motor units to units of activity. He discussed the idea that schemas organize the overall form but not the specifics of action. For example, we all have our own recognizable handwriting, whether it is on a small piece of paper or on a blackboard. Clearly, different sets of muscles, and therefore neurons, are in action, even though a basic interrelationship is maintained.

An important question to be asked in relation to schemas is how they develop. We suggest that, when an organism goes beyond its basic, built-in pattern of behavior, REM sleep plays a significant role and that this role is reflected in dreams. Consideration of this role can help us understand dreams.

To develop this idea, we shall use evidence from studies of REM sleep and dreams. We should note, therefore, that the psychological events in dreams and the physiological events in REM sleep represent different aspects of the same activity. This is analogous to the fact that the electrocardiogram and the sounds heard through the stethoscope are both manifestations of the sequential activities of the heartbeat and assist our understanding of what the heart is doing. Evidence for this assertion begins with the fact that dreams and REM sleep normally occur together. Awakenings from REM sleep lead to reports of mental activity which we recognize as dreams. In addition, while there have been a number of negative studies, some significant experiments have shown a clear relationship between dream content and such physiologic components of REM sleep as eye movements and small muscle twitches (Roffwarg et al., 1962), middle ear muscle activity (Roffwarg et al., 1975), and penile erections (Fisher, 1978). In view of this close relationship between REM sleep and dreaming, it is important to include evidence from studies of REM sleep physiology, REM deprivation, and dreams in the effort to develop a complete picture. Because all mammals show great similarities in the physiologic measurements made during REM sleep, the results of animal experiments can also help us understand REM sleep and dreams in humans.

Neurophysiology

Let us begin with the activity of the smallest units, the neurons. The brain is extremely active during REM sleep (Steriade and Hobson,

1976). Neurons are firing at a high rate, but this is not at random. Some areas of the pons shut off while others increase their rate of discharge. Hippocampal recordings show a kind of activity seen only in the awake, aroused animal (Passouant and Cadhilac, 1962). Cortical activity is increased, and this also shows certain specific patterns. For example, Steriade (1978) has shown that short interneurons, which may play a role in memory formation, have a marked increase in firing rate during REM activity. Thus, while some investigators have suggested that the pons is the source for all this activity (Hobson and McCarley, 1977), these studies suggest a complicated interaction among different levels of the nervous system. This is also consistent with the formulation of function by Luria noted earlier. Lesion studies have also contributed to this picture. In both humans (Greenberg, 1966) and animals (Jeannerod et al., 1965), destruction of certain cortical areas affects normal REM patterns with marked diminution of eye movements following damage to the visual association areas. Thus, brain activity during REM sleep suggests a highly activated system with complex interconnections hard at work. To what end, we shall see.

Effects of REM Deprivation

Next we will consider the role of REM sleep in the interaction between the animal and its environment. Here, REM deprivation studies have provided some interesting findings. A classical method for studying the nervous system has been to remove an area and to observe the resultant defects in behavior. In the case of REM deprivation (REMD), a particular form of nervous system activity is removed, and the effects are noted. A number of studies have been conducted using different animals, different means for producing REMD, and different measurements of behavioral effects. Both positive and negative results contribute to the picture.

Initial studies involved mainly observation of the animals. Some observers concluded that the animals' behavior suggested heightened drive pressure following prolonged REMD, as manifested by aggressiveness, hypersexuality, and ravenous hunger. However, when specific measures of the intensity of drive pressure were used, and artifactual effects of the REMD procedure were excluded, this idea was contradicted (Pearlman, 1981). Some studies suggested that emotionality (fear motivation) was actually reduced following REMD (Hicks and Moore, 1979). Other experiments then focused on the effects of REMD on learning. Simple tasks, such as one-way avoidance or simple position learning, were unaffected. More complicated tasks such as difficult discriminations or learning sets, to name a few, were clearly impaired when REMD followed learning trials (Pearlman, 1981). Of particular interest to psychotherapists was the impact of REMD on the effects of brief socialization for mice reared in social isolation (Watson and Henry, 1977). Isolation during infancy has profound disruptive effects on adult behavior. Brief periods of socialization prevented these effects, but when the socialization was followed by sleep and REM deprivation, the animals behaved just like the totally isolated ones.

Responsiveness of REM Sleep to Experiences

Having found that certain tasks were sensitive to REMD, experimenters turned to the examination of the effect of such tasks on REM sleep. If REM is required to master a task, will it respond to demand? Animals who were being trained in REMD-sensitive tasks showed increased REM following training, if they were learning. When the task was fully learned, REM returned to baseline levels (Hennevin and Leconte, 1977; Smith, 1985).

REM Studies in Humans

All these animal studies suggested involvement of REM sleep in the learning of unfamiliar tasks. Studies with humans have developed similar findings with regard to REM sleep but have added a dimension involving dreams. As mentioned before, the physiology—including EEG, eye movements, and loss of muscle tone—is similar to that in animals. REM deprivation can be produced by monitoring the EEG, and waking subjects at the beginning of REM periods. Initial studies were observational, and as in animals, the first interpretation suggested increased drive pressure and tension (Dement, 1960). Later studies failed to confirm this initial impression and instead have focused on the performance of certain tasks or activities. Again, there have been negative as well as positive findings. Simple word lists, used as tests of memory, have not shown any effect of REMD (Greenberg et al., 1970). Recently, we used a more sophisticated test of recent memory scanning, the Sternberg paradigm, and also found no effect (Greenberg et al., 1983). On the other hand, tests of more complicated information-processing have shown effects. Tasks requiring creative thinking and problem-solving were impaired by prior REMD (Lewin and Glaubman, 1975; Glaubman et al., 1978). Projective tests, such as the Rorschach, showed that REMD led to changes in the capacity to deal with recently aroused emotional material, suggesting that without REM sleep the usual mechanisms for dealing with such material were impaired (Greenberg et al., 1970). In a study using a modified TAT (Thematic Apperception Test) task, we found that connections to emotionally meaningful childhood memories were not developed without REM sleep (Greenberg et al., 1983). Another approach, involving adjustment to an unpleasant laboratory situation, also found decreased adaptation with REMD (Cohen and Cox, 1975).

Human studies have also shown a responsiveness of REM sleep to task demands. Thus, in an intensive foreign language course, students whose language performance improved showed increased REM sleep, while those who failed to improve showed no such increase (DeKonnick et al., 1977). Shortening of REM latency (the time asleep from sleep onset to the first REM period) was found in a subject who was in a state of heightened need for processing emotional material, and higher REM times were associated with a decrease in disturbance of emotional equilibrium from presleep to postsleep measurements (Greenberg and Pearlman, 1975).

Dreams

These findings must now be considered in connection with studies of dreams. The classical psychoanalytic view of dreams includes ideas about drive discharge, censorship, disguise, and indifferent manifest content. The foundation for the psychoanalytic view has been Freud's hypothesis that the dream provided an opportunity for discharge of potentially sleep-disturbing drives through wish fulfillment. While this seemed more possible in sleep, however, there was still, according to Freud, some barrier to the open expression of unacceptable wishes. The dream censor monitored the dream wishes and insured that they did not emerge in too direct a fashion. When a drive got expressed, it was in a disguised fashion. Supposedly, this disguise took the form of attaching the unacceptable material to inconsequential experiences from the previous day, the so-called indifferent day residues. Thus the manifest dream was considered to be composed of images from the previous day, which had no emotional significance in themselves. The research we have described raises some questions about these ideas. Availability of extensive dream material collected in sleep laboratories allows further reexamination of these beliefs. Most striking has been the finding that the manifest content is very meaningful in and of itself. The correspondence of manifest content and emotionally important waking experiences has become eminently clear. Such connections have been demonstrated in a study of a patient in psychoanalysis (Greenberg and Pearlman, 1975), in a study of our own dreams (Greenberg and Pearlman, 1980), and also, without the benefit of a sleep laboratory, in a reexamination of Freud's Irma dream (Greenberg and Pearlman, 1978). Some examples of these findings might be helpful to the reader. The psychoanalytic patient, for example, was struggling in one session with painful feelings about his father's death. He was attempting to talk about this without getting too upset. That night he dreamed that he was involved in a process of transferring some of his father's possessions from one refrigerator to another. In our reconsideration of the Irma dream, we took into account material involving a complicated surgical procedure preformed on Freud's patient, Emma, by Wilhelm Fliess, who was Freud's close confidant and major supporter. The operation and Freud's feelings about it were described vividly in letters Freud wrote to Fliess. The dream gave a vivid portrayal of Emma's symptoms following the operation and can readily be understood as Freud's attempt to exonerate Fliess in order to maintain his highly important and positive relationship with him. Other examples of the clear correspondence between waking concerns and manifest dreams have been shown in presurgical patients and subjects in intensive group therapy situations (Breger et al., 1971). For example, one patient was faced with an operation on a plugged artery. He dreamed of repairing plumbing.

A possible paradigm for the significance of the manifest content is seen in a posttraumatic nightmare. Here, the connection between the dream content and the emotionally important waking experience is portrayed literally. We would suggest that in these dreams only the problem is seen. On the basis of the research we have cited we feel this represents an example of a failed dream. That is, the task of integration has not taken place. In the usual dream, the problem is presented together with some evidence of efforts to deal with it in a more or less satisfactory fashion. The evidence of some processing or integration may be seen in the symbolism of the dream and in the kind of resolution to the manifest problem in the dream.

Some Implications of Research Findings

In this section on research, we have presented a number of studies relating dreams to REM sleep and adaptation to emotionally important situations. A more detailed discussion of this and related work can be found in a review by Pearlman (1982). For purposes of this discussion, it should be noted that most of the studies cited have been replicated in more than one laboratory. We see, therefore, that REM sleep is an activity ideally suited for developing the type of complex interconnections proposed by Luria and Gallistel. Such interactions form the basis for schemas that guide tasks but not the specifics of action. In order to do this, memories must be connected with current experiences, so that the animal or human can deal with the present by using past experience without being rigidly controlled by the past.

Many of the studies we have cited showed impairment of this process when REM sleep was not available. Dreams, then, might be viewed as showing the dreamer's struggles to make effective connections. In the nightmare there is obvious failure. A traumatic element cannot be integrated, as indicated by the dream that shows only the traumata and has no content from other aspects of the dreamer's life experience. In the nontraumatic dream, on the other hand, we can begin to look for evidence of *integration*. We thus can approach the content of the dream by formulating the problems in the dream and considering how the dreamer is faring in the struggle to make meaningful connections for currently active problems in waking life. This approach to dreams is, we feel, more consistent with the findings from REM sleep studies than the traditional view of dreams as a vehicle for discharge of drive tension and of attempts to disguise or censor. It is also consistent with two other recent theories of REM function. Rotenberg (1983), a Russian investigator, has conducted some creative studies of REM sleep that explored the role of REM sleep in resistance to toxic substances or in the lowering of seizure thresholds. He also studied the role of REM sleep in students' ability to cope with the anxiety related to examinations. As a result of his findings, as well as those already mentioned in this chapter, he has developed a theory that suggests that REM sleep serves the function of restoring search activity to the nervous system. This is an activity involving the quest for solutions to problems, be they intellectual or emotional. Without this activity the animal or human is resigned and vulnerable to nervous or physiologic disorders. For example, anaphylactoid edema of the muzzle of an animal after injection of an irritating substance was more severe in the absence of search behavior. Cobalt-induced seizures lasted longer when search behavior was reduced.

A second researcher, Palombo (1978), uses a somewhat different language to capture a similar idea. He sees REM sleep or dreaming as providing the opportunity to store recent memories by matching them with memories from the past, thus providing a sense of integration and continuity. Both these writers also discuss the problem of failure or success in the REM process in dreams. Palombo introduces the idea of the correction dream as an event that occurs when a previous dream fails to make an appropriate match. Rotenberg considers the role of REM deprivation or REM exhaustion in the renunciation of search, and therefore, its role in the development of depression or neurotic disorders. We will discuss the issue of success or failure in dreams after presenting further clinical material.

Integration with Earlier Clinically Based Theories

We have presented a theory of the adaptive function of dreaming that has evolved from research in sleep laboratories. While we have raised questions about the classical psychoanalytic formulations of dream function, there have been some psychoanalytic thinkers who have introduced modifications quite consistent with our perspective. In a paper entitled "The Dream Problem," Maeder (1916) went beyond Freud's view of dreams as drive discharge and introduced the idea of a prospective function for dreaming. He demonstrated how the dream showed evidence of the dreamer's struggle to find solutions to problems and that the nature of the solutions predicted subsequent waking behavior and affect. Thus, he added to libido theory and considered the dream to be an accurate reflection of the dreamer's more or less successful efforts to come to terms with important emotional issues. Years later French and Fromm (1964) presented very similar ideas. These stemmed from French's concept of the focal conflict. They suggested that every dream showed evidence of a particular conflict that was closely related to the dreamer's current waking concerns. The dream also showed the dreamer's efforts to find a more or less comforting resolution of the conflict. While focusing on the dreamer's current life, Maeder and French and Fromm did not ignore the past but related concerns of the present to unresolved past issues.

Also of importance to our discussion of dreaming is how, within their theoretical framework, these authors dealt with the problem of understanding the dream and especially the fact that the manifest dream contains a great deal of information. This then leads us to the next section in which we will consider the relation of the theory to dream interpretation and to the clinical use of the reported dream.

Integration of Theory and Practice

In his paper "Dream Interpretation and the Psychology of Dreaming," Jones (1965) discusses the importance of distinguishing between the two aspects of the title. He pointed out that dream psychology is the science of dreaming and can be subject to study, experimentation, and validation in an objective manner. Dream interpretation, on the other hand, is subjective and usually involves collaboration between two people attempting to understand the meaning of a dream to the dreamer.

Our discussion up to now has been concerned with the work that provides the basis for a psychology of dreaming. We feel this provides a basis for dream interpretation and for the clinical work with dreams, but it does not tell the whole story. Work with dreams during psychotherapy takes place within an ongoing process of treatment that has its own theoretical framework. In order for effective treatment to take place, there has to be some congruence between the approach to dreams and the overall clinical orientation. Freud showed this clearly by first demonstrating the meaningfulness of dreams and then using his understanding of dreams toward a better understanding of the unconscious processes involved in the patients' conflicts. While we have questioned the validity of his orientation toward drive discharge, we feel the basic idea of the dream as a window through which one can see most clearly what the patient is struggling with is crucial.

The thrust of the studies we have described underlines the centrality of the dream for understanding what is currently of major concern for the dreamer and how the patient is integrating or coping with these major issues. Furthermore, our research suggests that the manifest content should be taken seriously as representing in pictorial language the problems of the dreamer (Greenberg and Pearlman, 1980). Recently, we have investigated this idea more extensively and have found that the manifest problems in the dream correlate very closely with those seen in analytic material (Greenberg et al., 1992).

This work has involved the material we collected in the sleep laboratory from a patient who was also in psychoanalysis. We had transcripts of the sessions preceeding and following the sleep lab night. During twelve of the nights we awakened the patient at the end of REM periods and tape-recorded his dream reports. In our curent study of this material, we have scored the dreams for the appearance of problems in the manifest dream, and we also scored the analytic hours for problems. We then compared the dream problems with the problems in the hours. Some examples of what we found will illustrate how much the dream problems corresponded to those in the analytic hours.

One night the patient dreamed that he was in a love-making situation with a young woman. A yakking dog kept interrupting them. He shooed the dog away. We formulated the problem as something interfering with his sexual activity. In the hour before this dream the patient had been talking about an impending trip, in the company of a woman friend. He kept bringing up concerns about possible problems in his sexual performance. In the hour he dismissed each problem as it arose. As one can see, the problem and the solution in the dream are very similar to what was seen in the hour. Another example, referred to earlier, occurred on a night following an analytic hour in which the patient had been struggling with feelings about his dead father. He was having trouble containing his sadness. He then had a dream in which he was a prisoner of two men. They had the task of transferring his father's possessions from one refrigerator to another. As the dream progressed he became part of a very efficient line that moved things from one refrigerator to the other. He was very impressed by the smoothness of the operation. In this dream the problem continues, but the solution feels much more satisfactory to the patient.

It should be clear at this point that we are discussing dreams in a manner that fits with a psychodynamic perspective. While not totally consistent with a classical psychoanalytic understanding of the patient, it is consistent with more modern psychoanalytic approaches, such as those described by Kohut and associates. Although it is not possible in this discussion to provide a detailed discussion of self psychology, a few words might be appropriate. Kohut (1977) has introduced the idea that the development of a cohesive sense of self is superordinate in personality development. This occurs through the interaction of parental figures and the child and, in the normal course of events, leads to the important psychologic functions of self-esteem, initiative, ambition, and life goals. Treatment is focused on enhancing the arrested development of these functions by the analysis of transferences that reflect past difficulties in the parental self-object functions. Thus, while the focus is away from traditional conflicts related to libidinal issues, it includes the importance of transference and of the role that past experience plays in the understanding of present difficulties. Furthermore, Kohut emphasizes the idea that this theory is an experience near one in contrast to the metapsychology of traditional psychoanalysis. The clinical application is thus much closer to the theoretical foundation. The role we have formulated for dreaming meshes perfectly with this clinical orientation, in that it considers the dream as a vivid portrayal of what the patient is experiencing in relation to self and to important self-objects.

With what has preceded as a necessary foundation, we feel at this point that, just as the dream often captures better than words what is going on, some clinical examples can provide a better illustration of the application of these ideas than further theoretical discussion can.

Clinical Examples

A young woman had been in treatment for about a year and a half because of profound dissatisfaction with what life offered her, despite a succesful career and marriage. She also suffered from periodic severe anxiety. She had improved considerably, and currently, her main concerns are her inability to get pregnant (she has one child) and her growing awareness of intense feelings about the therapist, which she finds very discomforting. She began the hour by indicating that she had a cough from a cold she was getting over. She took the day off and made stuffing and cookies with her daughter. The latter were hard work, and her daughter got tired of it. She then mentioned that she had a dream a couple of days ago.

She was looking in the mirror and looked very pregnant, more than when she had been actually pregnant. She said that she couldn't be and then realized that she was leaning back. [This was followed by the description of another dream which she had had the night before.] She came to her session and worked on a dollhouse. She was coughing. The therapist didn't even comment on her cough. There were two other things they worked on, but she couldn't remember them.

She then said that actually her daughter has a dollhouse that the whole family works on, building new parts for it. She felt the interpretation was obvious, and she didn't like it. She had awakened irritated with the therapist and with herself for having the dream. She thought it meant she wants to be his daughter but can't. "Why doesn't she pick someone else? This is an unreal relationship." She was really irritated after the dream. The therapist focused on the problem in the dream by noting the fact that she was irritated in the dream because of his failure to comment on the cough. She then proceeded to bring up several times that he had failed to comment on things about her and instead had only dealt with what she brought up. This led to her talking about her disappointment in her father and father-in-law. Although dissappointed, she had not given up completely on her father, but she had on her mother. It made her nervous to talk about this. She doesn't want to still be wanting a father. The therapist questioned whether her nervousness in general stemmed from the fact that she did not have a father who helped her feel safe from her mother's superstitions. The hour then proceeded with further material about her fantasies and mixed feelings about the therapist.

In this hour the therapist dealt with the dream by commenting on the problem. His assumption that this was of importance to the patient was borne out by the fact that the patient was able to discuss her feelings about the therapist more openly than before. By focusing on the problem in the dream, she was helped to move from an intellectual interpretation to much more affect-laden material that was currently active in the treatment process. The connection between past and present is clearly seen in the similarity of affect toward the therapist and her father, both in her sense of disappointment and in her reluctance to acknowledge such feelings.

The second patient is a single woman in her middle twenties. She began treatment about a year before because she was depressed and unable find any direction for her life. She was involved in a long-term relationship with a man that did not seem to be going anywhere. She was not working, and although she had completed college, she had no idea about what she wanted to do. Of significance in her past history was the fact that her parents were divorced when she was six. Her mother developed cancer a couple of years later and, after a long illness, died when the patient was nine. The patient remembers little, if any, help in understanding what was happening and dealt with these events by denying they had any impact on her. She did not grieve and did not want anyone to feel sorry for her. She focused on looking good and trying to be popular. She described her father as being very involved in her life in a controlling and insensitive manner. The dream was reported in a session that followed a two-week interruption resulting from a visit to her father and step-mother. The first of the two missed hours was canceled at the last minute because of a sudden change in travel plans. Just before she left, she had been expressing dissatisfaction about the fact that she and the therapist had not been able to arrange a second hour to add to her regular weekly sessions.

She began the hour by asking why she had been billed for the first of the two missed hours. She seemed to accept the explanation that it had been done at the last minute and was perhaps related to a discussion last time about her wanting to pull back because she felt the therapist did not want to give her an additional weekly hour. She talked about having had a good time socially while away but also feeling very aware of the lack of any good feeling about herself. She didn't feel things went very well with her father. She was about to relate something she was telling him when she recalled a dream. She remarked that she rarely remembers dreaming.

Her parents (father and stepmother) were in their bedroom in the apartment in Florida. She was in the bathroom, in the shower, smoking. She's not allowed to smoke in the house. Robbers came in the house and started shooting. Suddenly the dream changed so that now her father was away in New York and only her stepmother was in the house when the robbers came in. They came into

the bathroom and started to shoot through the shower door. She was hiding be-
hind the bathroom door, and they didn't see her. She then realized that father was
coming back. The robbers were in the dining room, so she was able to go out into
the hall to meet father and stepmother, who was somehow still alive. She told her
father he'd better go downstairs and not risk his life by going into the apartment
to try to save things from the robbers. She told him that if he went in she would
get herself killed by going downstairs and getting herself run over. So he went
downstairs. It was the only way to get him to listen, that is, to threaten him with
the loss of her own life.

The therapist commented on the problem of not being able to get
her father to listen to her. She responded by relating it to what reminded
her of the dream in the first place. She had been asking her father about
his life in the past, and he had dismissed her questions and her interest
in getting to know him better. She also said that she had been thinking
last night about whether she could survive if her father were to die. The
therapist continued to focus on the problem of getting through to her
father and how important he is to her. She became more sad than she
had ever been during an hour. She was surprised at the strength of her
feelings. With the help of the therapist, she talked about her never feeling that what she felt was valid. She always had to hide her crying. The
therapist commented on her having to hide in the dream.

The issue of the robbery was also discussed, and in connection
with this, the loss of her mother came up. Her sister had quit therapy
when strong feelings about her mother's death began to emerge. No one
in the family had talked with the patient (who is the youngest) about
her mother's illness and death, and nothing had been explained. She
expressed her sense of the unfairness of her life in a much more direct
manner than she had ever done before.

Again, in this example, a manifest problem in the dream was
connected to a central and active concern of the patient. This was expressed in the dream in a manner that was overt and also in a symbolic
form that captured a great deal of affect. Work with the dream involved
an understanding of the patient, including her past, and of the therapeutic process.

Both these examples have been presented in a manner that we
hope will allow the reader to develop some sense of our clinical orientation and of how work with the dream fits into the work of a therapy
hour. Since every therapist has his or her own particular style, we feel
that presenting the major themes of the hour and the focus of the therapist's comments captures the essence of our thinking. Both examples
are summaries of the whole hour in which discussion moved back and

forth between the dreams and the problems in the dreams and the issues that were raised by these problems.

Discussion

We have attempted to provide a foundation for the clinical use of dream material. Recent research points to an understanding of the function of dreaming. This function can be formulated as the integration of current experiences into existing programs or memory systems, when such recent experiences require adaptation. We have also shown how this concept and the research on which it is based suggest modifications of classical psychoanlytic dream theory, while retaining a psychodynamic framework. Other clinical theoreticians have presented ideas that match very well with this approach. We have also suggested that one must have not only a theory of dreaming but also a clinical theory within which it fits. With this in mind, let us spell out some of our guidelines for thinking about a dream when it comes up in a therapy hour.

The main point is that the dream represents the dreamer's effort to cope with a currently meaningful issue. Thus the manifest dream is the royal road to what is important and not just a set of benign daily residues. Furthermore, we would suggest that a problem appearing in the manifest dream is a direct expression of the patient's problem and provides a unit with which to approach discussion of the dream. These problems are presented in the language used in the dream. Since this is perceptual, it is not always portrayed in an easily understood fashion, if one is thinking in waking verbal terms. Thus, some translation is required. If one thinks of translation, then the concept of disguise is not required. Since the dreamer is also searching for ways to cope with the problems, solutions may also be apparent in the dream, and in fact, the solutions, if successful enough, may even obscure the problem. This may also lead to the fact that the dream is not always readily understandable. The solutions in the dream may be new to the patient or may be the institution of old methods of coping, that is, defenses. The difference we see between our approach and the usual one is that the defenses are not there to hide meaning but are an example of the dreamer's method of coping with the problem.

To this point we have only considered the dream as illustrative of a current problem. In our clinical examples, however, we also related the dreams to the patient's past. We feel this is important because it allows us to seek an understanding of why the present experience is a problem. It is here, then, that the patient's associations to the dream become meaningful. Through them we can learn the *significance* of the problem in terms of the patient's unique life experiences. As we do this, we can appreciate the ways in which the dream integrates past and present in the dreamer's attempts to make sense out of what is happening. For example, although we did not discuss it during the hour, the robbery dream has some very clear connections with the patient's past. She grew up in the New York area, and at the time of the original robbery, mother's death, father was not there since he had remarried and was living in a nearby suburb. Finally, this approach to dreams also helps us understand how dreams can be more or less successful and more or less direct in their expression of the dreamer's situation and experience of it. Thus, the two examples from our research present two solutions that differ greatly in their effectiveness. In the first, the ineffective denial during the hour is merely repeated as a shooing away of the dog, while in the second an effective operation in which the patient is an active participant is instituted to keep her father's effects in cold storage.

It is our opinion that the integration of research and clinical experience is an important model for any approach to dreaming. Clinical work requires a theory that is not purely derived from clinical experience and yet at the same time is consistent with clinical realities. Experimental proof in our field is rarely possible. However, if we find that we develop similar ideas from different data bases, we can begin to feel that our ideas have some validity and are not subject just to a current therapeutic fashion.

References

Breger, L., Hunter, I., and Lane, R. (1971). The Effect of Stress on Dreams. *Psychological Issues.* New York: International Universities Press.

Cohen, D., and Cox, C. (1975). Neuroticism in the Sleep Laboratory: Implications for Representational and Adaptive Properties of Dreaming. *Journal Abnormal Psychology* 84:91-108.

DeKonnick, J., Proulx, G., King, W., and Poitras, L. (1977). Intensive Language Learning and REM Sleep: Further Results. *Sleep Research* 7:146.

Dement, W. (1960). The Effect of Dream Deprivation. *Science* 131:1705–7.

Fisher, C. (1978). Experimental and Clinical Approaches to the Mind-Body Problem Through Recent Research in Sleep and Dreaming. In *Psychopharmacology and Psychotherapy: Synthesis or Antithesis?* ed. N. Rosenzweig and H. Grissom. New York: Human Sciences Press.

French, T., and Fromm, E. (1964). *Dream Interpretation*. New York: Basic Books.

Gallistel, C. R. (1981). The Organisation of Action: A new synthesis. *Behavioral Brain Science* 4:609–19.

Glaubman, H., Orbach, I., Aviram, O., Frieder, I., Frieman, M., Pelled, O., and Glaubman, R. (1978). REM Deprivation and Divergent Thinking. *Psychophysiology* 15:75–79.

Greenberg, R. (1966). Cerebral Cortex Lesions: The Dream Process and Sleep Spindles *Cortex* 2:357–66.

Greenberg, R., Pearlman, C., Fingar, R., Kantrowitz, J., and Kawliche, S. (1970). The Effects of REM Deprivation: Implications for a Theory of the Psychologic Function of Dreaming. *British Journal of Medical Psychology* 43:1–11.

Greenberg, R., Pillard, R., and Pearlman, C. (1972). The Effect of REM Deprivation on Adaption to Stress. *Psychosomatic Medicine* 34:257–62.

Greenberg, R., and Pearlman, C. (1975). A Psychoanalytic Dream Continuum: The Source and Function of Dreams. *International Review of Psychoanalysis* 2:441–48.

——— . (1978). If Freud Only Knew: A Reconsideration of Psychoanalytic Dream Theory. *International Review of Psychoanalysis* 5:71–75.

——— . (1980). The Private Language of the Dream. In *The Dream in Clinical Practice*, ed. J. Natterson. New York: Jason Aronson.

Greenberg, R., Pearlman, C., Schwartz, W., and Youkilis, H. (1983). Memory, Emotion, and REM Sleep. *Journal of Abnormnal Psychology* 92:378–81.

Greenberg, R., Katzx, H., Schwartz, W., and Pearlman, C. (1992). A Research-based Reconsideration of the Psychoanalytic Theory of Dreaming. Journal of the American Psychoanalytic Association 40:531–550.

Hennevin, E., and Leconte, P. (1977). Études des relations entre le sommeil paradoxal et les processus d'acquisition. *Physiology and Behavior* 18:307–19.

Hicks, R. A., and Moore, J. D. (1979). REM Sleep Deprivation Diminishes Fear in Rats. *Physiology and Behavior* 22:689–92.

Hobson, A., and McCarley, R. (1977). The Brain as a Dream State Generator: An Activation Synthesis Hypothesis of the Dream Process. *American Journal of Psychiatry* 134:1335–48.

Jeannerod, M., Mouret, J., and Jouvet, M. (1965). Étude de la motricité oculaire au cours de la phase paradoxale du sommeil chez le chat. *Electroencephalography and Clinical Neurophysiology* 18:554–66.

Jones, R. (1965). Dream Interpretation and the Psychology of Dreaming. *Journal of American Psychoanalytical Association* 13:304–19.

Kohut, H. (1977). *The Restoration of The Self.* New York: International Universities Press, Inc.

Lewin, I., and Glaubman, H. (1975). The Effect of REM Deprivation: Is It Detrimental, Benificial or Neutral? *Psychophysiology* 12:349–53.

Luria, A. (1980). *Higher Cortical Functions in Man.* New York: Basic Books.

Maeder, A. (1916). The Dream Problem. *Nervous and Mental Disease.* New York: The Nervous and Mental Disease Publishing Co.

Palombo, S. (1978). *Dreaming and Memory.* New York: Basic Books.

Passouant, P., and Cadhilac, J. (1962). Les rythymes theta hippocampiques au cours du sommeil. In *Physiologie de l'hippocampe,* ed. P. Passouant. Paris: Centre National de la Recherche Scientifique.

Pearlman, C. (1981). Rat Models of the Adaptive Function of REM Sleep. In *Sleep Dreams, and Memory,* ed. W. Fishbein. New York: Spectrum Publications.

———. (1982). Sleep Structure Variation. In *Biological Rythyms, Sleep and Performance,* ed. W. Webb. London: John Wiley & Sons.

Roffwarg, H., Dement, W., Muzio, T., and Fisher, C. (1962). Dream Imagery: Relationship to Rapid Eye Movements. *Archives of General Psychiatry* 7:235–38.

Roffwarg, H., Herman, J., and Lamstein, S. (1975). The Middle Ear Muscles: Predictability of Their Phasic Activity in REM Sleep and Dream Material. *Sleep Research* 4:165.

Rotenberg, V. (1984). Search Activity in the Context of Psychosomatic Disturbance of Brain Monoamines and REM Sleep Function. *Pavlov Journal of Biological Science* 19:1–15.

Smith, C. C. (1985). Sleep States and Learning: A Review of the Animal Literature. *Neuroscience and Biobehavioral Review* 00:000–000 9:157–168.

Steriade, M. (1978). Cortical Long-Axoned Cells and Putative Interneurons during the Sleep-Waking Cycle. *Behavioral Brain Science* 3:465–514.

Steriade, M., and Hobson, J. A. (1976). Neuronal Activity during the Sleep-Waking Cycle. In *Progress in Neurobiology* 6:155–376.

Watson, F., and Henry, J. (1977). Loss of Socialized Patterns of Behavior in Mouse Colonies Following Sleep Disturbance during Maturation. *Physiological Behavior* 18:119–23.

LIST OF CONTRIBUTORS

John E. Beebe, M.D.; Jungian Analyst; private practice in San Francisco; member of C.G. Jung Institute; editor, *The San Francisco Jung Institute Library Journal*; co-author with C. Peter Rosenbaum, *Psychiatric Treatment: Crisis, Clinic and Consultation*, and author of *Integrity in Depth*.

Erik Craig, Ed.D.; Director of the Santa Fé Center for the Study of Dreams; Director, Center for Existential Studies Worcester, Massachusetts, and Santa Fe, MN. Psychologist in private practice in Worcester, and Santa Fé Past President and member of the original Board of Directors of the Association for The Study of Dreams. Senior Editor of *Dreaming*, Journal of the A.S.D. Core Faculty member, Southwestern College. Editor of *Psychotherapy for Freedom*. President of the division for Humanistic Psychology, of the American Psychological Association.

Gayle Delaney, Ph.D.; Founding President, Association for the Study of Dreams. Co-Director of the Delaney & Flowers Dream and Consultation Center in San Francisco. Author of *Sexual Dreams, Break Through Dreaming*, and *Living Your Dreams*.

Loma Flowers, M.D.; Associate Clinical Professor of Psychiatry at the University of California, San Francisco; Vice-President and Chairman of the original Board of Directors of the Association for the Study of Dreams; Co-Director of the Delaney and Flowers Dream and Consultation Center in San Francisco. Psychiatrist in private practice in San Francisco.

Ramon Greenberg, M.D.; private practice in Brookline, Massachusetts; Visiting Professor of Psychiatry, Harvard Medical School at Massachusetts Mental Health Center, author of: "If Freud only knew: a reconsideration of psychoanalytic dream theory," in: *Int. Rev. Psychoanal.*

Milton Kramer, M.D.; Medical Director of the Sleep Disorders Center of greater Cincinnati at Bethesda Oak Hospital, Ohio; author, *Dream*

Psychology and New Biology of Dreaming and *Dimensions of Dreams;* member of the original Board of Directors of the Association for the Study of Dreams. 1986 President of the Association for the Study of Dreams. Volunteer Professor of Psychiatry University of Cincinnati Clinical Professor of Psychiatry, School of Medicine Wright State University, Dayton, OH, Adjunct Professor of Psychiatry, University of Cincinnati. Joseph Natterson, M.D.; Clinical Professor, Department of Psychiatry, University of Southern California School of Medicine; training analyst, Southern California Psychonalytic Institute; Attending Psychiatrist, Cedars-Sinai Medical Center; co-author, *The Sexual Dream,* with Bernard Gordon; editor of *The Dream in Clinical Practice;* member of the original Board of Directors for the Association for the Study of Dreams.

Chester Arthur Pearlman, M.D; Consulting practice in Brookline, Mass.; Assistant Chief, Psychiatry Service, Veterans Administration Medical Center, Boston; Associate Clinical Professor at Tufts University School of Medicine; Assistant Psychiatrist and Consultant to Sleep Disorders Clinic, Beth Israel Hospital, Boston.

Montague Ullman, M.D.; Clinical Professor of Psychiatry, Albert Einstein College of Medicine; Life Fellow of the American Psychiatric Association; member of the faculty of the Westchester Center for the Study of Psychoanalysis and Psychotherapy, author of *Behavioral Changes in Patients with Strokes* and co-author of *Dream Telepathy* and *Working With Dreams.*

Stephen J. Walsh, M.D.; Associate Clinical Professor, Department of Psychiatry, University of California, San Francisco; Former Editor (San Francisco Medicine) and Past President of the San Francisco Medical Society, Fellow of the American Psychiatric Association, Past President, Assoc. of the Clinical Faculty, Univ. of California, San Francisco, private practice of general psychiatry, San Francisco and Mill Valley; member of the original Board of Directors of the Association for the Study of Dreams; author of "The Existential Approach in Psychiatry," in: *Review of General Psychiatry,* Howard Goldman, ed.